100
MASTER GAMES
OF MODERN CHESS

100
MASTER GAMES
OF
MODERN CHESS

BY

Dr. S. TARTAKOWER

AND

J. du MONT

DOVER PUBLICATIONS, INC.

NEW YORK

Published in Canada by General Publishing Company, Ltd., 30 Lesmill Road, Don Mills, Toronto, Ontario.

Published in the United Kingdom by Constable and Company, Ltd., 10 Orange Street, London WC 2.

This Dover edition, first published in 1975, is an unabridged and unaltered republication of the work originally published by G. Bell and Sons, Ltd., London, and Charles Scribner's Sons, New York, in 1955. It is reprinted by special arrangement with G. Bell and Sons, Ltd., York House, Portugal Street, London WC2A 2HL.

International Standard Book Number: 0-486-20317-4
Library of Congress Catalog Card Number: 74-75267

Manufactured in the United States of America
Dover Publications, Inc.
180 Varick Street
New York, N.Y. 10014

PREFACE

This collection of games is intended to link up with the present day the first two volumes published under the title of *500 Master Games of Chess*. Nevertheless, the reader will easily perceive that the present volume is complete in itself.

The period of the war was practically barren, but soon after its conclusion chess had a tremendous revival which made the task of selection for this book one of no little difficulty. Luckily, contemporary chess strategy unites the beauties of combinative play with the depth of a general plan and so provides many outstanding games.

The authors hope that the examples selected pay due attention to the many innovations in opening theory which occurred during the period they cover and also that their original annotations will throw some fresh light on these games. If, therefore, the present volume succeeds in presenting a living survey of contemporary chess, while at the same time adding to the reader's knowledge and his æsthetic enjoyment, the authors would consider this the finest reward for their labours.

Thanks are due to Messrs. D. Castello, L. E. Fletcher and A. R. B. Thomas for undertaking the onerous task of reading the proofs.

S. TARTAKOWER
J. DU MONT

CONTENTS

PART I OPEN GAMES

1. GIUOCO PIANO

PART II   SEMI-OPEN GAMES

12. FRENCH DEFENCE

13. CARO-KANN DEFENCE

14. SICILIAN DEFENCE

15. CENTRE COUNTER

16. ALEKHINE'S DEFENCE

17. NIMZOWITSCH'S DEFENCE

PART III CLOSED GAMES

18. QUEEN'S GAMBIT ACCEPTED

19. ALBIN COUNTER-GAMBIT

20. QUEEN'S GAMBIT DECLINED

INDIAN DEFENCES

29. OLD INDIAN DEFENCE

30. KING'S INDIAN DEFENCE

31. GRÜNFELD DEFENCE

32. QUEEN'S INDIAN DEFENCE

33. NIMZO-INDIAN DEFENCE

34. CATALAN SYSTEM

35. BUDAPEST DEFENCE

VARIOUS OPENINGS

36. ENGLISH OPENING

37. RÉTI–ZUKERTORT

38. BIRD'S OPENING

PART I

OPEN GAMES

1. GIUOCO PIANO

1

TARTAKOWER — EUWE
(Venice, 1948)

If it were necessary to demonstrate that, in an age of fluctuating fashions, chess still remains an art and that the spirit of Morphy still inspires even scientific play, the following game provides the irrefutable proof.

1 P—K4	P—K4
2 Kt—KB3	Kt—QB3
3 B—B4	B—B4
4 P—B3	Kt—B3

A staunch defence. In connection with his next move, this *preventive retreat* (or first 4 .... Q—K2;) enables Black to maintain his centre, for now, after 5 P—Q4, he need not exchange his KP, which exchange is forced if Black plays 4 .... P—Q3; or 4 .... Kt—B3.

5 P—Q4	Q—K2
6 Castles	

Development first! The impulsive sacrifice of a pawn by 6 P—Q5, Kt—Kt1; 7 P—Q6, is unconvincing.

6	P—Q3
7 P—KR3	Kt—B3
8 R—K1	Castles
9 Kt—R3	

Here 9 P—QR4, P—QR3; 10 P—QKt4, is not unusual, but this continuation fails to make an impression on the hostile formation. That is why White has recourse to play by pieces rather than by pawns: his QKt is to make for QB4, in order to eliminate Black's KB, or, perhaps, to reach the dominating square Q5, via QB2 and K3.

This is one of Morphy's ideas, which he tried out in a game against Arnous de Rivière, *Paris*, 1863.

9	Kt—Q1

Another defensive plan could be 9 .... P—QR3; 10 B—Q3, R—K1; 11 Kt—B4, B—R2; and Black succeeds in maintaining his KB on its present diagonal.

Playable also is 9 .... K—R1; regrouping his forces by .... Kt—KKt1; and .... P—KB3.

10 B—B1	

More effective is the restricted retreat 10 B—Q3, which would achieve the same object—namely, vacating QB4. Good also is 10 Kt—B2, followed eventually by P—QKt3, and B—QR3.

10	Kt—K1

To all appearances, 10 .... Kt—Q2; is more natural.

In a game Rossolimo–Dunkelblum (*Match France v. Belgium*, 1948), Black played 10 .... P—B3; and the game continued: 11 Kt—B4, B—B2; 12 P—QKt3, P—B4 (this forestalls the threat 13 B—R3, but prematurely gives up the strategic point at White's Q5 to his adversary. Preferable is 12 .... P—QKt3); 13 P×KP, P×P; 14 Kt—K3, P—QKt3; 15 Kt—Q5, Kt×Kt; 16 P×Kt, P—B3; 17 Kt—Q2, Kt—B2; 18 P—KB4, Q—Q1; 19 Kt—B4, P×P; (19 .... B—Kt2; is better) 20 P—Q6 (beginning a combination of the highest class), 20 .... B×QP; 21 Q—Q5, B—R3; 22 Kt×B, B×B; 23 R—K8 ("the bull in the china shop"), 23 .... Q×Kt; 24 Q×R, and White, emerging from this hot encounter the exchange to the good, won easily.

11 Kt—B4	

The immediate "gain" of a pawn by 11 P×P, P×P; 12 Kt×P, Q×Kt; 13 Q×Kt, would be premature and deceptive, for the consequence would be: 13 .... B×P; 14 Q×R, Kt—Q3; 15 Q×R ch, K×Q; 16 P×B, Q—Kt6 ch; and Black wins. This variation demonstrates that, already with his preceding move, Black had an *active defence* in view.

11	P—KB3

And here again—a puzzling move which looks like an oversight, for Black now loses a pawn. The sequel, however, tends to show that it is part of a deep-laid plot!

12 P—QR4	P—B3
13 Kt×B	P×Kt
14 Q—Kt3 ch	Kt—K3
15 Q×P	P—Kt4

The note to move 11 is now clear—White has won his pawn. But observe that Black is now ready for an offensive on the K side, in which his pawns will play a major part, while White's Queen is stranded far away from the scene of action, and will not be able to resume an active rôle throughout the game.

16 B—QB4
Faulty judgment: White deprives the King's field of an important defensive piece. He should aim at consolidation, and a more useful plan would be 16 P—KKt3, followed by B—Kt2.

16 ......   P—R3
17 P—R4
Faulty temperament: not satisfied with the gain of a pawn, he thinks he can also secure the initiative.
Wisdom demanded 17 B—K3, or 17 Q—Kt3.

17 ......   K—R2
18 P × KtP
Faulty perspective: it is not White but his opponent who will benefit from the opening of the KR file.

18 ......   RP × P
19 P × P   QP × P
20 B—K3
Here—or on the next move—White might well have begun his trek to the Q side with K—B1—K2, etc.

20 ......   R—R1
21 P—KKt3   K—Kt3
22 K—Kt2
This calls forth the storm. Essential is the defence of the King's field by 22 B—KB1, followed by B—Kt2.

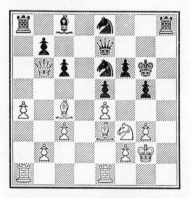

22 ......   Kt—B5 ch
Before White can oppose the occupation of the open file by R—R1, Black strikes the first blow.

23 P × Kt   B—R6 ch
But not at once 23 .... KtP × P; because of 24 R—R1, and White is safe.

24 K—Kt3
The white King is compelled to venture forth from his quarters, for if 24 K—Kt1, KtP × P; 25 B—KB1, Q—R2; and Black's attack succeeds.

24 ......   KP × P ch
25 B × P   Q—Q2
A splendid *interim manœuvre* which threatens mate in two. White had not foreseen this beautiful turn in his calculations (at move 22) thinking that after 25 .... P × B ch; 26 K × P, he would be out of all danger.

26 Kt—R2   P × B ch
27 K × P   R—R5 ch
28 K—K3
If 28 K—Kt3, R—Kt5 ch; 29 K—B3 (29 K × B, R—Kt4 dis ch), 29 .... B—Kt7 ch; followed by 30 .... R × P ch; or 28 K—B3, B—Kt7 ch; 29 K × B, Q—R6 ch; etc.

28 ......   B—Kt7
29 Kt—B3   R × P ch
In full cry.

30 K × R   Kt—Q3 ch
31 K—Q3   Q—B4 ch
32 K—Q4   Q—B5 ch
33 K—Q3
If 33 K—B5, Q × B ch; 34 K × Kt, Q—Q4 ch; 35 K—K7, R—R1; and wins.

33 ......   Q × B ch
34 K—B2   B × Kt
35 P—Kt3
A stronger resistance results from 35 Q—Q4. However, after 35 .... Q × Q; 36 P × Q, Kt—B4; 37 K—B3, R—Q1; Black wins the QP and, with two minor pieces for a Rook, has good winning chances.

35 ......   B—K5 ch
36 K—Kt2   Q—Q6
A beautiful move, which threatens 37 .... Q—B7 ch; 38 K—R3, Kt—B5 ch; 39 P × Kt, R × P mate.

37 R—Kt1 ch   K—B2
38 QR—QB1
A passive defence. Also insufficient would be 38 Q—B7 ch, K—K3; 39 QR—Q1, Kt—B5 ch; and wins.
Instead of the text-move, 38 KR—QB1 makes things more difficult for Black (e.g.

38 .... Q—Q7 ch; 39 K—R3, Kt—Kt4 ch;
40 K—Kt4, etc.).

| 38 ...... | Q—Q7 ch |
| 39 K—R3 | |

Now, at last, White appears to be safe.
But the fireworks begin afresh and with
redoubled brilliance.
After 39 K—R1, Black also plays 39 ....
Kt—B5; 40 P×Kt, R×P mate.
If instead 40 Q×P ch, K—K3; and it is
quite remarkable that, on an open board,
White has no practicable check! E.g.
41 R—Kt1, Q×P ch; 42 K—R2, R×P ch;
and mate next move.

| 39 ...... | Kt—B5 ch |
| 40 P×Kt | R×P ch |

The climax!

| 41 K×R | Q—R7 ch |

It is clear now that, on his thirty-eighth
move, White should have played his KR to
QB1.

| 42 K—Kt4 | Q—Kt7 ch |
| Resigns. | |

A spectacular victory by the former world
champion.

2

ROSSOLIMO   MÜHRING
(Hastings, 1948-9)

*What is the secret of contemporary master-
ship in chess? Is it the depth of strategical
conception or the subtlety of tactical manœuvres? We would say that it is a skilful
fusion of the two—as illustrated in the
following beautiful game.*

1 P—K4	P—K4
2 Kt—KB3	Kt—QB3
3 B—B4	B—B4
4 P—B3	Q—K2
5 P—Q4	B—Kt3

The inversion of Black's fourth and fifth
move is of little importance. It is true
that White, instead of 5 P—Q4, could have
played 5 P—Q3, the *Giuoco Pianissimo*, but
even then Black's fourth move has its uses.

6 Castles	P—Q3
7 P—KR3	Kt—B3
8 R—K1,	Castles
9 Kt—R3	Kt—Q1
10 B—Q3	

A shrewd manœuvre.

| 10 ...... | P—B3 |

If 10 .... P—B4; relinquishing the control of the strategic point at his Q4, then
11 Kt—B4, B—B2; 12 P×KP, P×P;
13 Kt—K3, followed by Kt—Q5, gives
White a clear positional advantage (Rossolimo–Snaevarr, *Reykjavik*, 1951).

| 11 Kt—B4 | B—B2 |
| 12 P—QKt3 | |

A very ingenious move intending
B—QR3, seriously hampering Black's position.

| 12 ...... | P—QKt4 |

Here 12 .... P—QKt3; would afford
Black better chances against the danger
mentioned above; e.g. 12 .... P—QKt3;
13 B—R3, P—B4. When attempting to
drive away a piece, it is essential to make
sure that there is no *interim manœuvre*
available to the other side.

| 13 P×P | P×P |

With reference to the preceding note, if
now, instead of the text-move, 13 ....
P×Kt; 14 P×Kt, Q×BP; 15 B×P, Q×P;
Black is in a hazardous situation.

14 B—R3	P—B4
15 Kt—K3	B—R4
16 Q—B2	B—Kt2
17 Kt—Q5	

Forcing the opening of lines. Of no
value would be the gain of a pawn after
17 Kt—B5, Q—B2; 18 B×KtP, because
18 .... Kt—K3; 19 QR—Q1, QR—Q1;
and Black's counter-chances must not be
under-estimated.

17	B×Kt
18 P×B	B—B2
19 Kt×P	B×Kt
20 P—KB4	P—Kt5
21 R×B	Q—Q3
22 B—Kt2	P×P

Otherwise there follows 23 P—B4, and
White would not only maintain his gain
(the QP) but his Bishops on the open
diagonals would become irresistible.

| 23 B×P | P—KR3 |

To prevent 24 R—Kt5.

| 24 R—KB1 | Kt—Kt2 |

Not 24 .... Kt×P; 25 R×Kt, Q×R;
26 B—K4, and wins.

25 B—B4	QR—Q1
26 R—B3	Q—Kt3
27 R—Kt3	Kt—Q3

Threat: .... Kt—Kt4—Q5; intercepting
the long black diagonal.

28 Q—Q3　　　P—R3

With the text-move, Black wishes to prepare for the simplifying transaction: 29 .... Kt—Kt4; 30 B × Kt, P—B5 dis ch; 31 Q—Q4, Q × Q ch; 32 B × Q, P × B; etc. But it would be better to pay attention to the consolidation of his King's field by playing 28 .... KR—K1.

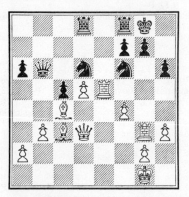

29 R × P ch

The long-expected blow has fallen. Mate or loss of Queen cannot be avoided.

29 ......　　　K × R

Forced.

30 Q—Kt3 ch　　　K—R2

In reply to 30 .... K—R1; 31 R—R5, is clearly decisive.

31 B—Q3 ch　　　Kt(Q3)—K5
32 R × Kt　　　P—B5 dis ch
33 B—Q4　　　P × B
34 B × Q　　　R × P

Or 34 .... Kt × R; 35 Q × P, QR—K1; 36 P—Q6, P—B4; 37 P—Q7, and wins easily.

35 R—Q4　　　Resigns

3

CORTE　　　JACOBO BOLBOÇHAN

(Parana, 1946)

In the following brief encounter we witness the triumph of creative mind over mere matter.

1 P—K4　　　P—K4
2 Kt—KB3　　　Kt—QB3

3 B—B4　　　B—B4
4 P—B3　　　Kt—B3

The classical reply.

5 P—Q4　　　P × P
6 P × P　　　B—Kt5 ch
7 Kt—B3

The famous *Greco continuation.* More prosaic is: 7 B—Q2, B × B ch; 8 QKt × B, P—Q4; 9 P × P, KKt × P; 10 Q—Kt3 (or 10 Castles, Castles; 11 R—K1, etc., with a slight frontal pressure), 10 .... QKt—K2; 11 Castles, Castles; 12 KR—K1, P—QB3; 13 P—QR4 (or 13 Kt—K4, Kt—QKt3; 14 Kt—B5, etc., with a slight lateral pressure), 13 .... Q—Kt3; 14 P—R5 (or 14 Q—R3, B—K3; 15 P—R5, Q—B2, and Black holds his own), 14 .... Q × Q; 15 Kt × Q, B—B4; 16 Kt—K5, KR—B1 (or, as in a game O'Kelly–Dr. Euwe, *Amsterdam*, 1950, 16 .... Kt—Kt5; 17 QR—B1, and White has secured a slight positional advantage); 17 QR—B1, K—B1; 18 P—Kt4 (playing his trumps without delay. In a game Rossolimo–König, *Hastings*, 1948-9, the more dilatory 18 P—R3, was played, and Black succeeded in throwing back the hostile cavalry by 18 .... P—B3; 19 Kt—B3, P—QKt3, etc.), 18 .... B—Kt3; 19 Kt—B5, and White's pressure becomes dangerous, which shows that the whole of this variation (7 B—Q2), although reputed to be quiet, or even inoffensive, contains subtle possibilities.

7 ......　　　KKt × P
8 Castles　　　Kt × Kt

Black here rebels against theory which prescribes as the best continuation on both sides: 8 .... B × Kt; 9 P—Q5 (the *Möller Attack*), 9 .... B—B3; 10 R—K1, Kt—K2; 11 R × Kt, P—Q3; 12 B—Kt5, B × B; 13 Kt × B, Castles; 14 Kt × RP, K × Kt; 15 Q—R5 ch, K—Kt1; 16 R—R4, P—KB4; 17 Q—R7 ch, K—B2; 18 R—R6, R—KKt1; 19 R—K1, Q—B1; 20 B—Kt5, R—R1; 21 Q × R, P × R; 22 Q—R7 ch, K—B3; 23 Kt × R, Q × R; 24 Q × RP ch, K—K4; 25 Q—K3 ch, K—B3; 26 Q—R6 ch, with perpetual check. To avoid this humdrum termination, analysts actively seek improvements for either side.

Taking the position in the following diagram, after White's fourteenth move Kt × RP, the continuation in a game Kildal–Hunte, 1951, was as follows: 14 .... B—B4; 15 R—R4 (obstinacy: by continuing simply 15 R × Kt, Q × R; 16 Kt × R, R × Kt; 17 Q—Q2, R—K1; 18 B—Kt5, B—Q2; 19 B × B, Q × B; 20 R—K1, etc. White can again bring about equalisation), 15 .... R—K1; 16 Q—R5 (if 16 Kt—B6 ch, P × Kt;

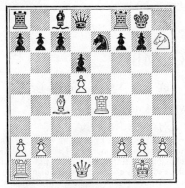

Position after White's 14th move Kt × RP in the variation

17 Q—R5, Kt—Kt3; parrying all threats), 16 .... Kt—Kt3; 17 Kt—Kt5, Q—B3 (Black keeps perfectly cool. If 17 .... Kt × R; 18 Q × P ch, and White secures the draw by perpetual check); 18 Q—R7 ch, K—B1; 19 B—Kt5, Q × P (decisive); 20 Q—R8 ch, Kt × Q; 21 R × Kt ch, K—K2; 22 R—K1 ch, K—B3; White resigns.

9 P × Kt   B × P
10 B—R3
A critical moment. Greco demonstrated that 10 Q—Kt3, wins forcibly against the covetous 10 .... B × R. But the wily Dr. Bernstein showed (about 1922) that the counter-thrust 10 .... P—Q4; saves the situation, and probably the former Argentine champion counted on this when playing his eighth move .... Kt × Kt.
The ingenious move in the text is of recent Italian origin and illustrates the tireless work of theoretical investigators.

10 ......   P—Q4
What was Black to do? After 10 .... P—Q3; comes 11 Q—Kt3, or as was indicated by Dr. J. M. Aitken, 11 R—B1, B—R4; 12 Q—R4, etc. After 10 .... B × R;

11 R—K1 ch, is decisive. Against 10 .... Kt—K2; there follows 11 R—B1, B—R4; 12 P—Q5, etc. or even 11 Q—Kt3, as suggested by Keres.

11 B—Kt5   B × R
12 R—K1 ch   B—K3
13 Q—R4
As can be seen, the contest now centres around White's QB6.

13 ......   R—QKt1
In order to reply to 14 B × Kt ch, P × B; 15 Q × P ch, with 15 .... Q—Q2; without losing the Rook; but White need not hurry to force a decision.

14 Kt—K5
A decisive reinforcement.

14 ......   Q—B1
Providing the unfortunate black King, rooted in the middle, with a flight square.

15 B × Kt ch   P × B
16 Q × P ch   Resigns
For if 16 .... K—Q1; White wins prettily by 17 Kt × P ch, B × Kt; 18 B—K7 mate.

Final position

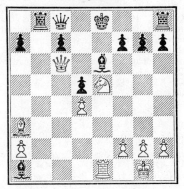

2. EVANS GAMBIT

4

A. R. B. THOMAS — UNZICKER
(Hastings, 1950-1)

Modern theory is ever on the look-out for variants, which tend to deprive the good old Gambits of their charm. Nevertheless, the chess muse, at times, rebels and shows that these Gambits, or, at least, the ideas which animate them, remain eternally young.

1 P—K4	P—K4
2 Kt—KB3	Kt—QB3
3 B—B4	B—B4
4 P—QKt4	B×P

Declining the gambit hardly lightens Black's task, as is shown, for instance, in the following superb brevity, Helms–Tenner, *New York*, 1942 at 10 seconds a move; 4 .... B—Kt3; 5 P—QR4 (against 5 B—Kt2, Black's best is 5 .... Kt—B3), 5 .... P—QR3; 6 P—R5 (usual here is 6 Castles, or 6 B—Kt2, or 6 Kt—B3), 6 .... B—R2; 7 P—Kt5, P×P; 8 B×P, Kt—B3; 9 B—R3, Kt×KP; 10 Q—K2, Kt×BP (his only chance is 10 .... Kt—Q3). He evidently underrates the aggressor's resources); 11 Kt×P, Kt—Q5; 12 Kt×QP dis ch (a most brilliant and attractive combination), 12 .... Kt×Q (against either 12 .... Kt—K3; or 12 .... Kt—K5; White has the same reply); 13 Kt—B6 mate.

5 P—B3	B—R4
6 P—Q4	P—Q3

The modern defence (due to Alapin). It also is the key move to *Lasker's Defence* which runs as follows: 6 Castles (instead of 6 P—Q4), 6 .... P—Q3; 7 P—Q4, B—Kt3 (instead of 7 .... P×P. Another idea of Alapin's here is 7 .... B—Q2); 8 P×P, P×P; 9 Q×Q ch, Kt×Q; 10 Kt×P, B—K3; and Black, having given back the pawn, has the superior end-game. We are far, however, from the lively exchanges which normally characterise this attractive opening.

7 Q—Kt3	

Other continuations are 7 Castles. 7 Q—R4, or 7 P×P. But 7 B—KKt5, holds out the greatest promise of a vigorous game, e.g. 7 .... Kt—B3; 8 Q—R4, etc., or 7 .... KKt—K2; 8 B×Kt, Q×B; 9 Castles, etc., or 7 .... P—B3; 8 Q—Kt3,

K—B1; 9 B—K3, etc., or, finally, 7 .... Q—Q2; 8 Castles, P—KR3; 9 B—R4, and White has the better game.

7	Kt×P

An obviously risky line, in which, at the cost of losing the option of castling, Black relies on maintaining his extra pawn. But Black is in an awkward situation in that he cannot play 7 .... Q—K2; on account of 8 P—Q5, Kt—Q5; 9 Kt×Kt, P×Kt; 10 Q—R4 ch, followed by Q×B. In order to avoid this untoward turn, Black at this point usually plays 7 .... Q—Q2; after which White still has some awkward threats, as shown in the following game from a qualifying tournament in the *World Junior Championship*, 1951: Malcolm Barker–W. Marshall, 8 P×P, B—Kt3 (if 8 .... P×P; 9 Castles, followed by R—Q1, and White's pressure becomes over-powering); 9 QKt—Q2 (or 9 Kt—R3, Kt—R4; 10 Q—Kt4, Kt×B; 11 Kt×Kt, and Black is still in difficulties), 9 .... Kt—R4 (here and even more so on the next move, Black should play .... Kt—R3); 10 Q—B2, Kt—K2; 11 B×P ch (tally-ho! the King-hunt begins), 11 .... K×B; 12 P—K6 ch, K×P; 13 Kt—Kt5 ch, K—B3; 14 P—K5 ch, P×P; 15 QKt—K4 ch, K—Kt3; 16 Kt—B3, QKt—B3 (or 16 .... Q—Q4; 17 P—B4, Kt×P; 18 Kt—B3 dis ch, B—B4; 19 Kt—R4 ch, etc.); 17 Kt—B5 dis ch, Q—B4; 18 Kt—R4 ch, and Black resigns.

8 Kt×Kt	P×Kt
9 B×P ch	K—B1
10 Castles	Q—K2

The immediate development by 10 .... Kt—B3; would be bad because of 11 P—K5, and if then, mechanically, 11 .... P×P; 12 B—R3 ch.

11 B—QB4	Kt—B3
12 P×P	Kt×P
13 Q—B3 ch	Kt—B3
14 Kt—B3	B×Kt

On the well-tried principle that, in a difficult defensive position, exchanges are to be recommended. If, instead, 14 .... P—B3; White plays 15 B—R3, followed by QR—K1, and Black's position is most precarious.

15 Q×B	B—B4

16 R—K1   Q—Q2
17 B—KKt5   Kt—K5

If, still in line with the principle enunciated above, 17 .... R—K1; there follows 18 B×Kt, R×R ch; 19 R×R, P×B; 20 Q—B3, P—B3 (in order to guard the QKtP and to prepare the thrust .... P—Q4. If 20 .... K—Kt2; 21 Q×P, and, in spite of dwindling material, White's advantage is decisive); 21 B—K6 (not 21 P—Kt4, because of the counter-thrust 21 .... P—Q4; 22 P×B, P×B; 23 Q—R3 ch, K—B2; etc., and Black is safe), 21 .... B×B; 22 Q×P ch, K—Kt1; 23 R×B, with a quick win for White.

18 R×Kt

The soundness of this *positional sacrifice* is based on the following logical consideration: White must maintain a situation in which the black King hinders the co-operation of his Rooks.

18 ......   B×R
19 R—K1   P—Q4

If he retires the Bishop to Kt3, there follows: 20 Q—B3 ch, B—B2; 21 R—K7 (or equally well 21 B—K7 ch), and wins. The text move appears to save the situation, but is refuted by White's brilliant rejoinder. On the whole, 19 .... Q—Kt5; provides the most promising defence, although, even then, 20 P—B3, Q×B; 21 P×B, etc., or, still more straightforwardly, 20 B—KB1, Q×B; 21 R×B, etc., would have set Black some difficult problems.

20 R×B

A second sacrifice of the exchange, and one of great beauty. With the black King unfavourably placed, the two mobile Bishops are superior to the disconnected Rooks.

20 ......   P×R (see diag.)

Compulsory, for if 20 .... P×B; 21 Q—B3 ch, wins at once (21 .... K—Kt1; 22 R—K7, or 21 .... Q—B2; 22 R—B4).

21 Q—KKt3

A pity! He overlooks that .... P—KKt3; makes all safe for Black—an instructive inadvertence.

In following up a plan, a player can easily fail to take advantage of a new possibility; that is why he should constantly review the

Position after 20 .... P×R

position independently of his previous intentions. Thus, here, he misses a win in the grand manner by 21 Q—Kt4 ch, Q—Q3 (forced, for if 21 .... K—K1; 22 Q×P, R—QB1; 23 Q×P ch, K—B1; 24 B—K6); 22 Q×P, R—K1; 23 B—Q2 (with the deadly threat 24 B—Kt4), 23 .... Q—Q1 (or 23 .... R—K2; 24 Q—B8 ch, R—K1; 25 Q—B5 ch, Q—B3; 26 B—Kt4 ch, R—K2; 27 Q—B8 mate. Incidentally, not 23 .... P—B4; 24 Q—B7 mate); 24 B—Kt4 ch, R—K2; 25 Q×KP (threatening 26 Q—B5 ch, K—K1; 27 B—Kt5 ch, R—Q2; 28 Q—K6 ch), 25 .... P—Kt3 (or 25 .... Q—Q2; 26 Q—R8 ch, Q—K1; 27 Q—B3 ch); 26 Q—K6, K—K1; 27 B—Kt5 ch, K—B1; 28 Q—B6 ch, K—Kt1; 29 B—B4 ch, with mate to follow.

21 ......   Q—Q3
22 Q—Kt4   P—KKt3

The magical saving clause mentioned in the preceding note.

23 B—R6 ch   K—K1
24 Q×KP ch   K—Q2
25 Q—Kt4 ch   K—K1

A see-saw motion by the King which, not unlike the flight of the King, at times helps to save desperate situations.

26 Q—K4 ch   K—Q2
27 Q—Kt4 ch   K—K1

Draw.

A most creditable performance by White, against the winner of the tournament.

3. TWO KNIGHTS' DEFENCE

5

KOVACS   LOKVENC
(Vienna, 1948)

Whenever Black succeeds early in assuming the initiative and in maintaining it to a successful conclusion, the sporting spirit of the chess lover feels gratified, because it shows that the resources of the game are far from being exhausted.

1 P—K4	P—K4
2 Kt—KB3	Kt—QB3
3 B—B4	Kt—B3
4 Kt—Kt5	

This variation, which for a time had fallen into disrepute, has been rehabilitated by recent analysis.

4	P—Q4
5 P×P	Kt—QR4
6 B—Kt5 ch	

De gustibus non est disputandum.

6	P—B3
7 P×P	P×P

There is nothing particularly new about all this; it is already found in *Polerio's MSS.* (about 1585).

8 Q—B3

A move originally suggested by Staunton which was much analysed a century later. Those who dislike adventure can retire the KB quietly to K2, or more artificially to Q3. Best is the retreat to QR4.

8	B—Kt2

There are possible drawbacks to this move: the QKt is deprived of its natural flight square and the QB renounces its primary original diagonal. A compensation is the fact that the adverse KB is forced to retreat immediately.

Other possible plans are:

(a) 8 .... Q—Kt3. The Queen leaves the centre too much to itself.

(b) 8 .... Q—B2. A more natural square for the Queen, which indirectly forces the retirement of White's KB (because of the threat 9 .... B—KKt5). Indeed if one way or another White delays the retreat of the threatened Bishop, or prefers to parry the threat 9 .... B—KKt5; by a preventive measure, 9 P—KR3, he lays himself open to possible surprises, as is shown by the following brevity, Sörensen–Jul. Nielsen, *Aalborg*, 1947: 9 P—KR3, B—Q3; 10 P—Q3 (he does not see what is coming; he should retire the Bishop, or at least play 10 Kt—B3), 10 .... P×B (confiscation); 11 Q×R, Kt—B3 (sequestration); 12 Kt—QB3, B—QKt5; White resigns, for if, e.g., 13 B—Q2, B×Kt; 14 B×B, P—Kt5; 15 B—Q2, Castles; etc., or 13 P—QR4, Castles; 14 P×P, B—Kt2, and the white Queen is lost.

(c) 8 .... B—Kt2; 9 B—R4, B—Q3; 10 Kt—B3, Castles; 11 P—Q3, etc.

(d) 8 .... QR—Kt1; 9 B—Q3, etc.

(e) 8 .... B—K2; 9 B×P ch, Kt×B; 10 Q×Kt ch, B—Q2; 11 Q—B4, Castles; 12 QKt—B3, and the extra pawn, will tell.

(f) 8 .... P×B; 9 Q×R (a continuation suggested by unbelievers), Q—Q2 (less convincing are other tries: 9 .... B—QB4; or 9 .... Kt—Kt2); 10 Q—B3 (a precipitate but necessary retreat, e.g. 10 Kt—QB3, Kt—B3; 11 P—QKt4, K—K2; with the mortal threat 12 .... B—Kt2; capturing the white Queen in broad daylight).

9 B—Q3

This semi-retreat is fashionable in all variations deriving from 6 B—Kt5 ch. An accessory idea of the text-move is to provide the Knight with an honourable retreat *via* K4. Not without drawbacks would be 9 B—R4, because of 9 .... B—K2; followed by .... Castles (e.g. 10 P—QR3, Castles; 11 P—QKt4, P—B4; and Black has the last word).

9	B—K2

White is in a difficult situation with his KKt "in the air," his Queen in line with Black's QB and his own KB temporarily obstructing his QP.

10 Kt—B3	P—KR3
11 KKt—K4	Kt—Q4
12 P—QR3	

He thinks that his move will not only prevent the intrusion 12 .... Kt—Kt5; but also threaten 13 P—QKt4, winning the hostile QKt, whose only flight square was cut off by Black's eighth move.

Nevertheless, White underestimates the vitality of Black's pieces.

In this fight for squares, White could not simultaneously guard the two danger points at QKt4 and KB4, but, against this, he could himself secure the important square QB5 by playing 12 Kt—R4. Better, in any case, than the slow text-move is the exchange of Knights: 12 Kt×Kt, P×Kt; 13 Kt—Kt3, P—K5; 14 B—Kt5 ch, K—B1; 15 Q—K2, and the battlefield is cleared somewhat.

12 ......   Kt—KB5
13 P—QKt4

Fatal would be the chastened retreat 13 B—B1, because of 13 .... P—KB4; 14 Kt—Kt3, P—B4; 15 Q—K3, Kt—B5; winning the white Queen in a comical manner (16 B×Kt, Kt×P ch).

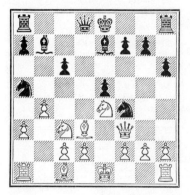

13 ......   Kt—Kt6

Very clever. After 14 R—QKt1, Kt—Q5; Black also obtains an overwhelming attack.

14 P×Kt   Kt×B ch
15 K—Q1   Q—Q2

Re-inforcing, just in time, the frontal pressure on the Q file.

16 K—B2   R—Q1
17 Q—K3   P—KB4
18 Kt—B5   B×Kt
19 P×B   Castles
20 P—B3   B—R3
21 R—Q1

In order to connect the Rooks by B—Kt2 without losing the QP.

21 ......   KR—K1
22 B—Kt2   Q—K2
23 P—QKt4

He wishes to preserve all his material including the QBP, but he again surrenders an important square (QB4).

23 ......   B—B5

24 Kt—R2   Q—K3
25 Kt—B1

White tries too late to eliminate this black Knight established within his lines.

25 ......   P—B5
26 Q—Kt1

A dismal retreat, but 26 Q—K4, would be no better. After 26 .... Kt×Kt; 27 K×Kt, B—Q6; 28 Q—K1, Q—Kt6; Black wins.

26 ......   B—Kt4
27 B—B3

He is now willing to throw over some ballast (the exchange), but Black wants more.

27 ......   B—R5 ch
28 K—Kt1   Kt×Kt
Resigns

Mate is forced, e.g. 29 K×Kt, Q—Kt6; etc., or 29 R×Kt, Q—Kt6 ch; 30 B—Kt2, Q—Q6 ch; 31 K—R2, B—Kt6 mate.

An attractive finish.

6

PRINS   J. PENROSE
(Southsea, 1950)

Modern scientists, such as in France, Henri Poincaré, Borel and others, in England, Whitehead, Bertrand Russell and others, excel in the calculation of probabilities. Similarly in chess it is sought, in certain risky variations, to establish and master the laws of chance.

1 P—K4   P—K4
2 Kt—KB3   Kt—QB3
3 B—B4   Kt—B3
4 Kt—Kt5   P—Q4

A startling variation here is 4 .... B—B4 (which the Americans attribute to researches of the Wilkes–Barre C.C. of Pennsylvania, while Czechoslovakians claim that K. Traxler is its spiritual father). The subtleties of this line are illustrated by the following brevity Rutka-Vesely (from the *Team-championship* at *Prague*, 1950): 4 .... B—B4; 5 Kt×BP (a plausible but detrimental reply. Weak also is 5 P—Q4, because of 5 .... P—Q4; 6 KP×P, QKt×P; 7 P—Q6, Castles, etc. Best is 5 B×P ch, K—K2; 6 P—Q4—instead of the immediate retreat 6 B—Kt3, R—B1; 7 P—Q3, P—Q3; 8 Kt—QB3, etc.—6 .... B×P; 7 P—QB3, B—Kt3; 8 B—Kt3, etc.), 5 .... B×P ch; 6 K×B (it is equally dangerous not to recapture, e.g. 6 K—B1, Q—K2;

7 Kt×R, P—Q4; 8 P×P, Kt—Q5, etc.),
6 .... Kt×P ch; 7 K—K3 (an unnecessary
journey. Much more prudent is 7 K—Kt1),
7 .... Q—K2 (most astute); 8 K×Kt,
Q—R5 ch; 9 P—Kt4, P—Q4 ch; 10 B×P,
B×P; 11 Q—K1, B—B4 db ch; White
resigns (if 12 K×B, Q—B5 ch; and mate
next move, or 12 K—K3, Q—B5 ch;
13 K—K2, B—Kt5 ch, followed by mate).

5 P×P   P—Kt4

Another risky variant is 5 .... Kt—Q5
(*Fritz*), for White has its refutation in
6 P—QB3, P—Kt4; 7 B—B1, Kt×P;
8 Kt—K4, etc., or, more quietly 6 Kt—QB3,
P—KR3; 7 Kt—B3, B—QB4; 8 P—KR3,
Castles; 9 P—Q3, etc.

The text-move, known under the name of
Ulvestad Variation, also aims at a counter-
attack, but in an improved form.

6 B—B1

The best continuation. The obvious
reply 6 P×Kt, P×B; 7 Q—K2, P—KR3;
8 Kt—K4, Q—Q4; is good for Black. On
the other hand, after 6 B×P, Q×P;
7 B×Kt ch, Q×B; 8 Castles, B—Kt2, etc.
Black's development is ample compensation
for his pawn.

6 ......   Kt×P

Instead of bringing about, with 6 ....
Kt—Q5; the *Fritz Variation* mentioned
above, Black accelerates his general mobilisation. If 6 .... Q×P; 7 QKt—B3, and now
the preventive nature of White's sixth move,
guarding the KKtP, becomes clear.

7 B×P   B—Kt2
8 Q—B3

More straightforward is the attempt to
develop by 8 P—Q4, P×P; 9 Castles, etc.
An alternative is 8 Kt—KB3, B—Q3;
9 P—Q4, P—K5; 10 P—B4, Kt—K2;
11 P—Q5, etc. (W. Korn's analysis, 1942.)
The text-move is tricky but superficial.

8 ......   Q—Q2
9 Kt—B3   Kt×Kt
10 QP×Kt   P—B3
11 Kt—K4   Castles

By simple means Black has steered clear
of all danger and his freedom of action is
well worth the pawn he has given up.

12 B—K3   P—B4

Black plays his trumps and White must
lose a piece.

13 Castles

For if 13 Kt—Kt5, P—KR3; 14 Kt—R3,
P—B5; 15 B—QB1, P—Kt4; and White

is clearly lost. More complicated is
13 Kt—B5, B×Kt; 14 B×B, Q—Q7 ch;
15 K—B1, Kt—Q5; 16 Q—Q3, Q—Kt4;
17 P—B3 (17 Q—Kt3, Q×Q; followed by
Kt×B), 17 .... P—K5; 18 Q—B4, Kt×B;
19 Q×Kt, P×P; 20 P—KKt3, Q—Q7;
21 B—B2, R—Q3; 22 P—B4, Q—K7 ch;
23 K—Kt1, KR—Q1; 24 R—KB1,
R—Q8; and wins.

13 ......   P×Kt
14 Q×P   Q—K3
15 Q—QR4   Q—Kt3

White has the semblance of an attack,
but must provide against Black's threat of
16 .... Kt—Q5.

16 P—B3

Not 16 B×P, Kt×B, and wins.

16 ......   P—K5
17 P—KB4   Kt—Kt1

A fine positional manœuvre, as will be
seen.

18 Q×RP

Or 18 R—B2, P—QR3; retreat of the
aggressor.

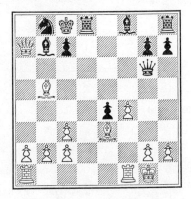

18 ......   R—Q7

A little brilliance thrown in. If 19 B×R,
P—K6; 20 P—KKt3, Q—K5.

19 R—B2   R×R
20 K×R   B—Q3
21 K—Kt1   Q—R4
22 B—B4

White is a piece down and must go on
attacking (threat: 23 B—K6 ch, Kt—Q2;
24 B×Kt ch, K×B; 25 Q×B). It is well
to remember that it is risky to place a piece
on an unguarded square.

22 ......   R—K1

23 Q—Q4   P—Kt4
24 Q—B6
This costs a piece, but there is no longer a valid defence.

24 ......   P×P
25 B×P   Q—B4 ch
26 K—R1   Q×B
27 B×B   P×B
28 Q×P   P—K6
Resigns

The white Queen in the enemy camp is curiously helpless.

An imaginative and fearless player, the Dutch master, in this game, was beaten with his own weapons by the young British fighter.

Max Lange Attack

7

CROWL   KLASS

(Correspondence, Australia, 1949)

The resources of this vibrant attack are many, and in spite of analyses by well-known theoreticians, their potentialities are by no means exhausted.

1 P—K4   P—K4
2 Kt—KB3   Kt—QB3
3 B—B4   Kt—B3
4 P—Q4   P×P
5 Castles   B—B4
6 P—K5   P—Q4
7 P×Kt   P×B
8 R—K1 ch   B—K3
9 Kt—Kt5   Q—Q4
10 Kt—QB3   Q—B4
11 QKt—K4   B—KB1

This move, introduced by Rubinstein, is not easy to refute. Early analysis was based on 11 .... B—Kt3. Later on the following line was suggested: 11 .... Castles QR; 12 Kt×QB, P×Kt; 13 P—KKt4, Q—K4; 14 P×P, KR—Kt1; 15 B—R6, B—Kt5 (or at once 15 .... P—Q6); 16 R—K2, P—Q6; etc.

12 Kt×BP
The only way to effect a breach. Little good would result from 12 P—KKt4, Q×KtP ch; and Black has the last word.

12 ......   K×Kt
13 Kt—Kt5 ch   K—Kt3
Against 13 .... K—Kt1; White continues with 14 P—KKt4, as his opponent cannot now reply 14 .... Q×KtP ch; 15 Q×Q, B×Q; because of 16 P—B7 mate.

The *Max Lange Attack* is full of similar surprises.

14 Kt×B
A far-sighted plan of attack. Theoreticians have given much thought to the following turn: 14 P×P, B×P; 15 R×B ch, B—B3; 16 P—KKt4, Q—Q4.

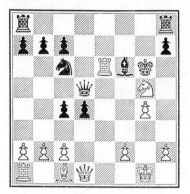

Here is a beautiful possible continuation: 17 P—B4 (proposed by the Hungarian expert, K. Torma), 17 .... P—KR4 (or 17 .... K—Kt2; 18 P—B5, Kt—K4; 19 B—B4, B×Kt; 20 B×Kt ch, etc.); 18 P—B5 ch, Kt—Kt2; 19 B—B4, K—K4; 20 R—Kt6 ch, K—B1; 21 B×B, Kt×B; 22 Kt—K6 ch, K—B2; 23 R—Kt7 ch, K—B3; 24 P—Kt5 ch (in this King-hunt, White has of course to burn his boats), 24 .... K×P; 25 Q—KB1 ch (note: if 25 Kt×P ch, then not 25 .... K—K5; 26 Q—K2 ch, K×Kt; 27 Q—B2 ch, K—K5; 28 R—K1 mate, but, ruthlessly, 25 .... Q×Kt ch; 26 Q×Q, Kt—B6 ch; with a substantial advantage for Black).

Instead of this *Torma Variation* (with 17 P—B4) there is another continuation, proposed by Tartakower as far back as 1924, which runs as follows: 17 Kt—R3, e.g. 17 .... K—B2; 18 Kt—B4, Q—QB4; 19 Q—B3, KR—KB1; 20 Kt—Q3 (not, recklessly, 20 R×B ch, K×R; 21 Kt—Q3 dis ch, K—Kt2; 22 B—R6 ch, K—R1; 23 B×R, Q×B; 24 Q×Q ch, R×Q, etc., and Black stands better), 20 .... P×Kt; 21 R×B ch, K—K2; 22 R×R, R×R; 23 Q—K4 ch, K—Q1; 24 P×P, etc., with advantage to White.

14 ......   P×P
15 P—KKt4   Q—QR4
16 B—B4   B—Q3
17 B×B
Far better than 17 Q—B3, QR—K1; etc.

17 ......   P×B

Black's position seems to become more secure.

18 P—Kt4

A fresh dagger thrust in his opponent's side.

18 ......   Kt×P

If 18 .... Q×KtP; 19 R—Kt1.

19 Q×P   P—Q4
20 Q—B4   QR—KKt1

If 20 .... P—Q5; 21 Q—K4 ch, P—B4; 22 P×P ch, Q×P; 23 Q—Kt2 ch, and White still breaks through.

21 Q—B5 ch   K—B2
22 P—Kt5   R—Kt3
23 P—KR4   KR—KKt1
24 K—R1   Resigns

(24 .... Q—Kt4; 25 P×P, P—KR3; 26 Kt—Kt5 ch, P×Kt; 27 R—K7 ch, followed by mate.)

8

SZABÓ   MÜHRING
(Zaandam, 1946)

In the following curious encounter, the black Queen is forced to execute extraordinary evolutions—a real danse macabre.

1 P—K4   P—K4
2 Kt—KB3   Kt—QB3
3 B—B4   Kt—B3
4 P—Q4   P×P
5 Castles   Kt×P

This is the *pseudo-Max Lange*, which is frequently played in contemporary contests.

6 R—K1   P—Q4
7 B×P   Q×B
8 Kt—B3   Q—KR4

Four other flight squares for the Queen have been tried—namely, QR4, Q1, KB4 and QB5. The most usual reply is 8 .... Q—QR4; with the following continuation: 9 Kt×Kt, B—K3; 10 QKt—Kt5 (after 10 B—Q2, B—QKt5; the pressure is eased), 10 .... Castles; 11 Kt×B, P×Kt; 12 R×P, and now 12 .... B—Q3; when White's best is 13 B—Kt5, QR—K1; 14 Q—K1 (if 14 Q—K2, Kt—K4), 14 .... Q×Q ch; 15 QR×Q, etc., which will give White a slight advantage for the end-game.

9 Kt×Kt   B—K3
10 B—Kt5

White must endeavour to keep the adverse King in the middle. After 10 QKt—Kt5, Castles; 11 Kt×B, P×Kt; 12 R×P, B—Q3, etc., Black has gained the initiative.

10 ......   P—KR3

An instinctive reaction which leads Black astray, for he now loses a valuable defensive tempo. Black envisaged only the white Bishop's retreat and not White's subtle reply.

As a consequence of Black's misconception, White's attack now takes a concrete form. Unsatisfactory also would be 10 .... B—K2; 11 B×B, Kt×B, 12 Kt—Kt3, Q—R3; 13 Q×P, Castles; 14 QR—Q1, etc., and White has the advantage in space. He should therefore have rested content with the continuation recommended by the books: 10 .... B—QKt5; 11 Kt×P (11 P—B3, P×P; 12 P×P, B—R4, etc.), 11 .... Q×Q; 12 KR×Q, Kt×Kt; 13 R×Kt, B—K2; 14 B×B, K×B; 15 Kt—B5, QR—Q1, etc., with complete equality.

11 B—B6

A nice turn, which had already occurred in 1860, in a correspondence game between Wesel and Orefeld.

White has now what de la Bourdonnais called *une petite position*, there being the Knight fork after .... P×B; which threat recurs several times in the course of the game.

11 ......   Q—Q4

Seeking more comfortable quarters for the lone Queen.

After 11 .... Q—R4; a beautiful continuation occurred in a game Rossolimo–Prins, *Bilbao,* 1951: 12 Kt×P (not 12 B×QP, Castles), 12 .... P×B (incredulity, but in

the game Wesel-Orefeld, mentioned above
12 .... Kt×Kt; 13 Q×Kt, etc., also
resulted in a win for White); 13 Kt×P ch,
K—K2; 14 P—QKt4 (pawn *ex machina*),
14 .... Kt×P (any move by the black
Queen would be equally disastrous);
15 Kt×B, K×Kt (or 15 .... P×Kt;
16 Q—Q7 ch, etc.); 16 Q—Q4 ch, K—Kt3;
17 Q×R, Kt×BP; 18 Kt×B ch, R×Kt;
19 Q×R, Kt×KR; 20 Q—Kt8 ch, K—B3;
21 Q—Q8 ch, K—Kt3; 22 Q—Q1, and
Black resigns, as his Knight is lost. This
game failed to gain the brilliancy prize
because the whole of the splendid combination occurred in an earlier game in the
U.S.S.R.—an unusual case of duplication.

12 P—B3   P—Q6
He again cannot capture the Bishop, but
he wants, at any rate and as far as possible,
to preserve what he has gained.

13 Kt—Q4   Kt×Kt
14 P×Kt   Q—QR4
15 Q×P   B—QKt5
And still he cannot effect the capture.
Observe 15 .... P×B; 16 Kt×P ch,
K—Q1; 17 P—Q5, B×P; 18 R—K8 mate,
or 16 .... K—K2; 17 P—Q5, K×Kt
(if 17 .... R—Q1; 18 Q—B5, R—Q3;
19 P—QKt4, etc., and if 17 .... B—Kt2;
18 Q—B5, Q—Kt3; 19 R×B ch, P×R;
20 R—K1, K—Q1; 21 R×P, Q—Kt4;
22 R—B6, with a knock-out); 18 Q—Q4 ch,
K—Kt3 (18 .... K—K2; 19 P×B, etc.);
19 Q×R (19 P×B, B—Kt2; or 19 R—K3,
B—Q3), 19 .... Q×QP; 20 QR—Q1,
Q×P; 21 R—Q3 (as can be seen, White's
attack has four open or semi-open lines
available), 21 .... P—KR4; 22 R—Kt3 ch,
B—Kt5; 23 P—R3, B—Kt5; 24 Q×R,
B×R; 25 Q—Kt8 ch, K—B3; 26 P×B, and,
after all this, White has the exchange and a
winning attack.

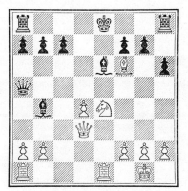

16 P—Q5
This and the following move, giving up
the exchange, show tactical skill of a high
order.

16 ......   Q×QP
Not 16 .... B×R; 17 P×B, P×P;
18 B×P, nor 16 .... P×B; 17 P×B,
R—Q1; 18 P×P ch, K×P; 19 Q—Kt3 ch,
and White has command of the situation.

17 Q—KKt3   B×R
Again the Knight fork follows the capture
of the Bishop.

18 R×B   Q—QR4
19 B—B3   Q—Q4
This is the black Queen's seventh move
and, what is worse, she is no better placed
than before.

20 Q×BP
Not 20 Q×KtP, after which Black castles
and obtains the better game, nor 20 B×P,
Castles; and Black, who threatens 21 ....
Q×Kt; obtains serious counter-chances.

20 ......   R—Q1
If 20 .... Castles; 21 Q—Kt3, and again
the fork is threatened—to say nothing of the
mate.

21 B—Kt4
An interesting moment: White prefers to
maintain his pressure, rather than to allow
the following liquidation: 21 B×P, Q×Kt
(an elegant way to avoid a *débâcle*);
22 Q×R ch, K×Q; 23 R×Q, R—R2 (after
23 .... R—Kt1; 24 B×P, with material
advantage to White); 24 B—B6 ch, K—Q2;
25 P—KKt4; P—KR4 (otherwise
26 P—KR4, and the black Rook remains
imprisoned); 26 P—Kt5, P—R5; and the
Bishops of opposite colours give Black
drawing chances.

21 ......   R—Q2
22 Q—Kt3   P—B3
Evidently neither 22 .... R—Kt1; nor
even 22 .... R—R2; again because of
23 Kt—B6 ch.

23 Q—Kt8 ch
Having weakened the hostile King's
ramparts, the white Queen continues her
harassing tactics. Very strong, however, is
here 23 Kt—B5, R—K2 (23 .... K—B2;
24 Kt×B, etc.; or 23 .... Castles; 24 Kt×R,
winning the double exchange!); 24 Kt×B,
R×Kt; 25 R×R ch, Q×R; 26 Q—Kt8 ch,
K—B2; 27 Q×R, Q×P; 28 Q—B8 ch,

K—Kt3;   29   Q—K8 ch,   K—R2;
30 Q—K4 ch, K—Kt1; 31 B—B3, and
White is a piece ahead.

23 ......   K—B2

He should resist with 23 .... R—Q1
(24 Kt—Q6 ch, Q × Kt, etc., or 24 Q × RP,
K—B2, or, finally, 24 Q—B7, R—Q2;
25 Q—B8 ch, R—Q1; 26 Kt × P ch, P × Kt;
27 R × B ch, K—B2; 28 R—K7 ch, K—Kt3;
29 Q—Kt4 ch, Q—Kt4; 30 Q—QB4,
Q—Q4, etc.).

But Black imagines he can trap the
Queen—

24 Q × R   R—Q1
25 Q—R7   B—B4

in this way, but White has seen a move
further.

26 Kt—Kt5 ch   BP × Kt
27 R—K7 ch   Resigns

Whatever Black plays, 28 Q × KtP, mates.

4. RUY LOPEZ

9

SMYSLOV   RESHEVSKY
(Radio Match, 1945)

The Second World War brought about an almost complete cessation of international competition.

A brilliant revival of these intellectual and peaceful contests was the sensational radio match which took place in 1945 between the U.S.S.R. and the U.S.A. This revealed not only the great playing strength of the Russian players, but also their profound theoretical knowledge.

1 P—K4	P—K4
2 Kt—KB3	Kt—QB3
3 B—Kt5	P—QR3

This is called the *Morphy Defence*, but with little justification, for he played it only a few times.

4 B—R4	Kt—B3
5 Castles	Kt×P

The so-called *open defence*, although it opens, for the time being, nothing. This variation, at one time under a cloud, has had a new lease of life in the last decade.

6 P—Q4	P—QKt4
7 B—Kt3	P—Q4
8 P×P	B—K3
9 P—B3	B—QB4

This move was tried in the *Vienna Tournament* of 1882. It is more ambitious than the modest 9 .... B—K2; and has not ceased to intrigue both theoretician and practical player.

10 QKt—Q2
He loses no time in undermining the enemy's advanced post.

Against 10 Q—Q3, known as the *Motzko Attack*, Dr. Euwe, the great expert in the open defence, recommends, not 10 .... Castles; 11 QKt—Q2, etc., but an immediate re-grouping of Black's forces by 10 .... Kt—K2; with a view to 11 .... B—B4.

10	Castles
11 B—B2	P—B4

Too little temperament is shown by the exchange 11 .... Kt×Kt; 12 Q×Kt, with a small but definite advantage to White; too

temperamental, on the other hand is the sacrifice 11 .... Kt×KBP (see following game).

12 Kt—Kt3
A positional diversion heralding a local struggle around the square Q4.

Less tense, but also less promising, is 12 P×P e.p., Kt×P(B3); 13 Kt—Kt5, B—KKt5; etc., or 13 Kt—Kt3, B—K2; and Black can equalise in either case.

12 ....   B—Kt3
More precise is 12 .... B—R2; for, after the text move, White could have played 13 P—QR4, P—Kt5; 14 P—R5, B—R2; 15 QKt—Q4, gaining in space, without any corresponding loss of time.

13 QKt—Q4   Kt×Kt
Here already (or on the next move) .... Q—Q2; avoids many dangers for Black and promises equality.

14 Kt×Kt   B×Kt
Or, as mentioned above, 14 .... Q—Q2 (e.g. 15 B—Kt3, P—B3; or 15 P—B3, Kt—B4).

15 P×B	P—B5
16 P—B3	Kt—Kt6

The famous *Mackenzie sacrifice*, which occurred in a similar position in a game Fleissig–Mackenzie, *Vienna, 1882.*

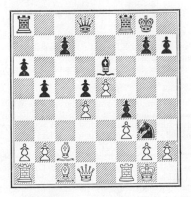

17 P×Kt

On the principle that the best refutation of a gambit is to accept it. Nevertheless, it is more prudent, in this case, to decline it by 17 R—B2. There follows: 17 .... Q—R5; 18 Q—Q3, R—B4 (if 18 .... B—B4; 19 Q—B3, B×B; 20 R×B, with advantage to White); 19 B×P, R×B (if 19 .... Q×B; 20 P×Kt, Q×KtP; 21 P—B4, Q—R5; 22 P—KKt3, Q—Kt5; 23 Q—KB3, White has the better game); 20 P×Kt, Q×P; 21 Q×P ch, K—B2; 22 Q—R5 ch, K—K2; 23 R—Q2—an important moment. A galaxy of high-grade analysts, Smyslov, Botvinnik, Bronstein, and others at this point considered only 23 R—Q1, which, after 23 .... R—R5; 24 Q—Kt6, QR—R1; 25 K—B1, R—Kt5; 26 Q—Q3, R—R8 ch; 27 K—K2, R—K5 ch; 28 Q×R, P×Q; 29 R×R, B—B5 ch; 30 K—K3, P—Kt4; etc., leads to the unexpected triumph of—Black!

The manœuvre which we suggest—23 R—Q2—fulfils the double function of guarding the pawn at Q4, the key to the position, and of giving the King breathing space, 23 .... R—R5; 24 Q—Kt6, and White's advantage becomes concrete.

17 ......   P×P
18 Q—Q3

In order to reply to 18 .... Q—R5; by 19 Q×P ch, with a favourable liquidation. If, however, 18 R—K1, Q—R5; 19 B—K3, then 19 .... B—Kt5; 20 Q—Q3, P—Kt3; gives Black an irresistible attack.

18 ......   B—B4

If 18 .... P—Kt3; 19 Q—K3, Q—R5; 20 Q—R6.

19 Q×B   R×Q
20 B×R   Q—R5
21 B—R3   Q×P ch
22 K—R1   Q×KP
23 B—Q2 (see diag.)

Or 23 R—QKt1, P—B4; 24 B—Q2, R—KB1; 25 KR—K1. We see here the eternal clash between quantity (the three white pieces) and quality (the black Queen).

23 ......   Q×P

The temptation was too great, but White will be able to eliminate, without difficulty and almost simultaneously, two scourges—namely, the terrible pawn at KKt3 and the dangerous passed QP.

Another plan here is 23 .... P—B4; as played in a game Cortlever–Dr. Euwe, *Amsterdam*, 1941. There can follow 24 QR—K1, Q×P; 25 B—B4, P—Q5; 26 B×P, Q—B6; with an uncertain issue.

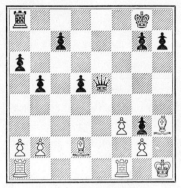

Position after 23 B—Q2

24 B—B4   P—B4

Too late! He has nothing better than to rely on the potentialities of his most advanced pawn by playing 24 .... P—Q5; e.g. 25 B×BP (or 25 B×KtP, P—Q6; 26 B×P, P—Q7, etc), 25 .... P—Q6; 26 B×P, P—Q7; 27 B—K6 ch, K—R1; 28 P—B4 (the counterblast!), 28 .... R—Q1; 29 QR—Q1 (or 29 P—B5, Q—B3; 30 QR—Q1, R—Q5, etc.), 29 .... Q—Q6; 30 R—B2 (if 30 B—B2, Q—B3; 31 P—B5, P—Kt4; etc. Kagan–Estrin, *correspondence*, 1947); 30 .... Q—Kt5; 31 B—R2, Q—K5; 32 B—Kt4, P—KR4 (unloading ballast, Baturinsky–Estrin, *correspondence*, 1946); 33 B×P, Q—K8 ch; 34 R—B1, R—K6; and Black has set up a fairly secure defence.

As can be seen, after having been dissected by various experts at various times, the *Mackenzie sacrifice* (16 .... Kt—Kt6;) represents the longest variant known to theory.

25 B—K6 ch

It is to be noted that Smyslov, who was thoroughly conversant with the ramifications of this line of play, used up six minutes for the first twenty-five moves, at which stage his opponent was already nearing the time limit.

25 ......   K—R1
26 B×QP   R—Q1
27 QR—Q1   P—B5
28 B×KtP

Thus Black's advanced pawns are being slaughtered.

28 ......   P—B6
29 B—K5   P—Kt5
30 B—QKt3   R—Q7
31 P—B4

Threatening 32 R×R, Q×R; 33 R—Q1, P—B7; 34 B×P, Q×B; 35 R—Q8 mate.

| 31 | ...... | P—KR4 |
| 32 | R—QKt1 | R—KB7 |

An ingenious artifice, which, however, cannot relieve the black Queen's compromised position.

33 KR—K1

The final struggle for the open files. If 33 KR—Q1, Q—K7; and Black can breathe again; but if Black after the text-move, were to try 33 .... R—K7; there follows 34 KR—Q1, and Black's Queen would be forced to the inglorious retreat to QR6.

| 33 | ...... | Q—Q7 |
| 34 | QR—Q1 | Q—Kt7 |

A more active defence is 34 .... R—K7; 35 R—KKt1, Q—K6.

| 35 | R—Q8 ch | K—R2 |
| 36 | B—Kt8 ch | K—Kt3 |

The mating net is tightening: observe 36 .... K—R3; 37 R—Q6 ch, P—Kt3; 38 R—Q7, P—Kt4; 39 R—Q6 mate, or 36 .... K—R1; 37 B—K6 dis ch, K—R2; 38 B—B5 ch, and mate follows.

37	R—Q6 ch	K—B4
38	B—K6 ch	K—Kt3
39	B—Q5 dis ch	K—R2

If 39 .... K—B4; 40 B—K4 ch, followed by mate in three.

| 40 | B—K4 ch | K—Kt1 |

Or 40 .... P—Kt3; 41 R—Q8, with mate to follow.

| 41 | B—Kt6 | Resigns |

If, in order to avoid 42 R—Q8 mate, Black plays 41 .... R—Q7; 42 B—Q4, and mate by one of the white Rooks, or 41 .... K—B1; 42 R—K6.

10

ESTELLES   DILWORTH
(Correspondence, 1941)

And here Black offers another sacrifice aiming at the break-up of the ramparts, reputed so solid, of the Ruy Lopez. Although known since 1887, this sacrifice has been revived and, as it were, polished by the efforts of Vernon Dilworth of Manchester.

1	P—K4	P—K4
2	Kt—KB3	Kt—QB3
3	B—Kt5	P—QR3
4	B—R4	Kt—B3
5	Castles	Kt × P

6	P—Q4	P—QKt4
7	B—Kt3	P—Q4
8	P × P	B—K3
9	P—B3	B—QB4
10	QKt—Q2	Castles
11	B—B2	Kt × KBP

Plunging into the beautiful adventure.

12 Q—K2

The *Dilworth Gambit deferred.* Much more to be recommended is the immediate acceptance of the gift: 12 R × Kt, P—B3; 13 P × P, Q × P; 14 Q—B1 (best. If, for example, 14 Kt—Kt3, the picturesque continuation in a game Nightingale–Ritson Morry, *correspondence*, 1944, was: 14 .... B × R ch; 15 K × B, Kt—K4; 16 Kt—B5, B—Kt5; 17 Q × P ch, K—R1; 18 Q—K4, P—Kt3; 19 K—Kt3, Kt × Kt; 20 Q × B, Kt—Kt8; 21 Kt—Q3, QR—Q1, etc.), 14 .... B—Kt5; 15 P—KR3 (an immediate counter-measure. Good also, according to Fine, is 15 Q—Q3. Too slow is the continuation in a game Smyslov-Botvinnik, 1944: 15 K—R1, B × R; 16 Q × B, QR—K1; 17 Q—Kt3, Kt—K4; 18 B—Q1, P—KR4; 19 P—KR4, Kt—Q6; etc., with the better game for Black), 15 .... B × Kt (or 15 .... B—R4; 16 Q—Q3, etc.), 16 Kt × B, Kt—K4; 17 B—Q1, etc., with a consolidated position.

| 12 | ...... | P—B3 |

Completing the idea of the sacrifice, the opening of the KB file in order to exert pressure on White's King's field.

13	P × P	Q × P
14	R × Kt	QR—K1
15	Q—Q3	P—Kt3
16	Q—B1	

In reply to hostile threats, the Queen makes a third move to occupy a square which she could have reached in one.

Thus White has lost two *tempi*, a fact of which Black takes skilful advantage.

| 16 | ...... | B—KKt5 |
| 17 | Kt—Q4 (see diag., p. 18) | |

White believes that his adversary has waited too long before capturing the Rook, and that now he can intercept the critical diagonal and thus preserve the whole of his gains.

| 17 | ...... | Kt × Kt |

A clever reply, as will be seen.

| 18 | R × Q | R × R |
| 19 | P × Kt | |

The point is that White cannot take the Rook. Observe 19 Q × R, Kt—B6 db ch;

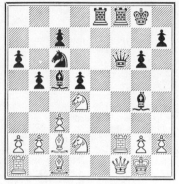

Position after 17 Kt—Q4

20 K—B1, R—K8 mate; or 20 K—R1, R—K8 ch, and mate one move later.

19	B×P ch
20 K—R1	R×Q ch
21 Kt×R	R—K8

The famous irruption on the "last rank." White's agony will be short.

22 B—Q3	B—KB4

With the direct threat to break down the last defence (23 B×B, R×Kt mate), and the consequent threat of occupying the dominant square, K5.

23 B—K2	R×KB
24 B—R6	B—K5
Resigns	

This game created something of a sensation when it was first published.

Botvinnik is one of the experts who have adopted the *Dilworth Variation* on several occasions.

11

SMYSLOV   EUWE

(World Championship, Moscow, 1948)

In both preceding games, we have seen attempts by Black to rebel against the supremacy of the move. Nevertheless, the Ruy Lopez continues to be one of the most popular openings. It is remarkable that, after the many thousands of games played with this opening and the enormous amount of analytical research which has been devoted to it, the experts should still find new lines and fresh ideas.

1 P—K4	P—K4
2 Kt—KB3	Kt—QB3

3 B—Kt5	P—QR3
4 B—R4	Kt—B3
5 Castles	Kt×P

As mentioned before, Dr. Euwe is a great exponent of the *open defence*.

6 P—Q4	P—QKt4
7 B—Kt3	P—Q4
8 P×P	B—K3

The *normal position* in the open defence. To recapitulate the main points of the respective positions: White has an objective in Black's advanced Knight. If he concentrates on this objective, Black will have to exchange the Knight with what amounts to the loss of a *tempo*, or retire it to QB4, still further obstructing the QBP.

Black's strategic aim is to advance his QBP to the fourth and, if he can achieve this without jeopardising his centre or his K side, he will have a positional advantage in his pawn majority on the Q side.

9 Q—K2

The modern continuation. It was originally thought essential for White to play 9 P—B3, in order to preserve the KB. White's strategy then aimed at the dislodgment of Black's outpost Knight by R—K1, or Q—K2, in conjunction with B—B2 or QKt—Q2, which takes much time. However, the retreat, ... Kt—B4, delays Black's important move .... P—QB4 for some time. The text-move, which permits the exchange of the terrible "Spanish Bishop," opens up a new vista.

9 ......   Kt—B4

Other moves have been tried here, 9 .... Kt—R4; 9 .... B—QB4; and particularly 9 .... B—K2. In spite of the seeming solidity of this last move, White can try to pierce the enemy lines as shown in the following game, played by *correspondence* in 1951 between Malmgren and Cuadrado: 9 .... B—K2; 10 P—B4 (a fine attacking idea, tried for the first time in a *correspondence game*, Adam–Malmgren, in 1939. If more quietly 10 R—Q1, as played in an earlier round in the same tournament, *Moscow*, 1948, between Keres and Dr. Euwe, which continued 10 .... Castles; 11 P—B4, KtP×P; 12 B×P, etc., the best continuation is 10 .... Kt—B4; 11 P—B4, P—Q5; an effective counter-advance of the QP), 10 .... KtP×P (if 10 .... QP×P; 11 R—Q1, etc. But the greatest presence of mind is shown by 10 .... Kt—B4, e.g. 11 P×KtP, Kt×B; 12 P×Kt, P×P; 13 R×R, Q×R; 14 Q×P, Castles; and Black's counter-chances are not to be underestimated); 11 B—R4, B—Q2; 12 Kt—B3,

Kt × Kt; 13 P × Kt, Kt—R2 (preferable is 13 . . . . Castles, in order to reply to 14 P—K6, by the pretty counter, 14 . . . . Kt—Q5, which saves the situation); 14 B—B2, Q—B1; 15 B—Kt5, Q—Q1; 16 B—B6 (Bravo!), Castles; 17 Kt—Kt5, P—R3; 18 Q—R5, Kt—Kt4 (sinking into the abyss); 19 Q × P, a thunderclap which forces Black's capitulation.

10 R—Q1
This re-grouping of Queen and Rook behind the lines constitutes a complementary point to White's preceding move.

10 . . . . . .   Kt × B
Or, as played in a subsequent round of the same tournament, *Moscow*, 1948, between Keres and Reshevsky: 10 . . . . P—Kt5; 11 B—K3, Kt × B; 12 RP × Kt, Q—B1; 13 P—B4, and still White has the better position.

11 RP × Kt   Q—B1
Evading the awkward opposition of the white Rook.

12 P—B4
A thematic advance.
In a game Keres–Reshevsky, played in a preceding round of this same tournament, *Moscow*, 1948, the less consistent continuation was: 12 B—Kt5, P—R3; 13 B—R4 (13 B—K3 is preferable), 13 . . . . B—QB4; 14 Kt—B3, P—Kt4; 15 B—Kt3, Q—Kt2; 16 Kt × QP, Castles QR; 17 Kt—B6, P—KKt5; 18 Kt—K1, Kt—Q5; 19 Q—B1, P—KR4; and Black has succeeded in building up an enduring counter-attack which brought about victory.
In the present game, however, instead of the problematical gain of a pawn, Smyslov has thought out a purely *positional sacrifice* of a pawn, with the only ostensible object of bringing his Queen into a commanding position. Incidentally, this is the first tournament game in which this ingenious break-through has been tried.

12 . . . . . .   QP × P
Preferable is 12 . . . . KtP × P; 13 P × P, Kt—Kt5; declining the Greek gift.

13 P × P   B × P
If 13 . . . . P—Kt5; White can still play 14 Q—K4, and have full control of the centre as well.

14 Q—K4   Kt—K2
Now Black is thoroughly bottled up and White has full value for his pawn, which Black gives back without a struggle. Neither

14 . . . . Q—Kt2; 15 Kt—Q4, etc., nor 14 . . . . Q—K3; 15 R—Q6, etc., nor 14 . . . . Kt—Q1; 15 B—Kt5, etc., is satisfactory. He should have tried to defend himself with 14 . . . . Kt—Kt5; 15 B—Kt5, B—B4 (not 15 . . . . B—K2; 16 B × B, K × B; 17 P—QKt3, winning); 16 R—Q8 ch, Q × R; 17 B × Q, R × B; etc.

15 Kt—R3   P—QB3
If 15 . . . . B—K3; 16 Kt × P.

16 Kt × B   P × Kt
17 Q × BP   Q—Kt2
What can he do? If, for example, 17 . . . . Kt—Q4; 18 Kt—Q4, K—Q2; 19 Kt × P, with gain in material. And if 17 . . . . Q—K3; 18 Q × Q, P × Q; 19 Kt—Kt5, winning the KP.
The text-move is to offer the exchange of Queens by . . . . Q—Kt4.

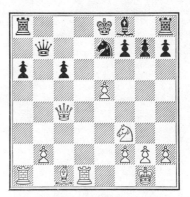

18 P—K6
A death-blow. One must admire the seemingly so simple means with which Smyslov obtains the maximum effect.

18 . . . . . .   P—B3
If 18 . . . . P × P; 19 Kt—Kt5, and Black's position is hopeless.

19 R—Q7   Q—Kt4
20 Q × Q   BP × Q
He hopes to attain a certain relief in the tension of the battle, but White gives him no time to breathe.

21 Kt—Q4
With the terrible threat, 22 Kt × P, with 23 Kt—B7, or Kt—Q6 mate.

21 . . . . . .   R—B1
The only move.

| 22 B—K3 | Kt—Kt3 |

If 22 .... Kt—B3; 23 R—QB1, Kt—K2; 24 R × Kt ch, followed by R × R:

| 23 R × RP | Kt—K4 |
| 24 R—Kt7 | B—B4 |

The Bishop arrives too late.

| 25 Kt—B5 | Castles |
| 26 P—R3 | Resigns |

A humorous finish. There is no reply to 27 B × B, followed by the doubling of Rooks on the seventh.

12

YANOFSKY   BOTVINNIK
(Groningen, 1946)

The following game is remarkable on several counts. Far from being an example of monolithic art, it is rather a jewel of many facets. Black treats the opening in superior fashion, as can be expected from that great connoisseur Botvinnik. His young adversary, the Benjamin of the tournament, Yanofsky, develops his forces a little superficially. Black's thirty-fourth move—a rare occurrence with Botvinnik—is too hasty and the whole scene changes: the "loss" of a white pawn is transformed into a deep "sacrifice"; Yanofsky harasses his great opponent and even effects on the forty-ninth move an elegant turn which brings him victory and the Brilliancy Prize.

1 P—K4	P—K4
2 Kt—KB3	Kt—QB3
3 B—Kt5	P—QR3
4 B—R4	Kt—B3
5 Castles	B—K2

The resources of this *closed defence* are many.

6 R—K1	P—QKt4
7 B—Kt3	P—Q3
8 P—B3	Castles
9 P—KR3	QKt—R4
10 B—B2	P—B4
11 P—Q4	Q—B2
12 QKt—Q2	

A well-known "book position." Against 12 P—QR4, 12 .... R—R2; can be recommended.

| 12 ...... | BP × P |

Above all, Black thus secures a base for action on the QB file. Less active is the immediate 12 .... Kt—B3; 13 P—Q5, Kt—Q1; 14 Kt—B1, Kt—K1; 15 P—KKt4,

P—Kt3; 16 B—R6, Kt—KKt2; 17 Kt—Kt3, P—B3; etc., with a long and arduous defence of a cramped position. Other tentative lines are 12 .... B—Q2; or 12 .... B—Kt2; or, again 12 .... Kt—Q2; manœuvring on inner lines (13 Kt—B1, Kt—Kt3; 14 P—QKt3, Kt—B3; 15 P—Q5, Kt—Q1; 16 P—KKt4, P—B3; 17 Kt—Kt3, Kt—B2; etc.).

| 13 P × P | Kt—B3 |
| 14 P—Q5 | |

Practically forced, for neither 14 Kt—B1, P × P; 15 B—Kt3, Q—Kt3; etc., nor 14 Kt—Kt3, P—QR4; etc., is satisfying for White.

14	Kt—QKt5
15 B—Kt1	P—QR4
16 Kt—B1	

Nonchalantly, White prepares for action on the K side, without paying overmuch attention to what happens on the opposite wing. Normally, White loses no time in chasing away the intruding Knight with 16 P—R3.

| 16 ...... | B—Q2 |
| 17 B—Q2 | KR—B1 |

If, first, 17 .... Kt—R3; 18 B—B2, KR—B1; 19 R—B1, and the localised contest for preponderance on the QB file tends to end in White's favour.

| 18 B × Kt | |

If, instead 18 P—R3, Black can already play 18 .... Kt—B7.

18	P × B
19 B—Q3	B—Q1
20 Q—Q2	Q—R4
21 Kt—K3	

Threatening to win the contested pawn by 22 Kt—B2, but Black has a fine rejoinder at his disposal.

| 21 ...... | P—Kt6 |
| 22 P—R3 | |

Neither 22 P × P, Q × R; 23 R × R, R × R ch; etc., nor 22 Q × Q, B × Q; 23 KR—Q1, P × P; 24 R × P, B—Kt3; etc., would be any better for White.

| 22 ...... | Q—R5 |
| 23 Kt—Q1 | P—Kt5 |

"Striking while the iron's hot." He threatens 24 .... R—B7; 25 B × R, P × B; 26 Kt—K3, P—Kt6; with a formidable position.

| 24 Kt—K3 | P × P |
| 25 R × P | Kt × KP |

Thanks to the patrol work of his doubled KtP, Black has effected a favourable clearance of the battlefield. Now White cannot reply 26 R × Q, because of 26 .... Kt × Q; 27 R × R, Kt × Kt ch; followed by .... R × R.

26 Q—Q1	Q—Kt5
27 R × P	Q—R5
28 B—B2	Kt—B4
29 R—B3	Q—Kt4

Instead of Black's QKtP, it is White's QKtP which is seen to be weak and exposed. White must now try to create some counterchances.

30 Q—Kt1	P—Kt3
31 R—B4	Q—Kt2
32 P—QKt4	Kt—R3
33 R × R	R × R
34 B—Q3	

The pawn cannot be saved, and White tries a diversion in the shape of a trap.

| 34 ...... | Kt × P |

Too rash. He should first play 34 .... R—Kt1; after which the contested pawn would fall of its own accord.

| 35 R—K2 | B—R4 |

This defence of the pinned Knight is scarcely economical, as the power of Black's KB is thereby impaired. By playing 35 .... R—Kt1; 36 R—Kt2, P—K5; 37 B × P, B—KB3; etc., Black could avoid much trouble.

| 36 R—Kt2 | R—Kt1 |
| 37 Kt—Q2 | |

With the threat 38 KKt—B4. Naïve would be, at once, 37 Kt—B4, Q × P.

37	Q—R2
38 Kt(Q2)—B4	Q—B4(R5)
39 Kt × B	Q × Kt
40 Kt—B2	Kt × B

The drama of the *pin* is resolved by Black's loss of the exchange.

41 R × R ch	K—Kt2
42 Kt—K3	Q—Q7
43 Q—KB1	Kt—B4

Black's QP cannot be held. He could have sought revenge on White's QP by 43 .... Kt—B5; e.g. 44 R—Q8, B—R5; 45 R × P, B—Kt6.

| 44 Q—Q1 | Q—B6 |

A less ambitious player than Botvinnik would have told himself that here the exchange of Queens would be the lesser evil.

| 45 R—Kt6 | B—R5 |
| 46 Q—B3 | Q—K8 ch |

He could have tried 46 .... Q—B8 ch; 47 K—R2, P—B4; 48 R × P, P—B5; but then White answers neither 49 Kt—B5 ch, P × Kt; 50 Q—R5, P—B6; etc., nor 49 Kt—Kt4, B—Q8 (capturing the Queen in broad daylight); but, elegantly, 49 R—Q8, P—R4; 50 P—Q6, and White must win.

| 47 K—R2 | P—B4 |
| 48 R × P | P—B5 |

| 49 Kt—B5 ch | |

Forced, but also forcing.

| 49 ...... | K—B2 |

If 49 .... P × Kt; 50 Q—R5, wins.

50 Q—Kt4	Kt—K5
51 Q—R4	P × Kt
52 Q × P ch	K—K1
53 Q—Kt8 ch	Resigns

Downfall of a Colossus.

13

BRONSTEIN   PANOV
(Moscow Championship, 1946)

To be taken by surprise by a prepared variation without losing his head but, adapting himself to the new circumstance, to redress the balance and to exploit his own chances to the end—that is the mark of the great player.

1 P—K4	P—K4
2 Kt—KB3	Kt—QB3
3 B—Kt5	P—QR3
4 B—R4	Kt—B3

5 Castles	B—K2
6 R—K1	P—QKt4
7 B—Kt3	P—Q3
8 P—B3	Castles

"Castle first and philosophise afterwards." This principle may be too sweeping, but its neglect brought about an early catastrophe in the following *correspondence game* played in 1951 between Gracs and R. Berger: 8 .... Kt—QR4; 9 B—B2, B—Kt2 (Black thinks he can immediately solve the problem of his QB. The reasoned continuation of the *Tchigorin system* is 9 .... P—B4; 10 P—Q4, Q—B2, etc.); 10 P—Q4, P—Q4 (too venturesome); 11 Kt×P, Kt×P; 12 Kt—Q2, Kt—KB3 (if 12 .... P—KB4; 13 Q—R5 ch, P—Kt3; 14 Kt×P, Kt—KB3; 15 Kt×B dis ch, Kt×Q; 16 Kt—B6 dis ch, and wins); 13 Kt—B1, Castles; 14 Kt—Kt3, Kt—K1; 15 Q—Q3, P—Kt3; 16 B—R6, Kt—Kt2; 17 B×Kt, K×B; 18 Kt—B5 ch (brilliant), 18 .... K—B3 (if 18 .... P×Kt; 19 Q×BP, is decisive, or 18 .... K—Kt1; 19 Kt×B ch, Q×Kt; 20 Kt×KtP, etc.); 19 Kt—Kt4 ch, K—Kt4; 20 Q—K3 ch, followed by mate in two.

9 P—KR3	QKt—R4
10 B—B2	P—B4
11 P—Q4	Q—B2
12 QKt—Q2	B—Kt2

The development of Black's Bishop at QKt2 in this variation was refuted by Teichmann in two memorable games against Schlechter and Rubinstein, *Carlsbad*, 1911. But the positions were rather different, for Teichmann in both cases played P—Q3, and not P—Q4, and against Rubinstein he played P—KR3, much later and against Schlechter not at all. The principle, nevertheless, remains the same, and in both the games mentioned a white Knight eventually landed on KB5 with devastating effect. It will be seen in this game that Black was aware of this, but *a new idea* underlies the Bishop's move.

13 Kt—B1
Continuing on his way. For 13 P—Q5, see the next game.

13	BP×P
14 P×P	QR—B1
15 B—Q3	

This reply, natural as it appears, has the drawback of obstructing the Q file, which enables his opponent to disorganise the centre. Doubtful also is 15 B—Kt1, and even against 15 R—K2, which strengthens the second rank, Black can effect, as in the present game, the counter-thrust ....

P—Q4; e.g. 15 R—K2, P—Q4; 16 QP×P, Kt×P; 17 Kt—Kt3, P—B4; 18 P×P e.p., B×P; etc., or 16 KP×P, P×P (if 16 .... P—K5; 17 Kt—Kt5); 17 Kt×P, Kt×P, etc., with equality. After 15 Kt—K3, there can follow 15 .... Kt×P; 16 Kt—B5, Q×B; 17 Kt×B ch, K—R1; 18 Q×Q (or 18 Kt×R, Q×BP ch, followed by .... R×Kt, with advantage to Black), 18 .... R×Q; 19 P×P, P×P; 20 Kt×P, P—B3; and Black has the initiative.

15 ......   P—Q4
This counter-idea is due to Panov himself. It is a complement to Black's twelfth move, and extends the range of his QB on the long White diagonal.

16 QP×P
A crucial moment. The main complication occurs when White plays 16 KP×P, e.g. 16 .... P—K5 (a pawn sacrifice which White must accept); 17 B×KP, Kt×B; 18 R×Kt, Kt×P; 19 R—K1, Q—Kt2 (if 19 .... B—KB3; 20 Kt—K3, etc. A very useful preparatory measure here is at once 19 .... KR—Q1; 20 Kt—K5, Q—Kt2, etc.); 20 B—B4, KR—Q1; and Black develops some energetic counter-play (Verlinsky–Panov, *Moscow*, 1945). On the other hand, if 16 Kt×P, P×P; Black gains space.

Bronstein recognises all these dangers and, while renouncing the gain of a pawn, engages in an open battle in the centre.

16 ......   Kt×P
17 Kt—Kt3
Not 17 Kt—K3, because of 17 .... KR—Q1.

17 ......   KR—Q1
The aim of reinforcing the advanced Knight could be attained in a far more concentrated manner with 17 .... P—B4; e.g. 18 P×P e.p., B×P (with enduring counter-play on widely open terrain). Psychologically, it can be said that Bronstein's reply (16 QP×P, in place of 16 KP×P) took his opponent by surprise and upset his plans.

18 Q—K2   B—Kt5
Now it is too late for .... P—B4; because Black's KB would be attacked twice after 19 P×P e.p., Kt×P(B3).

19 R—B1   Q—B3
He strives with all his forces to maintain his Kt at K5, but White's brilliant reply forces the position, frees the centre and opens the flood-gates of his direct attack.

20 Kt—Kt5	Kt × Kt(Kt5)
21 B × Kt	R—K1
22 Q—Kt4	

This brings the Queen into a commanding position, taking advantage of the unprotected position of Black's KB and Kt.

22	B—B1

For, if 22 .... R × P; 23 Q × B, R × B; 24 Q × Kt, P—Q5; 25 B—K4, and wins.

23 QR—B1	Q—QKt3
24 Kt—R5	R × R
25 R × R	Q—K3

If 25 .... R × P; 26 Kt—B6 ch, K—R1; 27 Kt—Q7. In one way or another Black must lose material.

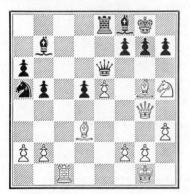

26 B—B5

A tremendous deployment of force in front of the hostile King. Note how the square KB5 has come into its own.

To be objective, however, it must be said that, according to M. Andor, a Parisian amateur, White, instead of merely gaining material, could already undertake the final assault and overrun the enemy lines with 26 B × P ch, e.g. 26 .... K × B; 27 Q—KR4 (more precise than at once 27 Kt—B6 ch), 27 .... K—Kt1; 28 Kt—B6 ch, P × Kt; 29 B × P, B—Kt2; 30 Q—Kt5, forcing mate at KKt7, or 26 .... K—R1; 27 Q—KR4, Q × KP; 28 Kt—B6, Q × B; 29 Q × Q, P × Kt; 30 Q × P ch, B—Kt2; 31 Q—R4, winning easily.

26	Q × P
27 Kt—B6 ch	K—R1
28 P—B4	

He is not content with the simple and immediate gain of the exchange by 28 Kt × R, Q × Kt; 29 B—B8, etc. He prefers to drive the Queen away from the Bishop, the threat being, e.g. 28 .... Q—K6 ch; 29 K—R2, Q × R; 30 Q—R5,

P—R3; 31 Q × P, P × B; 32 Q—R5, or Q—Kt8 mate, or 28 .... Q—Q5 ch; 29 K—R2, P × Kt; 30 Q—R5, P—R3; 31 Q × P, etc.

28	Q—K7

He avoids the trap and prefers a slow death.

29 Kt × R	Q × Kt
30 Q—R4	P—R3
31 R—K1	Q—B3

Or 31 .... B—B4 ch; 32 K—R2, Q—B3; 33 B—B6, K—Kt1 (not 33 .... Q × B; 34 R—K8 ch, nor 33 .... P × B; 34 Q × RP ch, nor 33 .... B—KB1; 34 Q × P ch, followed by mate); 34 B—B3, winning.

32 B—K7	B—B1
33 KB × B	Q × B
34 B × B	Q × B
35 Q—K7	K—Kt1
36 Q—Q7	Q—B4 ch
37 K—R2	Kt—B5
38 R—K8 ch	K—R2
39 Q—B5 ch	Resigns

The square KB5 at the last.

14

ALEXANDER   PACHMAN
(Zonal Tournament, Hilversum, 1947)

The winner in the following game, which gained the first Brilliancy Prize, is known as the scourge of Continental champions.

1 P—K4	P—K4
2 Kt—KB3	Kt—QB3
3 B—Kt5	P—QR3
4 B—R4	Kt—B3
5 Castles	B—K2
6 R—K1	P—QKt4
7 B—Kt3	P—Q3
8 P—B3	Castles
9 P—KR3	Kt—QR4
10 B—B2	P—B4
11 P—Q4	Q—B2
12 QKt—Q2	B—Kt2

A similar idea is to play first 12 .... BP × P; 13 P × P, and now, instead of 13 .... Kt—B3 (or 13 .... B—Q2); the fianchetto development, 13 .... B—Kt2; e.g. 14 P—Q5, B—B1; 15 Kt—B1, B—Q2; 16 B—K3, QR—B1 (or 16 .... KR—B1; 17 R—B1, Q—Kt2, etc.); 17 R—B1, Q—Kt1; etc., or 14 Kt—B1, QR—B1; etc., as in the preceding game.

13 P—Q5

It was one of Steinitz's axioms that the centre must be unassailable or fixed before an effective attack on the wings can be undertaken. This explains the text-move.

13 ......   B—B1

Black's plan is clear. He wanted White to lock up the centre, and hoped, with the QB on its original square, to resume his development, and if possible, to open up his game with .... P—KB4. But in effect White has received, as a gift, two *tempi* for his pending K side attack.

14 Kt—B1   R—K1
15 K—R2

In a game Boleslavsky–Smyslov, *Warsaw*, 1947, the white King retired to KR1. The positions were soon equalised.

15 ......   P—Kt3
16 Kt—K3   B—B1
17 P—KKt4

A style of attack well-known in this opening.

17 ......   B—KKt2
18 R—KKt1   K—R1
19 Kt—Kt5   R—B1
20 P—KR4   Kt—Kt1
21 Q—K2   B—Q2

Preferable is 21 .... P—R3.

22 B—Q2   Kt—K2

Both sides have proceeded according to plan, but, whereas Black could now play the desired .... P—B4; White seems to be debarred from playing Kt—B5, by Black's pawn at KKt3. However, Black should play 22 .... P—R3.

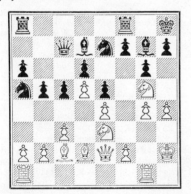

23 Kt—B5

A brilliant vindication of his strategy, which leads to beautiful and varied play.

Once again, this famous square is playing the star rôle.

23 ......   P×Kt

The first capture in the game. Capturing with the Bishop or Knight would expose Black to the same dangers on the KKt file, without any material compensation.

24 KtP×P   P—B3
25 Kt×P

A thunderclap. Had Black played 24 .... P—R3; White also sacrifices by capturing the BP; e.g. 24 .... P—R3; 25 Kt×P ch, R×Kt; 26 Q—R5, R—B3; 27 R×B, B—K1; 28 Q—Kt4, B—B2; 29 R—KKt1, and wins (29 .... R—KKt1; 30 R×R ch, and mate at Kt7, or 29 .... Kt—Kt1; 30 R—R7 ch, and mate at Kt7).

25 ......   B—K1
26 R×B

A third sacrifice!

26 ......   K×R
27 Kt×R   K×Kt
28 B—R6 ch   K—B2
29 Q—R5 ch

Here 29 R—KKt1, would have shortened Black's agony.

29 ......   Kt—Kt3

A sad necessity; he must close the terrible KKt file; the rest needs no comment.

30 P×Kt ch   K—Kt1
31 Q—B5   Q—K2
32 R—KKt1   Kt—B5
33 B—B1   B—Q2
34 Q—B3   R—KB1
35 P—Kt3   Kt—Kt3
36 P—R5   P—B4
37 B—Kt5   P×P
38 Q—K2   Q—K1
39 B×P   B—B4
40 B—R6   R—B3
41 Q—B3   Resigns

(41 .... Q—Q2; 42 R—Kt5.)

15

BRONSTEIN   KERES
(World Championship Candidates' Tournament, Budapest, 1950)

The following beautiful game had a dramatic background. Pitted against one of the strongest players of the time, Bronstein had to play for a win, for only thus could he equal the score of the tournament leader, Boleslavsky. The resulting tie match was won ·by him and enabled him to challenge Botvinnik for the Championship of the World.

1	P—K4	P—K4
2	Kt—KB3	Kt—QB3
3	B—Kt5	P—QR3
4	B—R4	Kt—B3
5	Castles	B—K2
6	R—K1	P—QKt4
7	B—Kt3	Castles
8	P—Q4	

He deliberately engages in a far more exigent line than the ordinary 8 P—B3, P—Q3; 9 P—KR3.

8 ......   P—Q3
Neither 8 .... Kt×QP; 9 B×P ch, followed by Kt×P; nor 8 .... P×P; 9 P—K5, etc., is satisfactory.

9 P—B3
The *coup juste.* If 9 P×P, P×P; 10 Q—K2, B—QB4; Black has a very good game, as is also the case after 9 Kt—B3, Kt—QR4.

9 ......   B—Kt5
Black wishes to solve the problem of his awkward QB. If first 9 .... P×P; 10 P×P, and now only 10 .... B—Kt5; there follows (as was demonstrated in a neo-classical game Dr. Lasker–Bogoljubow, *Mährisch-Ostrau*, 1923) 11 Kt—B3, and White has the better centre.

10 P—KR3
A critical moment. Having had the choice of several moves, Bronstein unhesitatingly chooses the most courageous (and incidentally, the least analysed).
The other possibilities are: 10 P—Q5, the most solid; 10 B—Q5, interesting; 10 B—K3, weak; 10 P×P, flabby; 10 P—QR4, troublesome.

10 ......   B×Kt
If 10 .... B—R4; there follows already, and the more tellingly 11 P—Q5, Kt—QR4; 12 B—B2, etc.

11 Q×B
A momentous decision. He avoids the ambiguous continuation 11 P×B, Kt—QR4; 12 P—KB4, Kt×B; 13 P×Kt, P—Q4; 14 BP×P, Kt×P; 15 P—B3, Kt—Kt6; 16 B—B4, Kt—B4; etc., and selects one even more tenebrous.

11 ......   P×P

12 Q—Q1
Thus White has "defended" his QP quite simply by abandoning it. He relies on the resulting practical chances, without troubling over-much whether this "sacrifice" will prove entirely sound in the light of subsequent analysis.

12 ......   P×P
13 Kt×P   Kt—QR4
14 B—B2   R—K1
And already Black hesitates to pursue his positional and material advantage on the Q side, by playing 14 .... P—B4; followed by .... P—B5; and eventually .... Kt—B3. Instead of this, he conceives a rather meticulous plan for taking purely defensive measures on the K side.

15 P—B4   P—Kt5
He tries to bring about liquidation, but disarranges his pawn phalanx. One would rather expect 15 .... B—B1.

16 Kt—Q5   Kt×Kt
17 Q×Kt   P—B3
18 Q—Q3   P—Kt3
A necessary weakening of the black King's field.

19 K—R1   B—B1
20 R—B1
Setting up again a base for action on the KB file.

20 ......   B—Kt2
21 B—Q2
Strategy of pinpricks on the Q side, preparing for more serious blows on the opposite wing.

21 ......   P—QB4
Having, on the sixteenth move exchanged his defensive Knight, he does not now wish to let go his defensive Bishop as well, or he might have preferred the following transaction: 21 .... B×P; 22 QR—Kt1, B—B6; 23 B×B, P×B; 24 Q×BP, Q—B2; and in spite of weak points in his forma.ion, Black has defensive chances, for his extra pawn represents some compensation.

22 B—R4   R—KB1
23 QR—Kt1   Q—Kt3
A distant expedition. The counter-measure 23 .... P—B4; is possible, but White would have continued his destructive work on the Q side with 24 P—R3, etc.

24 P—B5   B—Q5
25 Q—KKt3
Premature would be 25 P—B6, because of the counter-stroke, 25 .... P—Q4; but now

White already threatens 26 P—B6, and if then 26 .... P—Q4; 27 P—K5, Kt—B5; 28 B—B4, etc.

25	Kt—B5
26 B—R6	B—Kt2

The future is dark for Black. The lesser evil is the sacrifice the exchange by 26 .... B×P; etc.

27 B×B	K×B
28 P—B6 ch	K—R1

The King is in trouble.

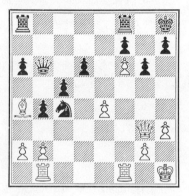

29 Q—Kt5

The final assault on the enemy fortress oegins. White's terrible threat is now R—B4, followed by Q—R6. Inaccurate would be 29 R—B4, at once, because 29 .... P—Kt4; would have eased Black's defence.

29 ......   P—Kt6

There is no saving clause. If 29 .... R—KKt1; 30 R—B4, Q—Q1; 31 R—R4, Q—KB1; 32 R—R6, with the pitiless sequel, 33 Q—R4.

30 P×P

He could already realise the main variation: 30 R—B4, P×P; 31 Q—R6, P×R(Q) ch; 32 K—R2, R—KKt1; 33 Q×P ch, K×Q; 34 R—R4 mate.

30	Q—Kt5
31 P×Kt	Q×B
32 R—B4	Q—B7
33 Q—R6	Resigns

For again, after a "spite check" by 33 .... Q×R ch; 34 K—R2, mate at KKt7 or KR7 is unavoidable.

16

KUPPE   RAUTENBERG
(Weidenau, 1947)

The spirit of attack for ever seeks—and finds—for Black, enterprising variations rich in practical chances and able to stand up even to analytical investigation.

1 P—K4	P—K4
2 Kt—KB3	Kt—QB3
3 B—Kt5	P—QR3
4 B—R4	Kt—B3
5 Castles	B—K2
6 R—K1	P—QKt4
7 B—Kt3	Castles

Reserving the option of advancing the QP one or two squares.

8 P—B3

He has no objections to Black's intentions, or he could have played (as in the preceding game) 8 P—Q4, P—Q3; 9 P—B3, B—Kt5.

Less good is 8 P—QR4, because of 8 .... B—Kt2. On the other hand, in a game Broadbent–Alexander, *Buxton*, 1950, White as a good psychologist, played the modest little move 8 P—Q3, trying successfully to nip his spirited antagonist's plans in the bud. Another sort of "anti-Marshall" continuation could be 8 P—KR3, still reserving the choice between P—Q4 and P—Q3.

8 ......   P—Q4

Or 8 .... P—Q3; with an ordinary normal development.

9 P×P

Accepting the challenge. The following might be termed the "Marshall Gambit Declined": 9 P—Q4, KKt×P; 10 P×P, B—K3; reverting to known variants of the open defence.

9 ......   Kt×P

A sort of intensified *Marshall Gambit* is here 9 .... P—K5. This attempt is met by 10 P×Kt, P×Kt; 11 P—Q4, P×P; 12 Q—B3, etc.

10 Kt×P	Kt×Kt
11 R×Kt	P—QB3

A modernised form of this Gambit, instead of 11 .... Kt—B3; played in the original game Capablanca–Marshall, *New York*, 1918.

12 R—K1

Or first 12 P—Q4, B—Q3; 13 R—K1, etc. Other defensive systems have been suggested, e.g. 12 B×Kt, P×B; 13 P—Q4, B—Q3;

14 R—K3, etc., or 12 Q—B1, B—Q3; 13 R—K1, Q—R5; 14 P—Kt3, Q—R4; 15 P—Q4, B—KKt5; 16 B—K3, etc., but Black will always have some attack for the pawn sacrificed.

12 ......   B—Q3
13 P—Q4

After 13 P—Q3, Black would follow the same scheme: 13 .... Q—R5; 14 P—Kt3, Q—R6; 15 B×Kt, P×B; 16 Q—B3, B—KKt5 (not 16 .... B—KB4; 17 B—B4); 17 Q—Kt2, Q—R4; and Black's pressure continues.

13 ......   Q—R5
14 P—Kt3

If 14 P—KR3, B×P.

14 ......   Q—R6
15 B—B2

At this critical moment, White dawdles instead of taking concrete precautionary measures. But wrong would be 15 R—K4, P—Kt4; 16 B×P, Q—B4; and Black wins a piece. Laborious would be 15 Q—B3, B—KKt5; 16 Q—Kt2, Q—R4; 17 B—K3, B—B6; 18 Q—B1, P—KB4; and this renewed activity gives Black equal chances.

More agile is the white Queen in the following variation: 15 Q—Q3, B—KB4; 16 Q—B1, reaching this important square in two *tempi* instead of three; nevertheless equality is again reached after 16 .... Q—Kt5; 17 B—K3, P—KR4; 18 Kt—Q2, P—R5; 19 B—Q1, Q—Kt3; etc. As the best solution, the following can be recommended for White: 15 B×Kt, P×B; 16 B—K3 (instead of 16 Q—Q3, B—KB4; 17 Q—B1, etc.), 16 .... P—KR4 (or 16 .... B—KKt5; 17 Q—Q3, or 16 .... B—KB4; 17 Kt—Q2, etc.); 17 Q—B3, P—R5; 18 Kt—Q2, and White has at least mobilised his reserves with some hope of holding the position.

15 ......   B—KKt5
16 Q—Q3   QR—K1

The concentration of the Black forces becomes overwhelming.

17 B—K3   P—KB4
18 Q—B1

If 18 P—KB4, B—B6; wins a piece. (19 Q—Q2, R×B; 20 R×R, Kt×R; etc. It is now seen that an early exchange, 15 B×Kt, etc., or even 12 B×Kt, etc., would have been justified.

18 ......   Q—R4
19 P—QB4

A vain attempt to counter the enemy's intentions. But 19 Kt—Q2, or even 19 B—Kt3, is answered in the same trenchant manner.

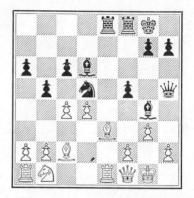

19 ......   P—B5

Black's assault is in full swing. The point of this advance is revealed on the next move.

20 P×Kt   KBP×P

Not 20 .... P×B; 21 P—B4, although even then White's position remains critical after 21 .... P—Kt4.

21 RP×P

After 21 Q—Kt2, there follows ruthlessly 21 .... P×RP ch; 22 K—R1, B—B6; winning the Queen.

21 ......   B—B6
Resigns

17

SIR G. THOMAS   G. WOOD
(Harrogate, 1947)

One is as old as one's nerves. In the following superb game (which won a brilliancy prize) the nerves of that glorious veteran, Sir George Thomas, are intact. The tension of the battle is brought to its maximum, after which the decision is reached by a devastating attack.

1 P—K4   P—K4
2 Kt—KB3   Kt—QB3
3 B—Kt5   P—QR3
4 B—R4   Kt—B3
5 Q—K2

The *Worrall Attack* one move ahead of time. It is usual to castle before playing the text-move.

5 ......   P—QKt4

This would be a good opportunity to play more actively 5 .... B—B4; as did Alekhine against Sir George Thomas, *Margate*, 1937. The text-move is, of course, quite sound.

6 B—Kt3   B—K2
7 P—B3   Castles
8 Castles   P—Q3

On 8 .... P—Q4; White need not embark on adventure by 9 P × P, B—KKt5; 10 P × Kt, P—K5; etc., for he can restrain Black's momentum.

9 P—Q4   P × P

Since the basic idea of the *Ruy Lopez* is to exert sustained pressure on the centre, Black should refrain as long as possible from liquidation. Otherwise White is in a favourable position for a King's side attack. That is why counter-action by 9 .... B—Kt5; is justified.

10 Kt × P

If 10 P × P, B—Kt5; would already have more concrete aims (control of White's Q4).

10 ......   Kt—QR4
11 B—B2   P—B4
12 Kt—B5

Less ambitious would be the retrogressive 12 Kt—B3. Note how the dissolution of Black's centre has benefited White. KB5 is a notoriously strong point for a white Knight in the *Ruy Lopez*. Black cannot afford to drive it away by .... P—Kt3; weakening his King's field. If he captures the Knight, White is well set for an advance of his K side pawns. Best would be to leave it alone for the time being by playing 12 .... R—K1; getting the Rook into play and threatening .... B—B1.

12 ......   B × Kt
13 P × B   P—Q4

Black starts a counter-demonstration on the Q side, where he has a pawn majority, quite a sound idea which fails only by reason of White's masterly handling of his K side pawns.

14 P—KKt4   P—R3

This is fundamentally unsound. White's P—Kt5, cannot be prevented, and so the text-move provides an additional target.

Better again is 14 .... R—K1; followed by B—Q3.

15 P—KB4

It is seldom possible to leave one's own King's position so bare without fear of consequences.

15 ......   R—K1
16 Q—Kt2   Q—Kt3
17 Kt—Q2   QR—Q1
18 P—Kt5   Kt—R2
19 Kt—B3

Splendid restraint. If 19 P × P, Q × P.

19 ......   P—Q5
20 P—B6   B—B1
21 Kt—K5   · Kt × KtP
22 P × Kt   R × Kt

The moment for big decisions has arrived. Black threatens 23 .... P—Q6.

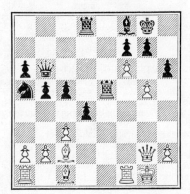

23 P—Kt6

The beginning of a most attractive combination, e.g. 23 .... KtP × P; 24 P × P db ch, K × P; 25 Q—Kt6 ch, K—K2; 26 Q—R7 ch, K—K3; 27 R × P ch, K × R; 28 Q—Kt6 ch, etc., or 23 .... BP × P; 24 Q × P, P—Q6; 25 P—B7 ch, again winning the Queen.

23 ......   P—Q6

Black seems to say, "Kismet."

24 P × P ch   K—R2
25 B × P ch   R × B
26 P × P   P—B5 dis ch
27 K—R1   B × P
28 Q × B ch   K × Q
29 P—B8(Q) ch   K—R2
30 R—B7 ch   K—Kt3
31 R—Kt7 ch   K—R4
32 Q—B7 ch   K—R5
33 Q—B4 ch   Resigns

18

KIRILOV   FURMAN
(U.S.S.R. Championship, 1949)

*The soundest opening, if treated super-
ficially, can give Black a chance to develop
his latent powers.*

1 P—K4	P—K4
2 Kt—KB3	Kt—QB3
3 B—Kt5	P—QR3
4 B—R4	Kt—B3
5 Q—K2	P—QKt4
6 B—Kt3	B—K2
7 P—QR4	

As the Black pieces are placed on inner
lines and Black has not yet played ....
P—Q3; this move is ineffective.

| 7 ...... | P—Kt5 |
| 8 B—Q5 | |

Beating the air. White has nothing better
than 8 P—Q3, followed by the time-honoured
manœuvre QKt—Q2—B1—K3 or Kt3.

8	Kt × B
9 P × Kt	Kt—Q5
10 Kt × Kt	P × Kt
11 Castles	

Better is 11 Q—K4, which attacks the
QP, but also threatens to win by P—Q6.
Worthy of consideration is 11 P—Q6, at
once, forcing the trebling of Black's QP,
followed by 12 P—Q3.

11	Castles
12 Q—B4	P—QB4
13 P × P e.p.	P × P
14 Q × BP	

Now White has won a pawn, but at the
expense of his development.

14	R—R2
15 Q—KB3	R—B2
16 P—Q3	B—Kt2

He is wise in not taking the pawn, which
would yield White an important *tempo* for
the development of his forces. If 16 ....
R × P; 17 Kt—Q2 (threatening 18 Kt—B4),
17 .... B—K3; 18 Q—Q1, and White gets
his pieces out.

17 Q—Q1	B—Q3
18 Kt—Q2	R—K1
19 Kt—B4	

This permits the famous *Two Bishops'
Sacrifice*, known through the games Lasker–
Bauer, *Amsterdam*, 1889, Nimsowitsch–
Tarrasch, *St. Petersburg*, 1914, Alekhine–
Drewitt, *Portsmouth*, 1924, and others.

However, even after 19 Kt—B3, he could
scarcely save the game: 19 .... Q—B3;

20 R—K1, R × R ch; 21 Q × R, R—K2;
22 Q—Q1, B × Kt; 23 P × B, Q—Kt3 ch;
24 K—R1, Q—R4; 25 Q—Kt1, R—K8;
knocking out his adversary.

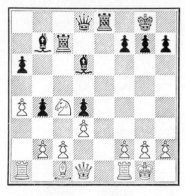

19	B × P ch
20 K × B	Q—R5 ch
21 K—Kt1	B × P

The *Two Bishops' Sacrifice*. The student
should be familiar with the conditions in
which it is likely to be sound: the defending
King must be exposed and his pieces not
readily available for defence. The attacker's
Rooks must serve a double purpose: to
prevent the King's escape to the other
wing and to take part in the final stages of
the attack without any loss of time. All
these premises obtain here in ideal fashion.

22 K × B	R—B3
23 B—B4	Q × B
24 R—R1	R—B3
25 R—KR2	R—Kt3 ch
Resigns	

For after 26 K—R1, R—K8 ch; 27 Q × R,
Q—B6 ch; is conclusive.
An exhilarating finale.

19

BRODERMAN   EDWARD LASKER
(Havana, 1950)

*The following game illustrates a well-
known fault, which occurs from time to time.
The Queen's great mobility is an incitement
to various expeditions: once the Queen strays
too far from the battlefield, it is not surprising
if the King's position collapses.*

| 1 P—K4 | P—K4 |
| 2 Kt—KB3 | Kt—QB3 |

3 B—Kt5	P—QR3
4 B—R4	Kt—B3
5 P—Q4	

A sidelight from history; this primitive continuation (at one time preferred by Morphy) has in our time experienced an intense revival, and was even "re-exported" to Europe by Reshevsky, as a "secret weapon" for the Olympiad at Dubrovnik in 1950. It also appears in a deferred form, as follows: 5 Castles, B—K2, and now, instead of the usual 6 R—K1, the proud advance in the centre, 6 P—Q4.

| 5 ...... | P×P |

Or 5 .... Kt×KP; 6 Castles, etc., leading into variations of the open defence. Of doubtful value is 5 .... Kt×QP.

6 Castles

Feasible is also, at once: 6 P—K5, Kt—K5; 7 Kt×P, etc. Less energetic is 6 Q—K2, here or on the next move.

| 6 ...... | B—K2 |

Too restless is first 6 .... P—QKt4; 7 B—Kt3, B—K2. Against 6 .... B—B4; White also secures the superiority in the centre by 7 P—K5, Kt—K5; 8 P—B3, etc.

7 R—K1

White prefers to complete some final preparations instead of playing out his trumps forthwith by 7 P—K5, Kt—K5; with the following continuations:
(a) 8 R—K1, Kt—B4; 9 B×Kt (or, more impetuously, 9 Kt×P, Kt×B; 10 Kt—B5, Castles; 11 Q—Kt4, P—KKt3; etc.); 9 .... QP×B; 10 Kt×P, etc.
(b) 8 Kt×P, Kt—B4; 9 Kt—B5 (this offer secures a fine attack for White, while simplification by 9 B×Kt, QP×B; 10 QKt—B3, Castles; leads to equality), 9 .... Castles (this wise decision was already applied in a game Zukertort–Mackenzie, London, 1883. Neither 9 .... Kt×B; 10 Kt×P ch, K—B1; 11 B—R6, K—Kt1; 12 Q—Kt4, etc., nor 9 .... B—B1; 10 R—K1, with the fine threat 11 Kt—Q6 ch, etc., is playable for Black); 10 Q—Kt4, P—KKt3; 11 B×Kt, QP×B; 12 Kt×B ch, Q×Kt; 13 Q—Kt3, and White maintains the pressure.

| 7 ...... | P—QKt4 |

If 7 .... P—Q3; White still plays 8 P—K5 (e.g. 8 .... Kt—KKt5; 9 Kt×P, etc.), with advantage to White. With the text-move, Black tries to utilise the respite afforded him in forestalling the various threats, and, if 8 B—Kt3, P—Q3; 9 P—KR3, Castles, etc., to lead the contest into smoother waters.

But White tries to prevent all this.

8 P—K5

Complications in the centre. The *Ruy Lopez* is astoundingly rich in alternative continuations.

| 8 ...... | Kt×P |

Little good comes of 8 .... P×B; 9 P×Kt, P×P; 10 Kt×P, etc., or 8 .... Kt—Q4; 9 B—Kt3, Kt—Kt3; 10 P—B3, etc., and White possesses a comfortable initiative.

9 Kt×Kt

The subtleties of 9 R×Kt, are well illustrated in the following brevity played in a match Wade–Schmid, *Bamberg*, 1950: 9 R×Kt, P×B (the right move is first 9 .... P—Q3; e.g. 10 R—K1, P×B; 11 Kt×P, B—Q2, etc., or, as in a game Reshevsky–Euwe, *Dubrovnik*, 1950, 10 R—Kt5, P×B; 11 R×P, Kt—R4; 12 R—Kt5, B×R; 13 B×B, P—KB3; 14 Kt×P, Castles, and Black emerged in the end the exchange to the good, and the American had to exert all his skill to escape with a draw); 10 Kt×P, Castles; 11 Kt—B5, R—K1; 12 B—Kt5, Kt—Q4 (the lesser evil is 12 .... P—Q3); 13 Kt×P (brilliant), 13 .... K×Kt; 14 Q×Kt, P—QB3; 15 Q—Q4, P—B3; 16 R—K3, P—B4; 17 B—R6 ch, K×B; 18 Q—KKt4, P—B4; 19 R—R3 ch, Black resigns.

A fine performance by the New Zealander.

| 9 ...... | P×B |
| 10 Q×P | R—QKt1 |

The text-move is an innovation. By playing the Rook thus early to the QKt file, Black gains a *tempo*, for White must provide against .... R—Kt5.

The continuation in a game Reshevsky–Unzicker, *Dubrovnik*, 1950, was: 10 .... Castles; 11 Q×RP, R—Kt1; 12 Kt—Q3, Kt—Q4; 13 B—Q2, B—B3; 14 Kt—R3, P—Q3; 15 Q—R5, B—Kt2; 16 P—QB4, Kt—Kt3; 17 Q—KB5, Kt—R5; 18 QR—Kt1, etc., with tactical complications which led to a draw.

11 P—QR3

This precautionary measure is a waste of time. Better is 11 Kt—Q3, guarding not only the square QKt4, but in addition the QKtP.

11	Castles
12 Q×RP	R—K1
13 R—Q1	

An instructive mistake. One should never make a threat which the opponent can parry with a developing move. The threat 14 Kt—B6, looks attractive, but to make it he has to move the Rook twice, and that after the Queen also has used up two *tempi* already. Better is 13 QKt—B3.

| 13 ...... | R—Kt3 |
| 14 QKt—B3 | |

If 14 B—K3, P—B4.

| 14 ...... | P—Q3 |
| 15 Kt—Q5 | |

This "threat," as was the one before, is a little crude (15 .... P×Kt; 16 Kt×Kt ch, etc.). Observe how Black meets the threat and then proceeds to exact penalties in many *tempi* lost by White.

15	Kt×Kt
16 R×Kt	B—B3
17 Kt—Q3	B—Kt2
18 R—KR5	R—K5
19 P—QB4	Q—K2
20 B—K3	

Since move fifteen, White has been continuously on the retreat, and now the time has come for Black to strike a heavy blow.

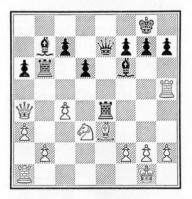

20	R×B
21 P×R	Q×P ch
22 Kt—B2	

If 22 K—R1, P—Kt3 (necessary to give his King breathing space); 23 R—K1 (a desperate attempt to save the situation, for neither 23 R—R5, Q×Kt nor 23 R—R3, Q×R is playable), 23 .... Q×Kt; 24 Q—K8 ch, K—Kt2; 25 R×P ch, K×R; 26 Q×P ch, B—Kt2; and White is lost.

| 22 ...... | R×P |
| 23 R—KB1 | B—Q5 |

With the threat 24 .... Q×Kt ch; 25 R×Q, R—Kt8 ch.

| 24 R—KB5 | Q—K5 |
| 25 R—B3 | R×Kt |

Resigns

For if 26 R(B3)×R, Q×P mate, and if 26 R(B1)×R, Q—K8 mate.

An entertaining game.

20

BROADBENT   AITKEN

(London, 1948)

There is no need to despair of contemporary style, nor the future of chess, as long as memorable games such as the following are produced.

1 P—K4	P—K4
2 Kt—KB3	Kt—QB3
3 B—Kt5	P—QR3
4 B—R4	P—Q3

In this variation, the *Steinitz Defence Deferred*, the idea of Black's sustaining his K4 shows the greatest vitality. Having prepared the repulse of the aggressor Bishop, Black avoids many drawbacks of the *Steinitz Defence* proper: 3 .... P—Q3 (4 P—Q4, etc.). Again, in what might be termed the "Steinitz Defence twice deferred," 3 .... P—QR3; 4 B—R4, Kt—B3; 5 Castles, P—Q3; Black gives up a choice of development of his KKt at KB3 or elsewhere.

5 B×Kt ch

He tries to solve the problem set by the *Steinitz Deferred* by simplification.

| 5 ...... | P×B |
| 6 P—Q4 | P×P |

The logical answer is 6 .... P—B3; preparing to hold on to his centre. However, even then Black must be prepared against the refinements of the opening, as is demonstrated by the following tragi-comic game, Feuer–O'Kelly, *Liége*, 1951: 6 .... P—B3; 7 Kt—B3, R—Kt1 (the development 7 .... P—Kt3; 8 B—K3, Kt—R3; 9 Q—Q2, Kt—B2; etc., is to be preferred); 8 Q—Q3, Kt—K2; 9 P—KR4, P—KR4; 10 B—K3, R×P (a moment of chess-blindness, rare in the Belgian champion); 11 P×P, QP×P (still chess-blind, but 11 .... BP×P; 12 Kt×P, etc., is not pleasant for Black); 12 Q×Q ch, K×Q; 13 Castles ch. Black resigns.

7 Kt×P

The situation now resembles the *Steinitz Defence* proper (3 .... P—Q3); but Black has prematurely abandoned the centre (his strong point at K4).

7 ......   P—QB4
A player full of imagination, the Scottish champion delights in experiments. The drawback of this impetuous move is that Black is practically forced to develop his Bishop at QKt2, which is the wrong diagonal. The following continuation is preferred: 7 .... B—Q2; e.g. 8 Castles, Kt—B3; 9 Q—B3, P—B4 (now necessary because of the threat 10 P—K5, P×P; 11 Kt×P); 10 Kt—B5, B×Kt; 11 P×B, B—K2; 12 Q—B6 ch, Kt—Q2; 13 Kt—B3, Castles; 14 Kt—Q5, R—R2; and Black's defence is artificial.

8 Kt—KB3
More resilient is 8 Kt—K2, e.g. 8 .... B—Kt2; 9 QKt—B3, Kt—B3; 10 Kt—Kt3, etc.

8 ......   B—Kt2
In a game Broadbent–Sergeant, *Felixstowe*, 1949, the battle-tried veteran executed a different plan of development: 8 .... B—K2; 9 Kt—B3, Kt—B3; 10 Castles, Castles; 11 Q—Q3, B—K3 (trying to make use of his Bishop on its original diagonal); 12 B—B4 (simpler is 12 P—KR3, followed by B—K3, or even P—KKt4), 12 .... Kt—R4; 13 B—K3, P—B4, and here is Black actually assuming the offensive.

9 Kt—B3   Kt—B3
10 Castles   B—K2
As long as the black King is not yet in safety, the capture of the KP (10 .... Kt×P; etc.) would clearly be reckless.

11 R—K1   Castles
12 Q—Q3
He defers 12 B—B4, because the reply 12 .... Kt—R4; would be awkward for him.

12 ......   Kt—Q2
13 B—B4   K—R1
Black pursues the wrong system. He still had a chance of retrieving the situation with 13 .... R—K1; followed by KB—B3; and Black's KB is as effective as its White counterpart.

14 QR—Q1   P—KB3
Now the KB is bottled up with little prospect of coming to life.

15 Kt—Q2

To avoid exchanges after .... Kt—K4; but also to allow P—KB4, at a later stage.

15 ......   Kt—K4
16 Q—K2   P—QR4
17 Kt—Q5   B—R3
He could not afford 17 .... B×Kt; 18 P×B, because White would have the run of the open K file and Black would have a hopelessly weak square at his K3.

18 P—B4   R—K1
19 B—Kt3   Kt—B3
20 P—B4   B—KB1
21 P—B5   B—B1
Returning to the diagonal which it should never have left. The immediate threat is 22 .... B×P; which is easily parried.

22 Q—R5
Threatening 23 Kt×QBP, Q×Kt; 24 Q×R, which accounts for Black's reply.

22 ......   R—R2
23 B—R4
Preparing for the final onslaught and also preventing .... Kt—K2.

23 ......   Kt—Kt5
This diversion does not alleviate Black's difficulties; relatively best is 23 .... Kt—K4; obstructing the centre.

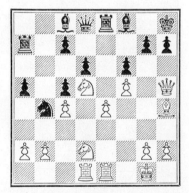

24 Kt×KBP   P×Kt
25 P—K5
The winning move, which Black tried hard to prevent. Much less effective would be 25 B×P ch, Q×B; 26 Q×R, B—Kt2; etc.

25 ......   R×P
A dramatic moment. If 25 .... B—KKt2; 26 P×BP, R×R ch; 27 R×R, etc., or 25 .... Q—Q2; 26 B×P ch, B—Kt2; 27 P—K6, Q—R5; 28 B×B ch, K×B;

29 Q—Kt5 ch, K—B1; 30 P—B6, R×P;
31 Q—Kt7 ch, K—K1; 32 R×R ch, with
an unavoidable mate by 33 Q—K7.

26 R×R   B—K2
If 26 .... QP×R; 27 Kt—K4.

27 R×B   Q×R
28 R—K1   Q—Q2
29 B×P ch   Resigns
A most impressive finish, not only on
account of its brilliance, but even more so
because it was the result of cumulative
strategy and not a fortuitous happening.

21

EUWE   KERES
(Moscow, 1948)

*The ability to create and to control the
tension of battle is perhaps the principal
attainment of the great player.*

1 P—K4   P—K4
2 Kt—KB3   Kt—QB3
3 B—Kt5   P—QR3
4 B—R4   P—Q3
5 P—B3
A violent attempt to gain space in the
centre.

5 ......   P—B4
The much-discussed *Siesta Variation*,
which has come to the fore since 1928.
Careful players prefer 5 .... B—Q2,
followed eventually by a King's fianchetto.

6 P×P
Best.

6 ......   B×P
7 P—Q4
Here 7 Castles avoids potential trouble.

7 ......   P—K5
8 Kt—Kt5
Here neither 8 Q—K2, B—K2; etc.
(Capablanca–Marshall, *fourteenth match
game*, 1909), nor 8 B—KKt5, B—K2; etc.
(A. Steiner–Capablanca, *Budapest*, 1928), has
given results satisfactory for White.

8 ......   P—Q4
This counter-idea, due to Znosko-
Borovsky, increases Black's chances. The
following are less satisfactory for the
defence: 8 .... P—R3; 9 Q—Kt3, P×Kt;
10 Q×P, etc., or 8 .... Kt—B3; 9 P—B3,
P—Q4; 10 Castles, etc.

9 P—B3
The former World Champion shows his
thorough theoretical knowledge, and his
positional advantage appears to be on the
way to consolidation.

9 ......   P—K6
A remarkable *positional sacrifice.*

10 P—KB4
An adequate reply, while 10 B×P, P—R3;
11 Kt—KR3, B×KKt; 12 P×B, Q—R5 ch;
brings the White camp into disorder.

10 ......   B—Q3
11 Q—B3
Here again 11 B×P, would lead to a fine
position for Black after 11 .... Q—K2;
12 Q—K2, Kt—B3; 13 Kt—B3 (if 13 Castles,
P—R3, to Black's advantage), 13 ....
B—KKt5; 14 QKt—Q2, Castles KR; etc.
A finesse, improving on the text-move,
would be 11 Q—R5 ch, P—Kt3; 12 Q—B3.

11 ......   Q—B3
Keres finds an improvement on the game
Horowitz–Fine, *Syracuse*, 1934, in which,
after 11 .... Q—Q2; 12 Q×P ch, Kt—K2;
13 Kt—B3, Castles KR; 14 Kt—K5, Black
had no compensation whatever for his pawn.

12 Q×P ch
Inferior to 12 B×P.

12 ......   Kt—K2
13 B×Kt ch
After the useless check, this useless exchange facilitates Black's counter-action.
The circumstances demanded the developing
move, 13 QKt—R3.

13 ......   P×B
14 Castles   Castles KR
15 Kt—Q2
In his anxiety to complete his mobilisation,
he misses the opportunity to strengthen his
position by 15 Kt—B3, followed by Kt—K5.

15 ......   Kt—Kt3
The storm-clouds gather.

16 P—KKt3   QR—K1
17 Q—B2
Note that 17 Q—B3, would lose the
Knight after 17 .... P—R3.

17 ......   B—Q6
18 R—K1   R×R ch
19 Q×R
He relies on 20 Q—K6 ch, to give him
breathing space at last.

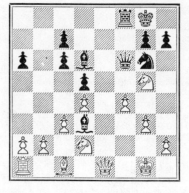

19 ......   B × P
The climax to a series of clever manœuvres.
White is overwhelmed before he is able to
complete his development.

20 P × B
If 20 Q—K6 ch, Q × Q; 21 Kt × Q,
B—K6 ch; 22 K—R1 (22 K—Kt2,
R—B7 ch), 22 .... R—B8 ch; 23 Kt × R,
B—K5 mate.

20 ......   Kt × P
21 QKt—B3   Kt—K7 ch
22 K—Kt2   P—R3
At last the Knight, unmolested for
fourteen moves, meets its fate.

23 Q—Q2   Q—B4
24 Q—K3   P × Kt
25 B—Q2   B—K5
Resigns
If 26 R—KB1, P—Kt5; and White is lost.

22

TARNOWSKI   KERES
(Szczawno Zdroj, 1950)

*In the following game Black develops the
utmost energy.*

1 P—K4   P—K4
2 Kt—KB3   Kt—QB3
3 B—Kt5   P—QR3
4 B—R4   P—Q3
5 P—B4
This move, which tries to control both
Q5 and QKt5, transfers, so to speak, to the
Steinitz Deferred an idea of Duras', which is
to be found in another variation of the *Ruy
Lopez* (3 .... P—QR3; 4 B—R4, Kt—B3;

5 P—Q3, P—Q3; 6 P—B4). Note that the
text-move was introduced by Keres himself
(against Alekhine, *Margate*, 1937), so that
the Esthonian has to contend here against
his own weapons!

5 ......   B—Q2
Here 5 .... B—Kt5; promises greater
freedom.

6 Kt—B3
White can well play 6 P—Q4, at this point.

6 ......   P—KKt3
7 P—Q4   B—Kt2
Holding the centre as far as possible.
Less judicious would be 7 .... P × P;
8 Kt × P, B—Kt2; e.g. in a game Boleslavsky–
Fine, *Radio Match, U.S.S.R. v. U.S.A.*, 1945;
9 Kt × Kt, P × Kt; 10 Castles, Kt—K2;
11 P—B5, and White succeeded in dis-
organising his opponent's forces.

8 B—K3   KKt—K2
And again 8 .... P × P; 9 Kt × P,
KKt—K2; would be injudicious, although
Black, having sufficiently supported his
QB3, can now hope for equality, e.g. Keres–
Capablanca, *Buenos Aires*, 1939: 10 Castles,
Castles; 11 P—KR3, Kt × Kt; 12 B × B,
Kt—K7 ch; 13 Kt × Kt, Q × B; 14 B—Q4,
B × B; 15 Q × B, Kt—B3; and the armistice
negotiations begin.
It is to be noted that the "flat" develop-
ment in the text is more elastic than 8 ....
Kt—B3; after which 9 P × P, P × P; 10 B—B5,
Kt—KR4; 11 Kt—Q5, etc., would hinder
the harmonious development of Black's
forces.

9 Q—Q2   Castles
10 P—KR3
As the tension in the centre cannot go on
indefinitely, 10 P × P, is preferable. The
text-move is intended to pave the way for
11 P—KKt4, but now Black himself opens
the offensive.

10 ......   P—B4
11 P × KP
He wants—but too late—to make a
clearance in the centre. Necessary is first
11 P × BP, Kt × BP; 12 P × P.

11 ......   BP × P
All of a sudden the battle is at its height.

12 Kt—KKt5
If 12 Kt × P, there follows 12 .... Kt × P;
13 B × B, Kt × Kt ch (but not 13 ....
Kt × P; 14 B—K6 ch, nor 13 .... R × Kt;

14 B—K6 ch, K—R1; 15 Kt—Kt5, etc.);
14 P×Kt, Q×B; with advantage to Black.

12	Kt×P
13 B—Kt3	Kt—Q6 ch

Driving a wedge into the hostile position.

14 K—B1	Kt—QB4
15 B—B2	Q—K1

Effecting a pressure—at present still hidden—on the K file.

15 R—Q1	Kt—B4
17 B×Kt	

He thinks he can win a piece, or at least ease the situation after 17 .... P×B; 18 Q×B, Kt—K6 ch; 19 K—Kt1, Kt×B; 20 Q×Q, QR×Q; 21 KKt×KP, etc. But Keres has reserved a little surprise for his adversary.

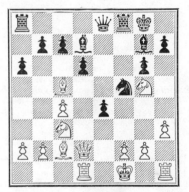

17	P—K6
18 Q—Q5 ch	K—R1
19 Kt—K2	

White notices with alarm that he cannot yet retire the QB, e.g. 19 B—R3, Kt—Kt6 ch; 20 K—Kt1, P×P ch; 21 K—R2, B—K4; 22 Kt—B3, Kt—B8 mate.

19	P×P

Without hurrying to recover his piece, Black proceeds to complete a mating net.

20 B—K4	B—QB3

If at once 20 .... P×B; White of course plays, not 21 Q×B, Kt—K6 mate, but 21 Q×BP.

21 Q—Q3	P×B
22 P—KKt4	

Or 22 B×B, Kt—K6 ch.

22	B×B
23 Kt×B	

Or 23 Q×B, Q×Q; 24 Kt×Q, Kt—K6 mate.

23	R—Q1
	Resigns

For the white Queen is attacked and cannot simultaneously defend the Rook at Q1, the Knight at K4 and the mating square K3.

An impressive victory for the black pieces.

23

P. MICHEL   ROSSETTO
(Mar del Plata, 1947)

A game in which a Queen is given up for, theoretically, insufficient material (in this case two minor pieces) will always give pleasure to beginners and experts alike.

1 P—K4	P—K4
2 Kt—KB3	Kt—QB3
3 B—Kt5	Kt—Q5

Bird's Defence, the most important and perhaps the soundest of the secondary defences. It is not generally realised that, on the third move, Black has a choice of no less than eighteen more or less acceptable replies. The three principal ones are *Morphy's Defence* (3 .... P—QR3), the *Berlin Defence* (3 .... Kt—B3), and the *Steinitz Defence* (3 .... P—Q3). All the others are more fanciful than sound.

4 Kt×Kt	P×Kt
5 Castles	P—KR4

Altogether too venturesome and quite unjustified. Normal continuations here are 5 .... P—QB3 (6 B—K2, P—KKt3; 7 P—Q3, B—Kt2; 8 P—KB4, etc.); or 5 .... P—KKt3 (6 P—Q3, B—Kt2; 7 Kt—Q2, Kt—K2; 8 P—KB4, P—QB3; 9 B—B4, P—Q4; 10 B—Kt3, etc.); or 5 .... B—B4 (6 P—Q3, Kt—K2; 7 Q—R5, B—Kt3; 8 B—Kt5, Castles; 9 Kt—Q2, etc.). As, however, all these variations give White the initiative and a comfortable game, modern tendency leans towards the more elastic 5 .... Kt—K2.

6 P—Q3	B—B4
7 Kt—Q2	P—QB3
8 B—B4	P—Q4
9 B—Kt3	K—B1

He is at least consistent. He cannot castle, but moves his King from the threatened K file (P×P and R—K1 ch) in order to keep up, for what it is worth, the attack initiated by 5 .... P—KR4.

10 P—QB4
With this fine flank attack, White vitalises the contest, whereas after 10 Kt—B3, B—KKt5; or 10 P—KB4, Kt—R3; Black could hope for a quiet life.

10 ......   P × P e.p.
11 P × BP   B—KKt5
He spends much ingenuity on an attack which, being fundamentally wrong, must needs bring its own refutation.

12 Q—B2   B—K7
13 R—K1   P × P
14 Kt × P
Of course, not 14 R × B, P × P; and Black wins.

14 ......   B × P
This was what Black was playing for: he has won a pawn, but . . .

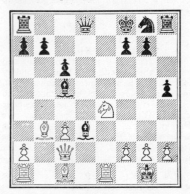

15 Q × B
. . . here comes retribution in the shape of a brilliant counter by White; fairly obvious if your instinct tells you it must be there, but not easy to calculate over the board.

15 ......   Q × Q
16 Kt × B
The point of the combination. The black Queen is attacked, but must keep control of her Q2 where mate is threatened by the white Knight.

16 ......   Q—B4
17 B—R3   Kt—R3 ·
Black feels safe now, as nothing is to be gained by a discovered check. But White takes advantage of the Queen's vulnerable position.

18 R—K5   Q—Kt3
Black cannot capture the Rook on this or the next move, as he would lose the Queen. If

at once 18 . . . . Q—R2; 19 QR—K1 (threatening mate in three by 20 Kt—Q7 db ch, etc.).

19 R—Kt5   Q—R2
20 Kt—K4 dis ch   K—K1
If 20 . . . . K—Kt1; 21 Kt—B6 mate.

21 R—K5 ch   K—Q1
22 R—K7   Kt—B4
23 R—Q1 ch   K—B1
24 R × BP   Resigns
The threat is 25 B—K6 ch, K—Kt1; 26 R × Kt, with a further threat of 27 B—Q6 mate. If 24 . . . . R—K1 (preventing 25 B—K6); White wins by 25 Kt—B6, and if 24 . . . . Q—Kt3; 25 R × Kt.
A brilliant finish to an exciting game.

24

O'KELLY
DE GALWAY   DENKER
(Mar del Plata, 1948)

He who ventures on a counter-gambit is playing with fire. This is shown in the following magnificent game, in which it is White who seizes the initiative and maintains it to the end without allowing his opponent a moment's respite.

1 P—K4   P—K4
2 Kt—KB3   Kt—QB3
3 B—Kt5   P—B4
The choice of the *Schliemann Defence* shows an aggressive spirit. The trouble is that, if you meet a level-headed opponent, the end can easily justify Boden's famous aphorism: "In a gambit you give up a pawn for the sake of getting a lost game."

4 Kt—B3
The development of pieces is more energetic here than other possible continuations, such as 4 P—Q3 or 4 P—Q4 or 4 P × P, or also 4 B × Kt, QP × B.

4 ......   P × P
More incisive than 4 . . . . Kt—B3; after which 5 P × P, P—K5; 6 Kt—KKt5, P—Q4; 7 P—Q3, gives White an advantage in the centre.

5 QKt × P   P—Q4
Evidently the former Champion of the U.S.A. has an aggressive temperament, but also an optimistic one. The text-move is very risky and not good enough for a strong masters' tournament. A normal continuation is 5 . . . . Kt—B3. Another

line, more or less "normal," is 5 .... B—K2; in preparation for the development of the KKt. That it is not without its dangers is shown in a game Kubanec–Wacker *correspondence*, 1939: 5 .... B—K2; 6 P—Q4, Kt—B3 (or more prudently 6 .... P×P; 7 Castles, Kt—B3, etc.); 7 Kt×Kt ch, B×Kt (if 7 .... P×Kt; 8 P×P, Castles; 9 B—KR6); 8 P×P, Kt×P (he should have resigned himself to the retreat, 8 .... B—K2; The text-move costs a piece in an instructive manner); 9 Kt×Kt, Q—K2 (on 9 .... B×Kt or even 9 .... P—B3; the attack by 10 Q—R5 ch wins); 10 Castles, B×Kt; 11 R—K1, K—B1 (if 11 .... Castles; 12 Q—Q5 ch, or 11 .... P—B3; 12 Q—R5 ch, or, finally, 11 .... K—Q1; there arises the amusing sequel, 12 Q—R5, B×P ch; 13 K×B, Q×R; 14 B—Kt5 ch, and Black is irretrievably lost); 12 Q—B3 ch, Q—B3; 13 R×B, Black resigns.

6 Kt×P
A splendid counter. Black will suffer from under-development in an open position.

6 ......   P×Kt
Otherwise 8 Q—R5 ch, and after 8 .... P—Kt3; 9 Kt×P, the defence 9 .... Kt—B3 is not available.

7 Kt×Kt   P×Kt
It is questionable whether the text-move is compulsory. It is true that after 7 .... Q—Kt4; White obtains a definite advantage after 8 Q—K2, Kt—B3; 9 P—KB4, etc. But 7 .... Q—Q4; is playable.

8 B×P ch   B—Q2
9 Q—R5 ch   K—K2
Not 9 .... P—Kt3; 10 Q—K5 ch, Q—K2; 11 B×B ch, K×B; and White can capture the KR or alternatively win the QR by 12 Q—Q5 ch.

10 Q—K5 ch   B—K3
11 P—Q4
This and the subsequent three moves

(attack with development) would have delighted Morphy.

11 ......   P×P e.p.
12 B—Kt5 ch   Kt—B3
13 Castles QR   K—B2
14 KR—K1   B×P
15 Q—R5
Gaining an important *tempo*.

15 ......   B—K3
16 B×Kt   Q×B
If 16 .... P×B; 17 R×P, followed by B×R, and a general rout of the black forces.

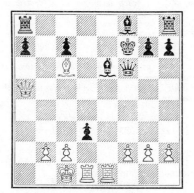

17 R×B
Brilliant! If now 17 .... Q×R; 18 B—Q5, and if 17 .... K×R; 18 Q—Q5 ch, K—K2; 19 Q—Q7 mate.

17 ......   Q×P
18 R×P   K×R
19 Q—Q5 ch   K—K2
20 Q—K5 ch   Resigns
If 20 .... K—B2; 21 B—Q5 ch, K—Kt3; 22 R—Kt3 ch, etc.

A piquant feature of this attractive fight is that the black QR remains *en prise* for twelve moves and is *en prise* at the end.

5. SCOTCH GAME

25

TARTAKOWER   G. WOOD
(Hastings, 1946-7)

Nearly every chess contest has its moments of danger. Frequently, the greatest danger occurs, not when a player is subjected to attack, but, on the contrary, when he himself believes that he has secured the initiative. For then, it is not merely a question of finding the coup juste, *but also of elaborating a whole series of plans which meets the situation, as otherwise there would come a troublesome reaction.*

This is what happens on Black's nineteenth move in the following game.

1 P—K4	P—K4
2 Kt—KB3	Kt—QB3
3 P—Q4	P × P
4 Kt × P	Kt—B3

This so-called modern defence is losing ground, while the ancient line, 4 .... B—B4; is gaining in popularity.

5 Kt × Kt
Sharper than 5 Kt—QB3, B—Kt5; etc.

5	KtP × Kt
6 Kt—Q2	

This new attack in the *Scotch Game* also has more "bite" than the usual 6 B—Q3, P—Q4; 7 P × P, P × P; 8 B—Kt5 ch, B—Q2; etc.

6 ......   P—Q4
Playable also is 6 .... B—B4.

7 P × P	P × P
8 B—Kt5 ch	

And so White has gained a very useful *tempo* (see note to White's sixth move).

8	B—Q2
9 B × B ch	Q × B
10 Castles	B—K2
11 P—QKt3	

The contest would be less incisive after 11 Kt—Kt3, followed by B—Kt5. But the most direct plan of action would be here 11 Kt—B3, Castles KR; 12 B—Kt5.

11	Castles KR
12 B—Kt2	Q—B4

In order to free his game at last by .... Kt—K5.

13 Kt—B3	Kt—K5
14 Q—Q3	KR—K1
15 QR—Q1	QR—Q1
16 Kt—Q4	

Nothing more than equality would result from 16 P—B4, P × P; 17 Q × P, B—B4; 18 B—Q4, B—Kt3, etc.

16	Q—Q2
17 P—KB3	

A binding but logical move which aims at repelling the hostile forces. If 17 P—QB4, P—QB3.

17 ......   Kt—Q3
Not 17 .... Kt—B3; 18 Kt—B5, etc., nor 17 .... Kt—B4; 18 Q—B3.

18 Kt—K2
Instead of this voluntary renunciation of territory, 18 B—R3, is worth considering.

18	Kt—B4
19 KR—K1	

He plays with fire instead of taking preventive measures by occupying the critical diagonal: 19 B—Q4, Kt × B; 20 Kt × Kt, B—B4; 21 K—R1.

19 ......   B—R5
Instead of indulging in pinpricks, Black should conceive some definite counter-plan. Less artificial would be 19 .... B—B4 ch; 20 K—R1, which maintains the solidity of the position with chances for either side.

20 P—Kt3	R—K6
21 Q—Q2	B—K2

A compulsory retreat. Insufficient is the sacrifice 21 .... R × BP; 22 P × B, Kt × P, because of 23 Kt—Q4 (23 .... Q—R6; 24 K—R1).

22 Kt—Q4
The key-move—compulsory, but sufficient.

22	R × R ch
23 R × R	B—B4

If 23 .... Kt × Kt; 24 B × Kt, P—QB4; 25 Q—K3, emphasising White's positional advantage.

24 K—Kt2 Kt×Kt
25 B×Kt B—Kt3
Or 25 .... B×B; 26 Q×B, P—QB3;
27 Q—B5, etc., or 25 .... Q—Q3; 26 B—K5,
and White maintains the initiative. In the
local contest for White's QB5, the text-move
appears to secure Black's prospects (for if,
e.g. 26 Q—B3, P—KB3; the situation is
stabilised), but appearances are deceptive.

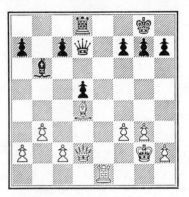

26 B×P
A solution as elegant as it is unexpected.
At the least, White wins a pawn.

26 ...... K×B
Against 26 .... R—K1; 27 Q—Kt5, is
decisive.

27 Q—Kt5 ch K—B1
28 Q—B6
This "quiet" move is one of the points of
White's combination.

28 ...... B—Q5
He is already forced to give up material,
for if 28 .... K—Kt1; 29 R—K7, Q×R
(compulsory); 30 Q×Q, R—Q3; 31 P—KB4,
White is in sight of victory.

29 Q×B K—Kt1
30 Q—KB4
An astute manœuvre.

30 ...... R—K1
After this instinctive reply, plausible
though it appears, Black is lost at once.
Necessary is 30 .... Q—Q3; after which
White continues with 31 R—K5.

31 Q—Kt4 ch
A bolt from the blue. Black resigns, for
after 31 .... Q×Q; 32 R×R ch, K—Kt2;
33 P×Q, he remains a Rook down.

26

BOGOLJUBOW LOTHAR SCHMID
(Bad Pyrmont, 1949)

*A game of chess can impress on various
counts: it may be brilliancy, intrinsic logic,
theoretical value or, finally, originality.
The following game belongs to the last
category.*

1 P—K4 P—K4
2 Kt—KB3 Kt—QB3
3 Kt—B3 Kt—B3
4 P—Q4
The *Scotch Four Knights'.*

4 ...... P×P
5 Kt×P Kt×P
A startling continuation which shows that
modern theoretical investigation does not
restrict itself to stable variations and does not
shrink from fanciful ideas. The usual continuation is 5 .... B—Kt5; 6 Kt×Kt,
KtP×Kt; 7 B—Q3, P—Q4; and Black has a
satisfactory game.

6 Kt×QKt
A violent continuation, in which White
relies on his advantage in development.
The best system for White, however, is the
capture of the other Knight: 6 Kt×KKt,
Q—K2, 7 Kt—Kt5 (not so good is 7
P—KB3, P—Q4; etc.), 7 .... Q×Kt ch;
8 B—K2, K—Q1; 9 Castles, etc., with com-
pensations for the mislaid pawn.

6 ...... Kt×Kt
7 Kt×Q Kt×Q
8 Kt×BP Kt×BP
These fantastic "desperado" manœuvres
by both opposing Knights give the game a
character of its own. At first sight the play
has the appearance of a light-hearted
skirmish between carefree amateurs, but
closer examination indicates that Black, who
starts the ball rolling, has at all times an
equal game.

9 Kt×R Kt×R
10 B—Q3 B—B4
Here 10 .... P—KKt3; would be unsatisfactory after 11 B—K3, B—Kt2; 12 Kt×P,
P×Kt; 13 B×P ch, followed by Castles.

11 B×P
White has recovered his pawn, but he
wants to get more for all his trouble and
worry.

11 ...... Kt—B7

12 B—B4   P—Q3

Black has no time for elaborate manœuvres, as his King is exposed to attack.

13 B—Kt6 ch   K—B1
14 B—Kt3

To 14 K—Q2, threatening 15 R—KB1,
the reply would be 14 .... Kt—Kt5;
followed by 15 .... Kt—B3; without
Black coming to any harm.

14 ......   Kt—Kt5
15 Kt—B7

A surprising error of judgment in so experienced a player as Bogoljubow. He could
have extricated his Knight without any
complications by 15 B—Q3, followed by
16 Kt—Kt6 ch, with a probable draw.

15 ....   Kt—K6
16 K—Q2   B—B4

The young German master seizes his
opportunity.

17 Kt—Kt5   B × B
18 Kt—K6 ch   K—K2
19 Kt × B

He expects 19 .... P × Kt; 20 K × Kt, etc.,
with equality.

19 ......   Kt × BP

An *interim manœuvre*. This is where
White's combination goes wrong. We again
have Spielmann's "desperado" Knights.

Position after 19 Kt × B

20 B—R4 ch   K—K1
21 Kt—K6   K—Q2

Better than 21 .... Kt × R; 22 Kt × BP ch,
K—Q2; 23 Kt × R, K—B1; 24 B—Kt3,
K—Kt1; 25 B × P ch, K × Kt; 26 B—K5,
and White gets two strong passed pawns for
the Knight, which makes a win for Black
problematical.

22 Kt—B4   Kt × R
23 Kt × B   R—K1
24 B—B2   Kt—B7
25 Kt—B4   Kt—Kt5
     Resigns

An original game in which the Knights
on either side exhibit a voracious appetite.

6. FOUR KNIGHTS' GAME

27

BOTVINNIK   RESHEVSKY
(Moscow, 1948)

In the following memorable game, Mikhaïl Botvinnik, playing in his own sober and precise style, made sure of the world's title, a worthy successor to his predecessor, Alexandre Alekhine.

1 P—K4	P—K4
2 Kt—KB3	Kt—QB3
3 Kt—B3	Kt—B3
4 B—Kt5	B—Kt5

Here Rubinstein's counter, 4 .... Kt—Q5; can be mastered, but is nevertheless full of pitfalls, as is shown by the following brevity, played by *correspondence* between H. Nebel and K. Hallmann 4 .... Kt—Q5; 5 B—R4, B—B4 (Black has to continue in gambit style); 6 Kt×P, Castles; 7 Kt—B3 (he should have combined attack and defence with the retreat, 7 Kt—Q3 B—Kt3; 8 P—K5, Kt—K1; 9 Castles, etc.), 7 .... P—Q4; 8 Kt×Kt, B×Kt; 9 P—K5 (at this point the move is a waste of time, but 9 Castles, P×P also is in favour of Black), 9 .... Kt—Kt5 (not 9 .... B×P; 10 P—Q4); 10 Castles (having gone astray on his seventh move, White's every attempt is one move late. Better, however, is 10 Q—B3), 10 .... Q—R5; 11 P—KR3, Kt×P; 12 R×Kt (or 12 Q—B3, Kt×P dis ch, etc.), 12 .... Q×R ch; 13 K—R2, B—Kt5; this superb final stroke forces White's resignation.

5 Castles	Castles
6 P—Q3	B×Kt

He rightly gives up symmetry, for after 6 .... P—Q3; 7 Kt—K2, the position becomes for Black more tricky than it looks.

7 P×B	P—Q3
8 B—Kt5	Q—K2

This move implies a re-grouping of three pieces, the Queen, QKt and KR, and is one of the soundest defensive systems for Black.

9 R—K1	Kt—Q1
10 P—Q4	Kt—K3
11 B—QB1	R—Q1

An important juncture. The text-move indirectly protects the KP. Other playable lines are 11 .... P—B3; 12 B—B1, Q—B2; etc., or, more incisively, 11 .... P—B4; which also indirectly guards the KP (for if 12 P×KP, P×P; 13 Kt×P, Kt—B2; wins a piece!).

12 B—B1
Without waiting to be compelled, White's other Bishop also returns to base and prepares, undisturbed, for fresh operations.

12 ......   Kt—B1
Continuing the re-grouping behind the front. Another plan could be 12 .... P—KKt3; 13 P—Kt3, Kt—R4; 14 B—KKt2, P—QB4.

13 Kt—R4
And again a move characteristic of Botvinnik's self-reliant strategy: usually this diversion is undertaken only after due preparation by 13 P—KKt3, but this immediate escapade renders his opponent's task more complicated, for if 13 P—Kt3, B—Kt5; and if first 13 R—Kt1, R—Kt1.

13 ......   Kt—Kt5
If Black tries to win a pawn by 13 .... Kt×P; 14 R×Kt, P—KB4; White obtains a formidable attack by 15 B—B4 ch, K—R1; 16 Q—R5, P×R; 17 B—KKt5, Q—Q2; 18 B—B7, P—QKt3 (if 18 .... P—KR3; 19 B×P, P×B; 20 Q×RP ch, Kt—R2; 21 Kt—Kt6 mate); 19 Kt—Kt6 ch, Kt×Kt; 20 B×Kt, P—KR3; 21 B×R, Q×B; 22 P×P, P×P; 23 B×P, R—Kt1; 24 R—Q1, and wins.
Instead of the text-move, Black should adopt the counter-measure 13 .... P—B4; but he thinks the moment favourable to capture the initiative.

14 P—Kt3   Q—B3
A double threat to White's KB2 and Q4.

15 P—B3	Kt—R3
16 B—K3	R—K1
17 Q—Q2	Kt—Kt3
18 Kt—Kt2	

Neither 18 B—KKt5, Kt×Kt; 19 B×Kt, Q—Kt3; 20 B—KKt5, P—KB3; etc., nor

18 B×Kt, Kt×Kt; 19 P×Kt, P×B;
20 Q—B2, K—R1; etc., is advisable, for
in either case Black obtains counter-chances.

18 ......   B—R6
Black also avoids a hornet's nest after
18 .... Q×P; 19 B—K2, Q—B3;
20 B—KKt5, Q—K3; 21 P—Q5, Q—Q2;
22 B×Kt, P×B; 23 Q×P, Q—R6;
24 Q—Kt5, etc., with advantage to White.
We see that the play on either side is full
of pitfalls, which require the most intricate
calculations.

19 B—K2   B×Kt
20 K×B
Thanks to scientific manœuvring, which
White has carried out with the greatest
composure over numerous quicksands, he
has consolidated his defences and preserved
the dynamic advantage of the "two Bishops"
on a mobile front.
He threatens both 21 P—Q5, followed
by B—KKt5 (mating the Queen), or
21 B—KKt5, Q—K3; 22 P—Q5, Q—Q2;
23 B×Kt, P×B; 24 Q×P, securing a footing in the hostile position.

20 ......   P—Q4
And now Black decides to sacrifice a pawn
in order to enlarge his field of action. He
hopes to recover the pawn, or at least to
seek safety in an ending in which the weakness of White's Q side may make itself felt.

21 P×QP   P×P
22 P×P
If 22 B×P, Q—Q3; 23 P—QB4, Kt—B4;
24 B—B2, P—QB3; and then .... KR—Q1.

22 ......   Kt—B4
23 B—B2   KR—Q1
24 P—QB4   P—KR4
25 P—KR4   P—Kt4
Another attempt at the devaluation of the
hostile mass of pawns would be 25 ....
P—B3.

26 Q—Kt5
This counteracts any prospective attack
against the white King.

26 ......   Q×Q
27 P×Q   P—R5
28 B—Q3   RP×P
29 B×P   Kt×P
The temptation to recover his material is
too great, otherwise he might play for simplification by 29 .... Kt×B; 30 K×Kt,
P×P; 31 B×P, when White keeps his extra
pawn, weak as it is.

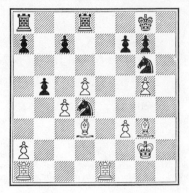

30 QR—Q1
Threatening to win a Knight by 31 B×Kt.

30 ......   P—QB4
If 30 .... Kt—B1; 31 B—K4, P—QB4;
32 P×P e.p., threatening P—B7.

31 P×P e.p.   Kt×QBP
If 31 .... P×P; 32 P—B7, R—KB1;
33 B×P, Kt—B4; 34 R—Q7, with an over-
powering position for White. Black has
now recovered his pawn, but this "success"
is not lasting, and the long range of the
"two Bishops" comes into play.

32 B—K4
Producing a double threat (33 B×Kt, and
33 P×P), which is more telling than 32 P×P,
Kt(B3)—K4; and Black avoids the worst.

32 ......   QR—B1
33 R×R ch   Kt×R
34 B—B5
Again stronger than the immediate
34 P×P.

34 ......   R—R1
35 R—K8 ch   K—R2
36 P×P
A ripe fruit falling.

36 ......   P—B3
Desperately, Black tries to evade the
stranglehold, but it would be simpler to
resign.

37 B—B7   Kt—K3
38 R×R
Instead of 38 R×Kt, White under time
pressure prolongs the agony.

38 ......   Kt×B
39 R×P   Kt×P
40 R—Q7   P×P
41 P—R4   Resigns

7. PHILIDOR'S DEFENCE

28

BARDEN   KLEIN
(Buxton, 1950)

In the following game the main feature, after an early exchange of Queens, is the struggle for space, in which White succeeds, in exemplary fashion, in gradually working his way into the enemy position.

Incidentally, and as in the preceding game, the manifold activities of the "two Bishops" are well to the fore.

1	P—K4	P—K4
2	Kt—KB3	P—Q3
3	P—Q4	Kt—Q2

The *Hanham Variation* proper. Against 3 .... Kt—KB3; the following is to be recommended: 4 P×P, Kt×P; and now 5 QKt—Q2,—development by opposition. Not to be commended, in any case, is the immediate and voluntary abandonment of the centre by 3 .... P×P; 4 Kt×P, etc.

4	B—QB4	P—QB3
5	Kt—B3	B—K2

After 5 .... P—KR3; 6 P—QR4, Black's game remains restricted.

6 P×P

An astute simplification. More energetic, however, is 6 Castles, P—KR3; 7 P—QR4, KKt—B3; 8 P—QKt3, Q—B2; 9 B—Kt2, etc., with a promising mechanism.

6	P×P

Naïve would be 6 .... Kt×P; 7 Kt×Kt, P×Kt; 8 Q—R5, and White wins a pawn, thanks to his double-threat against Black's KB2 and K4.

7 Kt—KKt5

He wisely strikes the iron while it's hot; if 7 Castles, P—KR3; Black's defences are already "over-protected."

7	B×Kt

An instinctive reply. By playing the correct 7 .... Kt—R3; he would lay himself open to a perpetual check after 8 B×P ch, Kt×B; 9 Kt—K6, Q—Kt3; 10 Kt×P ch, K—B1; 11 Kt—K6 ch, K—K1; 12 Kt—Kt7 ch, etc.

8	Q—R5	P—KKt3
9	Q×B	Q×Q
10	B×Q	Kt—B1
11	Castles QR	B—K3
12	B—K2	P—B3
13	B—K3	

White has had the better of the opening, and he has secured a nicely centralised position and the command of the open Queen's file.

13	Kt—K2

A more immediate plan for consolidation is 13 .... P—KR4; followed by .... R—R2; contesting the Q file at the earliest possible moment.

14	R—Q2	Kt—B1
15	KR—Q1	Kt—Kt3
16	R—Q6	P—KR4
17	P—QR4	Kt(Kt3)—Q2
18	P—R5	

An instructive technical point: White has asserted his command of the Queen's file, and in particular he will make good use of his Q6, as will be seen during the course of the game. A more incisive procedure, however, would be 18 P—QKt4—Kt5, and Black must allow the entry of the Knight or lose a pawn.

18	......	P—R3
19	Kt—R4	R—KR2
20	P—QKt3	R—K2
21	Kt—Kt2	K—B2
22	Kt—B4	K—Kt2
23	R(Q6)—Q2	Kt—R2
24	Kt—Q6	Kt(Q2)—B1
25	Kt—B4	Kt—Q2

Both players are getting short of time, which explains some unimportant repetitions of moves.

26	P—Kt3	R—QB1
27	Kt—Q6	R—QKt1
28	Kt—B4	R—QB1
29	P—R4	P×P
30	B×BP	Kt(Q2)—B1
31	B—Q6	R—KB2
32	B—R3	R—R1

Black is reduced to complete passivity and can do nothing but "wait and see" what plan his opponent will think out.

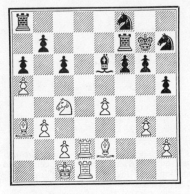

33 P—K5

Rupturing the centre. As indicated by Mr. Barden himself after the game, a more effective plan—and more in keeping with his methodical play up to this point—is 33 R—Q8, R × R; 34 R × R, followed by Kt—Q6, and R—QKt8, winning a pawn.

33	P × P
34 B—Kt2	K—R3
35 Kt × P	R—B7

| 36 B—KB3 | R × R |
| 37 R × R | Kt—Kt4 |

This attempt to break out is natural, but in no way improves Black's constricted position. He has a better chance with 37 .... R—K1; and a difficult ending, although White's Bishops and his strong Knight would still win.

38 B—Kt2	Kt—B2
39 Kt—Q3	Kt—Q2
40 R—K2	R—K1

An impulsive move just before the time control, a not unusual occurrence. But if 40 .... B—B4; 41 R—K7, and White must win.

| 41 Kt—B4 | Kt—Kt4 |

Nothing can save Black, for if 41 .... Kt—B4; 42 P—QKt4, or 41 .... Kt—B1; 42 B—QR3, or 41 .... Kt—Q1; 42 B—KR3, B—B2; 43 B × Kt.

42 P—R4

Winning a piece and the game, although Black struggled for some moves longer.

A splendid piece of deep positional play on the part of the victor against a formidable opponent.

8. PETROFF'S DEFENCE

29

FUDERER   KOSTIC
(Ljublana, 1951)

The following beautiful game represents a clash between the old guard and the new. One must admire the optimism which enables fresh talent to break through all obstacles.

1 P—K4	P—K4
2 Kt—KB3	Kt—KB3
3 Kt×P	

Steinitz's continuation 3 P—Q4, has its supporters. In a game, Broadbent-B. H. Wood, *London*, 1950, the continuation was 3 .... Kt×P (preferable is 3 .... P×P); 4 B—Q3, P—Q4; 5 Kt×P, B—Q3; 6 Castles, Castles; 7 P—QB4 (the accepted procedure against the *Petroff*, which aims at undermining Black's centre, one of the weak points of this defence), 7.... P—QB3; 8 Q—B2, and White has a strong initiative.

3	P—Q3
4 Kt—B4	

An unusual continuation, which was tried successfully by L. Paulsen–Schallopp, *Frankfurt*, 1887. The idea is that Black must capture the pawn, allowing White some advantage in development. The traditional variant is 4 Kt—KB3, Kt×P; after which White obtains no palpable advantage from the classic continuation, 5 P—Q4, P—Q4; 6 B—Q3, B—K2; 7 Castles, Kt—QB3, nor from the simplifying line, 5 Q—K2, Q—K2; 6 P—Q3, Kt—KB3; etc. (a line handled by Lasker with great virtuosity), nor from other variations, such as 5 Kt—B3, Kt×Kt; 6 QP×Kt, B—K2; etc., 5 P—Q3, Kt—KB3; 6 P—Q4, B—K2; etc.

4	Kt×P
5 Kt—B3	

In a game from the match Pilnik–Bogoljubow, *Zürich*, 1951, equality was reached after 5 Q—K2, Q—K2; 6 Kt—K3, P—QB3; 7 P—Q3, Kt—B3; 8 Kt—Q2, QKt—Q2; 9 P—QKt3. In the game mentioned above, L. Paulsen–Schallopp, 5 P—Q4, P—Q4; 6 Kt—B3, B—K3; 7 B—Q3, P—KB4; 8 Castles, B-Q3; etc., the game also is even.

5	Kt×Kt

He hardly has a choice. If 5 .... P—Q4, then not 6 Q—K2, B—K3; 7 Kt×Kt, P×KKt (Rossolimo–Pomar, *Gijon*, 1951); but rather 6 Kt×Kt, P×QKt; 7 P—Q4, P×P e.p.; 8 Q×P, Q×Q; 9 B×Q, and White has the superior development (O'Kelly–Pomar, *Gijon*, 1951). If 5 .... Kt—KB3; 6 P—Q4, B—K2; 7 B—Q3, Kt—B3; aiming at equality (Matanovic–Udovcic).

6 KtP×Kt	B—K2

Black has the choice of two other continuations in 6 .... P—Q4; 7 Kt—K3, B—K3; 8 R—QKt1, P—QKt3; 9 P—Q4, B—Q3; 10 Q—B3, P—QB3; with equality (Rossolimo–Alexander, *Birmingham*, 1951), or 6 .... P—KKt3; (best), as played in Matanovic–Alexander, *London*, 1951.

7 P—Q4	Kt—Q2

This development is more flexible than 7 .... Kt—B3; e.g. 8 B—Q3, B—B3; 9 Castles, Castles; 10 Kt—K3, P—KKt3; 11 P—KB4, Kt—K2; 12 P—B5, etc., after which White has a fine attack (Gligoric–Vidmar, *Yugoslav Championship*, 1951).

8 B—Q3	Kt—Kt3
9 Kt—K3	

A beautifully centralised Knight.

9	P—Q4

He cannot submit to 10 P—QB4, without resistance.

10 Castles	Castles
11 P—KB4	

Heralding the coming K side attack, but the move is a two-edged weapon. If this pawn is prevented from advancing further, White may be deprived of the use of his QB in future operations.

11	P—KB4
12 Q—R5	P—Kt3

White has provoked this move in order to provide himself with a future target for attack.

13 Q—B3	P—B3
14 P—Kt4	Kt—B5

He tries a diversion, hoping for 15 Kt×Kt, in which case 15 .... P×P; followed by 16 .... P×Kt; would ease the situation.

However, 14 .... B—K3; is less artificial.

15 P×P   Kt×Kt
If 15 .... B×P; Black loses a vital pawn
after 16 Kt×Kt.

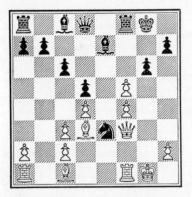

16 P×P
Imaginative play, even though practically
forced, as White has already burnt his
bridges. The obvious 16 B×Kt, leaves
Black with the superior game after 16 ....
B×P.

16 ......   Kt—Kt5

A picturesque situation. He resists the
temptation to add to his spoils because
White would win quickly after 16 ....
Kt×R; 17 Q—R5. But the text-move
enables White to force a win by an overwhelming accumulation of forces. The
better alternative is 16 .... Kt—B4; when
Black has every chance of a draw.

17 P—B5
The winning move, which releases the
QB and gets both Rooks into play.

17 ......   Kt—B3
18 B—KR6   R—K1
19 P×P ch   K—R1
A deceptive shelter.

20 K—R1   B—B1
21 B—KKt5   B—Kt2
22 R—KKt1   Q—K2
23 R—Kt2   B—Q2
This looks like consolidation! But, no,
the end is near.

24 QR—KKt1   R—KB1
25 B—R4   R—B2
26 R—Kt6   QR—KB1
27 Q—Kt2   Resigns
There is no reply to 28 B×Kt.

9. BISHOP'S OPENING

30

HEIKINHEIMO   CRÉPEAUX
(Dubrovnik, 1950)

This is an old-fashioned opening which runs counter to the modern tendency to develop Knights before Bishops (in application of the principle of the "least commitment"). The opening is rarely met in contemporary contests, particularly because it nearly always transposes into other openings such as the Vienna Game, the Giuoco Piano or the King's Gambit Declined, etc.

In the following game, however, the opening retains its distinctive character.

1 P—K4	P—K4
2 B—B4	Kt—KB3
3 P—Q4	

A vigorous move. Too quiet is 3 P—Q3 (3 .... P—B3; to be followed soon by .... P—Q4), and too impetuous is 3 P—B4 (3 .... P—Q4; if not 3 .... P×P; reverting to the *Bishop's Gambit*).

Alternatives are: 3 Kt—QB3, the *Vienna Game*, and 3 Kt—KB3, which after 3 .... Kt—B3; leads to the *Two Knights' Defence*.

An ancient continuation, preferred by Steinitz, is 3 Q—K2.

3	P×P
4 Kt—KB3	Kt×P
5 Q×P	

This prevents the logical and strong advance 5 .... P—Q4. Black now has won a pawn, but at the cost of a somewhat retarded development.

5	Kt—KB3

Best.

6 B—KKt5	B—K2
7 Kt—B3	P—B3

Black must build up his defences. A little premature is 7 .... Castles (8 Castles QR, P—B3; 9 Q—R4, etc.). Again 7 .... Kt—B3; 8 Q—R4, P—Q3; 9 Castles QR, B—K3; 10 B—Q3, offers little resistance and White's pressure goes on increasing.

8 Castles QR	P—Q4
9 Q—R4	

Less good is 9 KR—K1, B—K3; 10 B—Q3 Q—R4; 11 K—Kt1, QKt—Q2; and Black can prepare to castle on the Q side, where his King will enjoy greater safety.

9	Q—R4

Not good, although it looks tempting. Also after 9 .... B—KB4; 10 Kt—Q4, B—Kt3; 11 KR—K1. White's frontal pressure becomes too heavy, in view of which Black should organise his defence as follows: 9 .... B—K3; 10 B—Q3, QKt—Q2; 11 Kt—Q4, Kt—B4; 12 P—B4, Kt—Kt1; 13 KR—K1, K—B1; and Black, although he can no longer castle, has sufficient means of defence.

10 KR—K1	

With the obvious threat: 11 B×Kt, P×B; 12 Q×BP.

10	B—K3

Now the blockade of the K file proves to be insufficient.

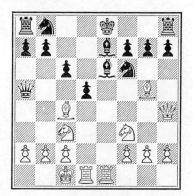

11 Kt—Q4	

White acts with dispatch and skill. His Bishop still cannot be taken, for if 11 .... P×B; 12 Kt×B, P×Kt; 13 R×P, K—B2; 14 QR—K1, R—K1; 15 B×Kt, B×B; 16 R×B ch, P×R; 17 Q×RP ch, K—B1; 18 Q—R8 ch, with swift destruction.

11	QKt—Q2

A desperate measure: Black returns the pawn, but the pressure remains.

12 Kt×B	P×Kt

13 R × KP   K—B2
If 13 .... P × B; 14 QR—K1.

14 QR—K1   QR—K1
15 B—K2

With this super-ingenious manœuvre White renders his attack irresistible. Black cannot well reply with 15 .... K × R; because of 16 B—R5 dis ch.

15 ......   B—Q1
16 B—Kt4   Kt × B
17 Q × Kt   B × B ch

All these exchanges fail to ease the situation.

18 Q × B   Kt—B3
19 R × Kt ch   Resigns

If 19 .... P × R; 20 Q—R5 ch, followed by R × R.

10. VIENNA GAME

31

PRINS   **RELLSTAB**
(Travemünde, 1951)

Here is one of the most original and startling games from contemporary practice.

1	P—K4	P—K4
2	Kt—QB3	Kt—KB3
3	B—B4	

Preventing 3 .... P—Q4. If 3 P—KKt3, P—Q4; 4 P×P, Kt×P; 5 B—Kt2, B—K3; Black has a very good game. Similarly, in the case of the *Vienna Gambit* proper, 3 P—B4, Black's best is the counter 3 .... P—Q4; and after 4 BP×P, Kt×P; 5 Kt—B3, B—K2; 6 P—Q4 (if 6 Q—K2, P—KB4, etc.), 6 .... Castles (or 6 .... B—QKt5; 7 B—Q2, with equality); 7 B—Q3, P—KB4; 8 P×P e.p., B×P; 9 Castles, Kt—B3; and the tension relaxes.

The text-move certainly is more imaginative than 3 Kt—B3, bringing about a *Three Knights'* or *Four Knights' Game*.

3	......	Kt×P

Accepting the challenge.

4	Q—R5	Kt—Q3
5	B—Kt3	

Simplification by 5 Q×KP ch, Q—K2; 6 Q×Q ch, B×Q; 7 B—Kt3, etc., does not conform with the Dutchman's spirited style.

5	......	Kt—B3

The play now becomes embittered, while 5 .... B—K2; can still lead to a peaceful issue after 6 Kt—B3, Kt—B3; 7 Kt×P, Castles; etc.

6	Kt—Kt5	

Opinion on this enterprise is divided; while it wins the exchange, it may unleash an attack by Black.

6	......	P—KKt3
7	Q—B3	P—B4
8	Q—Q5	Q—K2

Nolens volens, Black must be prepared for sacrifices. For tactical reasons 8 .... Q—B3; is inferior.

9	Kt×P ch	K—Q1
10	Kt×R	P—Kt3

11	P—Q3	Kt—Q5

The value of 11 .... B—QKt2; is still *sub judice*, e.g. 12 P—KR4 (or else 12 Kt—R3, or even, as suggested by a French amateur, B. Eliacheff, fearlessly 12 Kt—B3, P—B5; 13 Castles, Kt—Q5; 14 Q×B, Kt×Q; 15 Kt×Kt, P×Kt; 16 B×P, etc.), 12 .... P—B5 (or 12 .... P—KR3); 13 Q—B3 (or first, 13 Kt×P, P×Kt; 14 Q—B3), 13 .... Kt—Q5; 14 Q—R3, with a very uncertain issue.

12	Kt—R3	

An amusing continuation occurred in a simultaneous performance at *Amiens*, 1950, Tartakower-N.: 12 P—KR4, P—KR3; 13 Kt×P, P×Kt; 14 Q—R8, K—B2; 15 B—Q5, Kt×P ch; 16 K—Q1, Kt×R; 17 B—K3, and White retains the initiative.

12	......	P—KR3
13	P—QB3	B—QKt2
14	Q×B	

A compulsory sacrifice, for the Queen has no move; but White foresaw this contingency, as he comes out with Rook, Bishop and Knight for Queen and pawn, and, most important, his pieces are exceptionally mobile.

14	......	Kt×Q
15	P×Kt	Q—Kt5 ch

The beginning of Black's disappointments. He must forgo 15 .... P×P dis ch; 16 K—Q1, as the opening of the K file would benefit only his adversary.

16	B—Q2	Q×P
17	Castles KR	B—Q3 (see diag.,
		p. 50)

To take either pawn would leave the Queen dangerously exposed. Unfavourable too would be 17 .... P—KKt4; because of 18 B—B3, Q—Q3; 19 P—B4, etc. Similarly, if 17 .... B—Kt2; 18 B—B3, etc. The best in the circumstances is 17 .... Q—KR5; 18 B—B3, B—Q3; etc.

18	Kt—B4	

A brilliant turn. He can play this after all, for if 18 .... P×Kt; 19 B—B3, Q—B4; 20 B×R. The white pieces now get into full play.

18	......	Kt—R4

Position after 17 .... B—Q3

Had Black foreseen the coming machinations, he would have given preference to 18 .... Q×KtP; with the following continuation: 19 Kt×KKtP, R—R2; 20 QR—Q1, Q—Q5; 21 P—Kt3, etc., with chances for both sides.

19 B—K3	Q—Kt5
20 Kt—Q5	Q—KR5

Or 20 .... Q—Kt4.

21 QKt×P
The moribund Knight comes to life. Black cannot very well reply with 21 .... P×Kt (22 B×P ch, followed by 23 B×Kt); nor with 21 .... Kt×B (22 P×Kt, P×Kt; 23 R—R8 ch, with mate to follow).

21	P—B5
22 QR—B1	

Unperturbed, White carries out his plans.

22	Kt—B3
23 Kt—B4	

By skilful manœuvring White succeeds in saving the whole of his threatened material.

23	B—Kt1
24 B—B5	P—B6

But here is a fresh danger.

25 P—Kt3
Not 25 P×P, because of 25 .... P—K5.

25	Q—R6
26 Kt(Q5)—K3	

Faulty would be 26 Kt(B4)—K3, P—KR4; followed by .... P—R5. But after the text-move, the continuation 26 .... P—KR4; 27 Kt—Q2, P—R5; 28 Kt×P, P×P; 29 BP×P, P—K5; 30 P×P, B×P; 31 P×B, etc., would result in the exhaustion of the Black forces.

26	P—Q4

Or 26 .... Kt—Q5; 27 B—Q1. With the text-move Black has the satisfaction of gaining a piece, but at the cost of undermining the foundations of his position.

27 B—Q1	P×Kt
28 B×BP	Q—Q2

He has to parry the double threat, 29 B×Kt, and 29 B—KKt4.

29 R×P Kt—Q5
Side-stepping the new threat, 30 B×Kt, Q×B; 31 B—K7 ch.

30 B×Kt	P×B
31 B—Kt4	Q—QKt2

If 31 .... Q—KKt2; 32 Kt—Q5, again with the threat 33 R—B8 mate.

32 R×P ch
More dynamic than 32 R—B8 ch, Q×R; 33 B×Q, P×Kt; after which Black has some hope of a draw.

After the text-move, Black still is the exchange ahead, but White takes advantage of the mobility of his pieces with consummate skill.

32	K—K1
33 R—K1	R—R2
34 Kt—B5 dis ch	K—B1
35 R—Q8 ch	K—B2
36 R—K7 ch	K—B3
37 R—B8 ch	K—Kt4
38 R×Q	R×R
39 Kt—K3	P—KR4
40 P—R4 ch	K—R3
41 B—K6	Resigns

32

W. W. ADAMS   H. STEINER
(Hollywood, 1944)

Another fierce contest. It is surprising to note that the Vienna game, so sedate at first sight, can lead to the most turbulent variations in the repertoire of the openings—namely, the Hamppe-Allgaier (6 Kt—KKt5), the Pierce (5P—Q4) and the Steinitz (4 P—Q4) Gambits.

1 P—K4	P—K4
2 Kt—QB3	Kt—QB3

This gives White the opportunity of turning the opening into a real gambit, with all its attendant dangers and complications.

3 P—B4

Heralding the intended attack. Players of a less bellicose temperament can revert to a *Three Knights'* or eventually a *Four Knights' Game*, with 3 Kt—B3. Older masters, such as Louis Paulsen, Tchigorin, and later on Mieses, had a preference for 3 P—KKt3, which, however, promises no more than equality.

The *Vienna Game* proper occurs after 3 B—B4, and contains dangers for both sides, which we shall now examine in connection with a game played by *correspondence in South Africa*, 1946: St. John Brooks–Crous: 3 B—B4, B—B4 (3 .... Kt—B3); shows greater initiative); 4 Q—Kt4, Q—B3; 5 Kt—Q5, Q×P ch; 6 K—Q1, K—B1; 7 Kt—R3, Q—Q5; 8 P—Q3, B—Kt3 (in view of the threat, 9 P—B3, but he should first ease his position by 8 .... P—Q3; 9 Q—Kt3, B×Kt; 10 Q×B, etc.); 9 R—Kt1, P—B3 (not 9 .... P—Q3; 10 R×P ch, K×R; 11 Kt×B dis ch, K—B1; 12 Kt×B, Kt—B3; 13 Q—K6, etc., nor, as in a game, Alekhine–Lugovsky, 1931, 9 .... Kt—Q1; 10 P—B3, Q—B4; 11 Kt—Kt5, nor even 9 .... Kt—B3; 10 R×Kt, P—Q3; 11 Q×P çh, K×Q; 12 B—R6 ch, K—Kt1; 13 R—Kt6 ch, RP×R; 14 Kt—B6 mate); 10 Kt×KBP, Black resigns, for 10 .... Kt×Kt (10 .... P×Kt; 11 B×Kt); 11 R×Kt ch, P×R; 12 B—R6 ch, followed by 13 Q—Kt7, is devastating.

3	P×P
4 Kt—B3	P—KKt4
5 P—KR4	P—Kt5
6 Kt—KKt5	

The *Hamppe-Allgaier Gambit*. Although recognised as unsound, it yields a ferocious attack which is difficult for Black to meet.

6	P—KR3
7 Kt×P	K×Kt

The difference between this position and that occurring in the *Allgaier Gambit* is that here both QKts are developed. In consequence, Black can, in answer to B—B4 ch, reply .... P—Q4; B×P ch, K—K1; with comparative safety.

8 P—Q4	P—Q4

An alternative is 8 .... P—B6; 9 B—B4 ch, P—Q4; 10 B×P ch, K—K1; with good prospects for Black.

9 P×P

After 9 B×P, B—Kt5; Black should weather the storm as he then succeeds in consolidating his Q4, the critical square (10 B—QKt5, KKt—K2; etc., or 10 P—K5, B—K3; etc.), and that is why White tries

here to upset the balance in the centre. As we can see, even in an old-fashioned gambit modern research can modify the trend of play.

9	QKt—K2
10 B×P	Kt—Kt3

Black prefers not to recapture the QP, which would expose him to fresh dangers (10 .... Kt×P; 11 B—B4, P—B3; 12 Castles). He hopes to blockade the critical pawn by .... B—Q3; and to use it as a shield.

11 B—K5	B—Q3

A clever reply. It would be dangerous for White to take the Rook.

12 B—QB4	Kt×B

White's threat was 13 Castles ch.

13 P×Kt	B×P
14 Q—Q3	

An excellent move which keeps up the pressure and leaves White with a wide choice of moves.

14	Kt—B3

A more obdurate resistance was seen in a game from the *Pan-American Tournament* of 1947 between W. W. Adams and A. Sandin: 14 .... K—Kt2; 15 Castles QR, Kt—K2; 16 Q—K4, B—B3; with an improved defence for Black.

15 Castles QR	P—Kt4

Directed against the dangerous discovered check by P—Q6. At the same time Black hopes for some counter-play on the open QKt file. Nevertheless, such an incisive measure reveals a restless spirit. Far more collected is 15 .... K—Kt2.

16 Kt×P	K—Kt2
17 P—R5	B—B5 ch
18 K—Kt1	R—B1
19 P—KKt3	B—Kt4 (see diag., p. 52)

He may have intended 19 .... B—Q3; but it is not playable because of 20 Q—Kt6 ch, and 21 Q×P ch.

20 P—Q6	

Opening up dangerous lines for White's attack. It is clear that the attacking technique of contemporary masters is equal in every way to that of their glorious predecessors.

20	P—B3

It is manifest that 20 .... P×P; would be fatal after 21 Q—Kt6 ch, K—R1; 22 Kt×QP, and Black has no defence.

Position after 19 .... B—Kt4

21 Kt—B7   R—QKt1

22 QR—K1

The last act of the drama. The threat is
23 R—K7 ch, K—R1; 24 R—KB1, to which
there is no reply.

22 ......   Kt—Kt1

If 22 .... Kt—Q4; there follows
23 Kt × Kt, P × Kt; 24 R—K7 ch, B × R;
25 Q—Kt6 ch, K—R1; 26 Q × P ch, K—Kt1,
27 B × P ch, R—B2; 28 B × R ch, K × B;
29 Q—Kt6 ch, K—B1; 30 R—B1 ch, and
Black has no resource.

23 Q—Kt6 ch   K—R1
24 B—Q3   Kt—B3
25 R—K7   Q × R
26 P × Q   R—Kt1
27 P—K8(Q)   Resigns

A skilfully conducted attack.

11. KING'S GAMBIT

33

RAVN	**O'KELLY** **DE GALWAY**

(Southsea, 1951)

An aggressor thrown on the defensive, that is the motive of the following game.

1 P—K4	P—K4
2 P—KB4	

The young Dane follows in the footsteps of two contemporary grand masters, Keres and Bronstein, who, in our scientific age, still dare from time to time, to offer this gambit.

2	P×P
3 Kt—KB3	

Less aspiring is 3 B—B4, the *Bishop's Gambit*. More ambitious, however, is 3 Q—B3, known as the *Breyer Gambit*, although this was tried already by Charousek against Showalter, *Nuremberg*, 1896. The following brevity was played by *correspondence* in 1950, between Hoerner and Lorenz: 3 Q—B3, Kt—QB3 (a recognised reply); 4 Kt—K2 (in this opening it is essential for White not to obstruct his Queen. If 4 P—B3, Kt—B3; 5 P—Q4, P—Q4; 6 P—K5, Kt—K5; etc. The simplest is 4 Q×P), 4 .... B—B4 (here the soundest is 4 .... P—Q4); 5 P—Q3, P—KKt4 (White is unaware of his danger, and allows his Queen to be hemmed in more and more); 6 P—KKt3, Kt—K4; 7 Q—Kt2 (if 7 Q—R5, White loses his Queen or is mated after 7 .... Kt—KB3, etc.), 7 .... P—B6, White resigns. He loses at least a piece.

3	B—K2

The *Cunningham Gambit*, which for a long time was thought to be decidedly inferior, but which has successfully been modernised, and strengthened by some new turns. Nowadays, however, it has become the usual practice to adopt a more elastic defence by 3 .... P—Q4; or .... Kt—KB3.

4 B—B4	

Interesting is here the *Chaudé Gambit*, 4 P—KKt3. M. Bernard Chaudé, husband of the Lady Champion, Mme. Chaudé de Silans, is himself a player of parts.

4	Kt—KB3

The usual continuation is 4 .... B—R5 ch; 5 K—B1, P—Q4; 6 B×P, Kt—KB3; 7 Kt—B3, Castles; 8 P—Q4, P—B3; 9 B—B4, B—Kt5; 10 B—K2, B×Kt; 11 B×B, B—Kt4; 12 P—KKt3, and White intends to have the last word. That is why the text-move is more in the spirit of modern positional play. Its finer points have been analysed by Dutch players, especially by Dr. Euwe and H. Kmoch.

5 P—K5	

A natural reaction. White lets himself be tempted to this advance, which, however, can easily prove to be premature.

To be recommended is 5 Kt—B3, with the intended continuation 6 P—Q4, and Castles.

A superb illustration of this line of play is given in the following from the *Antwerp League Competition*, 1951, Devos–Borodine, 5 Kt—B3, Kt×P; 6 Kt—K5 (weak would be 6 Kt×Kt, because of 6 .... P—Q4. Too impetuous would be 6 B×P ch, K×B; 7 Kt—K5 ch, for then the black King takes a wise refuge by 7 .... K—Kt1; 8 Kt×Kt, Kt—B3, etc.), 6 .... Kt—Q3; 7 B—Kt3, Kt—B3; 8 P—Q4, Castles; 9 B×P, Kt×Kt; 10 B×Kt, P—QKt3 (Black is reduced to an artificial plan of defence); 11 Castles, B—Kt2; 12 Q—R5, P—Kt3; 13 Q—R6, Kt—K1; 14 Q×R ch (a thunderbolt), 14 .... K×Q (if 14 .... B×Q; 15 B×P mate); 15 R×P ch, and Black resigns, for he is faced with a pitiless mate in two.

5	Kt—Kt5

An important decision. Much inferior is 5 .... Kt—R4; 6 Kt—B3, P—Q3; 7 P—Q4, B—Kt5; 8 Q—Q3, and White stands considerably better.

6 Castles	

If 6 P—KR3, B—R5 ch; and White is in trouble.

6	Kt—QB3

By reinforcing the attack against White's advanced pawn this sound developing move is effected without loss of time.

Premature would be 6 .... P—Q4; 7 P×P e.p., Q×P; 8 P—Q4, Castles; 9 Kt—B3, worrying the black Queen.

7 P—Q4   P—Q4

Well timed! It is instructive to note how Black manages to develop his game and at the same time to hold on to his gambit pawn.

8 P×P e.p.

Not the retreat, 8 B—Kt3, Kt—K6; 9 B×Kt, P×B; etc., by which White would lose space and see his attack vanish into thin air before having properly begun.

8 ......   B×P

The key-move; Black does not fear the coming frontal attack.

9 R—K1 ch

The continuation in a game, Keres–Alatorzev, *Moscow*, 1950, was as follows: 9 Kt—B3, Castles; 10 Kt—K2, Kt—B3; 11 B×Kt, P×B; 12 P—QR3, Q—B3; 13 Q—Q3, Q—R3; 14 QR—K1, B—KKt5; 15 P—R3, B—R4; 16 Kt—B3, QR—K1; 17 Kt—Q5, P—K7; 18 R—B2, B—Kt6; White resigns.

9 ......   Kt—K2

The value of Black's sixth move now stands out clearly.

10 P—KR3   Kt—B3
11 Kt—B3

If 11 Kt—K5, B×Kt; 12 P×B, Q×Q; 13 R×Q, Kt—R4; 14 B—K2, Kt—Kt6; 15 B—B3, Kt—Kt3; with a poor outlook for White.

11 ......   Castles
12 Kt—QKt5   Kt—Kt3
13 Kt×B   P×Kt

Another instructive move. He submits to having an isolated pawn in order, at any cost, to guard his K4. And still the gambit pawn is guarded.

14 B—Q3   Kt—R4
15 P—B4   Q—B3
16 P—QKt4

Trying to create counter-chances wherever he can.

16 ......   Kt—Kt6
17 B—Kt2   B—B4
18 P—QR4   KR—K1
19 Q—Q2

He tries to make possible the advance 20 P—Q5, by connecting his Rooks and guarding his QB. Black's next move prevents this.

19 ......   B×B
20 Q×B   Kt—B4
21 Q—Kt3   Kt(Kt3)—R5

Again obstructing White's desire to open the long diagonal for his Bishop; for if 22 P—Q5, Kt×Kt ch; 23 P×Kt, Q—Kt4 ch; 24 K—R1, Q—Kt6; demolishing White's position.

22 Kt×Kt   Kt×Kt
23 Q—B2

In order to limit the damage after 23 .... Q—Kt4; by 24 Q—B2, e.g. 24 .... P—B6; 25 P—Kt3, Kt—B4; 26 K—R2, etc., or 24 .... R—K6; 25 R×R, P×R; 26 Q—K2, etc.

23 ......   P—B6

Driving a wedge into the hostile position. The whole defence against a dangerous gambit was conducted by Black with supreme ease.

24 P—Q5

At last he can make this advance, attacking the Queen. But before he can force a passed pawn by P—B5, Black's own K side attack will be in full swing.

If 24 P—Kt3, Kt—Kt7; 25 R×R ch, R×R; 26 P—Q5, Q—Kt4; and wins, thanks to his command of the open K file.

24 ......   Q—Kt4
25 P—Kt4   P—KR4

Demolition!

26 Q—B1   R×R ch
27 Q×R   P×P
28 B—B1   Q—B3
29 R—R3   P×P

Spoliation!

30 K—R2   P—B7
31 Q—B1   Q—K4 ch

Resigns

There is no reply to .... Q—K8. The chief characteristics of O'Kelly's play are logic and aggressiveness. These enabled him here to accept the gambit and then to wrest the initiative from his opponent.

King's Gambit Declined

34

KOCH   GEREBEN
(Zoppot, 1951)

Another example in which White's impet-uous strategy is mastered by the technique of modern defence.

1 P—K4	P—K4
2 P—KB4	B—B4
3 Kt—KB3	P—Q3
4 B—B4	

Or alternatively, 4 P—B3, or even first 4 P×P, P×P; 5 P—B3. In an amusing game, Soler–Almeda, *Madrid*, 1947, White played 4 P—Q4, and the continuation was 4 .... P×QP; 5 Kt×P (interesting is 5 B—Q3), 5 .... KKt—B3; 6 QKt—B3, Q—K2; 7 Q—Q3, Kt×P (too precipitate; 7 .... Castles, was essential); 8 Kt—Q5, Q—R5 ch; 9 P—Kt3, Kt×P; 10 P×Kt, Q×R; 11 Q—K2 ch, B—K3; 12 Kt×B, K—Q2; 13 Kt—B8 ch (a brilliant solution. If 13 Kt×B ch, K—B1; while now there follows a pitiless King-hunt), 13 .... R×Kt; 14 Q—K7 ch, K—B3; 15 Q×BP ch, K×Kt;   16   Q×KtP ch,   Kt—B3; 17 Q—Kt3 ch, K—K5; 18 Q—Q3 mate.

4	Kt—QB3
5 Kt—B3	Kt—B3
6 P—Q3	B—KKt5

The *normal position* in the *King's Gambit Declined*. The actual order of the moves as they occurred in this game was: 1 P—K4, P—K4; 2 B—B4 (*Bishop's Opening*), 2 .... KKt—B3; 3 P—Q3, B—B4; 4 QKt—B3 (the *Vienna Game*), 4 .... P—Q3; 5 P—B4, B—KKt5; etc.

7 QKt—R4
The accepted continuation. Against 7 P—KR3, Black's best is 7 .... B×Kt; 8 Q×B, P×P; etc.

7	Q—K2

Black here has quite a number of moves from which to choose, e.g. 7 .... B—Kt3; 7 .... P×P; 7 .... KKt—R4; 7 .... Kt—Q5; 7 .... B×Kt (8 Q×B, Kt—Q5).

8 Kt×B	P×Kt
9 Castles	

The great connoisseur of the open game (and particularly the *Vienna Game*), Weaver W. Adams, recommends here 9 B—Kt5, e.g. 9 .... P×P; 10 B×Kt ch, P×B; 11 B×P, Castles QR; 12 Castles, and White has the easier game.

9	Castles QR
10 Q—K1	B×Kt
11 P×B	

If 11 R×B, Kt—Q5; 12 R—B2, Kt—Kt5; 13 R—Q2, P×P; 14 P—B3, Kt—K3; 15 R—Q1, P—KKt4; and Black has not only maintained his extra pawn, but he is ready to launch a counter-offensive.

11	Kt—KR4
12 P×P	P—KKt4

A significant moment, and one which clearly illustrates the nature of the modern technique of defence. The recapture of the pawn is not urgent; the attack has priority, and for this it is essential to secure the necessary bases.

13 B—K3	KR—Kt1
14 B—Q5	Kt—Q5

As can be seen, Mr. Adams is right in recommending the elimination of this dangerous piece. Less active is 14 .... Kt×P; 15 P—Q4, P×P; 16 B×QP, and White has gained space.

15 Q—B2	R—Kt1
16 P—B3	Kt—K3
17 B×Kt ch	Q×B
18 P—Q4	

If 18 B×BP, Kt—B5; with the double threat 19 .... Kt—R6 ch; and 19 .... Kt×P. The advance in the text defends both the pawns at Q3 and K5. Nevertheless, Black finds an ingenious way of disrupting White's formation.

18	P×P
19 P×P	P—Kt5

Here it is! White is forced to open the KKt file, for if 20 P—B4, there follows 20   ....   P—Kt6;   21   P×P,   R×P ch; 22   K—R1,   R—R6 ch;   23   K—Kt1, R—Kt1 ch; and White is irretrievably lost.

20 P×P	R×P ch
21 K—R1	R×KP

Thus Black has recovered his pawn and secured a firm footing in the enemy camp.

22 Q—B3	Q—Q4

23 QR—K1 (see diag., p. 56)
Clearly not 23 Q×Kt, R—Kt5 dis ch; followed by mate. The text-move parries the threat 23 .... R×B; but does not prevent other inflictions. He should rather have tried to defend himself by 23 K—Kt1.

23	Kt—B5

Very pretty. In reply, White cannot play 24 B×Kt, R×R; 25 Q×Q, R×R ch; 26 K—Kt2, R×Q; 27 K×R, R×QP; and wins.

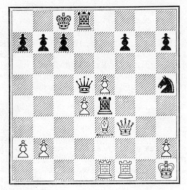

Position after 23 QR—K1

24 P—KR3	Kt—Q6
25 R—K2	Kt—B5

Before giving the *coup-de-grâce*, Black, by a repetition of moves, wins a little more time for reflection.

26 R(K2)—K1	Kt—Q6
27 R—K2	Kt × KtP

This Knight's manœuvres have been masterly. Again White can hardly reply 28 R × Kt, R × B; 29 Q × Q, R × Q; 30 R × BP, P—Kt3; 31 R—QB2, R—Q2; 32 R × R, K × R; 33 K—Kt2, R—K5; 34 R—B2, R × QP; 35 R—B7 ch, K—K3; 36 R × BP, R—QR5; 37 R × KRP, R × P ch; 38 K—Kt3, K × P; and Black must win.

We see that the *art of liquidation* is thoroughly mastered by players of to-day.

28 R—Kt2	Kt—B5
29 B—Kt5	R—Q2
30 Q—B6	P—Kt3
31 Q—R8 ch	K—Kt2
32 P—K6	R × KP
33 K—R2	R—Kt3
34 R(B1)—KKt1	Q × P
35 Q × Q	Q—K4 ch
36 K—R1	Q—Q4
37 K—R2	Kt—K4
Resigns	

And the terrible Knight has the last word.

Falkbeer Counter-Gambit

35

HORNE   A. R. B. THOMAS
(Felixstowe, 1949)

Here is a fine example of the open game. A feature of the King's *Gambit, whether*

accepted or declined, is that, should the mechanism of the defence falter ever so little, the consequence is a convincing and rapid collapse.

1 P—K4	P—K4
2 P—KB4	P—Q4
3 P × QP	P—K5

This counter-gambit was looked upon for many years as the refutation of the *King's Gambit*. Dangerous also is Nimzowitsch's idea, 3 .... P—QB3; which, however, is satisfactorily met by 4 Kt—QB3.

Not to be recommended is 3 .... Q × P; as is illustrated in the following game, Tolush–Alatorzev, from the *U.S.S.R. Championship*, 1948: 3 .... Q × P; 4 Kt—QB3, Q—K3 (the black Queen walks into trouble and the full retreat 4 .... Q—Q1; should be considered); 5 P × P (playable is even 5 Kt—B3, P × P dis ch; 6 K—B2, with the counter-threat, 7 B—Kt5 ch, followed by R—K1), 5 .... Q × P ch; 6 B—K2, B—KKt5; 7 P—Q4, Q—K3 (the transaction 7 .... B × B; 8 Q × B, Q × Q ch; 9 KKt × Q, would give White a considerable advance in development); 8 Q—Q3, P—QB3, 9 B—B4, Kt—B3; 10 Castles, B × B; 11 KKt × B, B—Q3 (Black is no longer able to make up for retarded mobilisation); 12 P—Q5 (on the principle: "Open more lines when in a superior position"), 12 .... Kt × P; 13 Kt × Kt, P × Kt; 14 Q—KKt3, B × B ch; 15 Kt × B, Q—KR3 (best, but not good enough); 16 KR—K1 ch, K—B1; 17 Q—R3 ch, Black resigns (to avoid being mated by R—K8.

More difficult to refute is the retarded acceptance of the Gambit by 3 .... P × P; which occurred in a game, Larsson–Englund, *correspondence*, 1942, as follows: 3 .... P × P; 4 Kt—KB3 (more subtle is 4 Q—B3, still defending his centre pawn), 4 .... Kt—KB3; 5 P—Q4 (better is 5 Kt—B3), 5 .... Kt × P; 6 P—B4 (a hasty move), 6 .... B—Kt5 ch; 7 QKt—Q2 (preferable is 7 B—Q2, and if 7 .... Kt—K6; 8 Q—Kt3), 7 .... Kt—K6; 8 Q—R4 ch (restless play. More rational is 8 Q—Kt3, at once), 8 .... B—Q2; 9 Q—Kt3, Q—K2; 10 K—B2, Kt—Q8 ch (well played: if 11 Q × Kt, Q—K6 mate); 11 K—Kt1, Kt—B6 (beautiful! Again 12 .... Q—K6 mate, is threatened); 12 P—KR3, B—R5; White resigns. In avoiding the mate, White loses the Queen. A sprightly display.

4 P—Q3	Kt—KB3
5 P × P	

Other continuations are less incisive, e.g. (a) 5 Kt—QB3, B—QKt5; and Black keeps up the pressure; (*b*) 5 Q—K2, an ancient continuation, played successfully by Blackburne against Marco, *Berlin*, 1897, and against which 5 .... B—Kt5; can be recommended; (*c*) 5 Kt—Q2, Keres' modern continuation. Its subleties are shown in a game Javelle–Dewacke, *correspondence*, 1951: 5 Kt—Q2, B—KB4 (after the accepted line, 5 .... P—K6; 6 Kt—B4, White obtains the better game. Or 5 .... P×P; 6 B×P, Kt×P; 7 Q—K2 ch, B—K2; 8 Kt—K4, Castles; 9 Kt—KB3, R—K1; 10 Kt—K5, P—KB3; 11 Q—R5, P×Kt; 12 Kt—Kt5, etc., with a winning attack); 6 P×P, Kt×KP; 7 B—Q3 (if 7 Q—K2, Q—K2; but more logical is 7 KKt—B3), 7 .... Q—R5ch (he could add to White's problems by 7 .... B—QKt5); 8 P—Kt3, Kt×P; 9 KKt—B3, Q—Kt5; 10 P×Kt, Q×P ch; 11 K—B1, B—B4; 12 Q—K2 ch, K—Q1; 13 B×B, R—K1; 14 Kt—K5, P—KB3, 15 Kt—B7 mate. Tableau!

5	Kt×KP
6 B—K3	

Reviving an old recipe of Dr. Krause's. More modern is Alapin's 6 Kt—KB3.

6	B—KB4

He probably discards the better continuation, 6 .... B—Q3; in order to have .... B—QKt5; in reserve, should White play Kt—QB3. No useful purpose is served by 6 .... Q—R5 ch; 7 P—Kt3, Kt×P; 8 Kt—KB3, Q—R3; 9 P×Kt, Q×R; 10 Q—K2, etc.

7 Kt—KB3	P—QB3

Sounder strategy would be 7 .... B—Q3.

8 B—B4	Q—R4 ch
9 P—B3	Kt—Q2
10 P×P	

Without fear of hostile action on the Q file and at the right time.

10	P×P
11 Castles	R—Q1
12 Kt—Q4	

A fine move which contains so many threats that there is no satisfactory reply.

12	Kt—Kt1
13 P—QKt4	Q—B2
14 Q—B3	Kt—Q3

On 14 .... Q—Q2; 15 Kt×B, Q×Kt; 16 P—Kt4, Q—Kt3; 17 P—B5, and Black must lose a piece.

15 Kt×B	Kt×Kt
16 Q—K4 ch	Q—K2

16 .... Kt—K2; is clearly hopeless. The finish is neat.

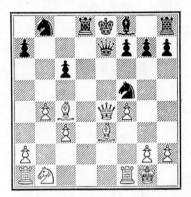

17 B×P ch

Black's ill-fated KB2 is beset by many afflictions.

17	K×B
18 Q×Kt ch	K—Kt1
19 B—Q4	Q—KB2

If 19 .... P—QR4; 20 Kt—Q2, R×B; 21 P×R, Q—K6 ch; 22 K—R1, and he cannot play .... Q×Kt; because of 23 Q—K6 mate.

20 Q×Q ch	K×Q
21 B×RP	Resigns

An anomalous situation: after a *King's Gambit*, an opening which promises so much turmoil and strife, White ends up simply with a material advantage of three pawns, collected in the heat of battle.

PART II

SEMI-OPEN GAMES

12. FRENCH DEFENCE

36

H. PILNIK   BENI
(Vienna, 1951-2)

*The mechanism of the sacrifice is well
illustrated in the following game.*

1 P—K4	P—K3
2 P—Q4	P—Q4
3 Kt—QB3	Kt—KB3
4 B—Kt5	B—K2
5 P—K5	KKt—Q2
6 B × B	Q × B

In this, the *normal position* of the *French*,
White has a wide choice of moves. True to
contemporary thought, which likes to
mingle logic and imagination, Pilnik decides
on a bold plan.

    7 Q—Kt4   Castles
Weaker is at once 7 .... P—KB4;
8 P × P e.p., Kt × P; 9 Q—R4, and White
already exerts considerable pressure.

    8 Kt—B3   P—QB4
    9 B—Q3   P—B4
Now necessary as White, according to a
well-known pattern, was threatening
10 B × P ch, K × B; 11 Kt—Kt5 ch, etc.

    10 P × P e.p.   Kt × P
Or alternatively, as in a game Dr. O. S.
Bernstein–Dr. Em. Lasker, *Zürich*, 1934,
10 .... R × P; 11 Q—R4, Kt—B1;
12 P × P, Q × P; 13 Castles KR, Kt—B3;
14 QR—K1, B—Q2; 15 Kt—K5, Kt × Kt;
16 R × Kt, Q—Kt3; and Black has succeeded
in obtaining equality.

    11 Q—R4   Kt—B3
    12 P × P   P—K4 (see diag.)
This counter-attempt is too impetuous
to be good. But resolute as well as imaginative strategy is required to prove this.
Black should have followed the lines of the
game Pilnik–Guimard, *Buenos Aires*, 1941,
as follows: 12 .... Q × P; 13 Castles QR,
Q—Kt5; trying to neutralise the momentum
of White's attack.

    13 Kt × QP
A *deflecting sacrifice* rich in additional
points.

    13 ......   Kt × Kt

Position after 12 .... P—K4

    14 Q × P ch   K—B2
    15 Q—R5 ch
An important check which forces the black
King to participate in the struggle in the
centre.

    15 ......   K—K3
    16 Castles QR
White has ample time to bring up the
bulk of his forces.

    16 ......   Q—B3
On 16 .... Q × P; White can without any
haste reinforce the pressure with 17 KR—K1.

    17 B—K4
White must continue his work with prob-
lem-like moves. 17 B—B4, is clearly inade-
quate against 17 .... Q—B5 ch; 18 K—Kt1,
Q × B; etc., while after the text-move White's
Bishop is safe because of Kt—Kt5 ch.

    17 ......   Q—B5 ch
    18 K—Kt1   Kt—B3
    19 Q—Kt6
With the threat of instant death by
20 Kt—Kt5 ch, K—K2; 21 Q × P ch,
K—K1; 22 B—Kt6 ch, followed by mate.

    19 ......   Q—R3
    20 R—Q6 ch   K—K2
    21 Q × Q
The defender has scored a moral success
in that he has brought about an exchange of
Queens while preserving his extra piece, but
Pilnik has seen a little farther.

21	P × Q
22 B × Kt	P × B
23 Kt × P	

Black's central line of defence lies devastated. Already now, with four pawns for the piece and the prospective gain of a fifth, it is White who has registered an advantage in material.

| 23 ...... | Kt—K5 |
| 24 R—Q4 | |

White keeps full control of the situation and allows his opponent no counter-chance. After 24 R × RP, R × P; Black could still offer resistance. 24 .... Kt × KBP; is not playable because of 25 Kt × P ch, K—B3; 26 R—B4 ch, K—Kt2; 27 R × R, Kt × R (or 27 .... K × R; 28 R—KB1, appropriating the Knight); 28 R—B1, B—Kt2; 29 Kt—R5, B × P; 30 R—Kt1, and wins.

24	B—B4
25 R—K1	Kt × QBP
26 Kt—Kt6 db ch	K—B3

Or 26 .... K—B2; 27 Kt × R, R × Kt; 28 R—K5, R—K1; 29 R × R (but not 29 R × B ch, K—Kt3; 30 P—QKt4, Kt—R5, etc.), 29 .... K × R; 30 R—QB4, Kt—K5; 31 R × P, Kt × P; 32 R × P, and White's advantage in material (the exchange and four pawns for a minor piece) is sufficient to secure an easy win.

| 27 R—Q6 ch | K—Kt4 |
| 28 Kt × R | |

The big harvest.

28	R × Kt
29 R × BP	Kt—K5
30 P—KB3	

The White pawn phalanx comes into play and Black's agony will be short.

30	Kt—B3
31 P—KKt3	P—KR4
32 R—K5	Resigns

A wise decision in an irretrievable situation, e.g. 32 .... R—Q1; 33 K—B1, or 32 .... K—Kt3; 33 P—KR4, etc. If 32 .... Kt—Q2; 33 P—R4 mate, and if 32 .... P—R5; 33 P—KKt4.

37

C. ALEXANDER   YANOFSKY
(Hastings, 1946-7)

This magnificent struggle, on which depended the first prize in the tournament, was won by the player who showed the greater "will to win."

1 P—K4	P—K3
2 P—Q4	P—Q4
3 Kt—QB3	Kt—KB3
4 B—Kt5	B—K2
5 P—K5	KKt—Q2
6 P—KR4	

The *Chatard–Alekhine Attack* which suits Alexander's style particularly well.

| 6 ...... | P—QR3 |

From several playable replies, the young Canadian selects one which aims at a Q side preponderance, but which has no particular effect on the K side, where White can operate virtually a *tempo* to the good. Analysis has shown that the immediate counter-demonstration, 6 .... P—QB4; is playable, e.g. 7 Kt—Kt5, P—B3; etc., or 7 B × B, K × B; etc., or 7 Q—Kt4, Kt—QB3; etc.

| 7 Q—Kt4 | P—KB4 |

More staidness is shown by 7 .... K—B1; first, and then only 8 .... P—KB4; in reply to 8 P—B4.

| 8 Q—Kt3 | |

A psychologically interesting moment. Anticipating prepared analysis, Alexander steers clear of the impetuous 8 Q—R5 ch, P—Kt3; 9 Q—R6. Lifeless would be 8 P × P e.p., Kt × P; 9 Q—K2, etc., which Alexander tried against Gudmunsson in the same tournament.

| 8 ...... | P—B4 |

He continues to bait his opponent on the Queen's wing.

| 9 B—K3 | |

A logical retreat which consolidates his position in the centre. An interesting skirmish could arise from 9 P × P, Kt—QB3; 10 B—KB4, Castles; 11 B—R6, R—B2; 12 Kt × P, QKt × P; and Black has strengthened his game.

| 9 ...... | Castles |
| 10 KKt—K2 | Q—Kt3 |

Black pays too much attention to his ventures on the Q side. The Queen is still required at Q1. A re-grouping by 10 .... R—K1; followed by .... B—B1; would reinforce his position. More solid also than the diversion in the text would be 10 .... Kt—QB3; e.g. 11 Kt—B4, Kt—Kt3; 12 Castles, P × P; 13 B × QP, Q—B2; and Black has defensive chances.

| 11 Castles | R—B2 |

Black's difficulties are on the increase. He cannot yet make the natural developing

move, 11 .... Kt—QB3; because of
12 B—R6, R—B2; 13 Kt×P, P×Kt;
14 P—K6, and wins.

12 Kt—B4   Kt—B1
13 B—K2
White makes straight for his target on the
K side, without allowing himself to be side-
tracked by other possible plans, as, for
instance, 13 K—Kt1, with threat 14 P×P,
etc.

13 ......   Kt—B3
If 13 .... P—Kt3; 14 P—R5, P—Kt4;
15 KKt×QP, P×Kt; 16 Kt×P, Q—Q1;
17 Kt×B ch, Q×Kt; 18 QB×P, and White's
attack is ample compensation for the piece
invested.

14 B—R5   P—Kt3
An interesting interlude here, according to
Alexander's own analysis, is 14 .... P×P;
15 B×R ch, K×B; 16 B×P, Kt×B;
17 Q—K3, B—B4; 18 Kt—R4, and Black
has lost the exchange in a bad position.
Note that if now 18 .... Kt—Kt6 ch;
19 Q×Kt.

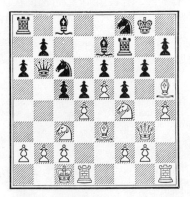

15 Kt×KtP
Brilliant and logical. "Strike while the
iron's hot." If, for instance, 15 QKt—K2,
K—R1; 16 B—B3, the struggle would die
away.

15 ......   P×Kt
16 B×P   Kt×B
Here 16 .... R—Kt2; 17 P—R5, K—R1;
would limit the damage as the KR file
remains closed.

17 P—R5   P—KB5
Black defends skilfully. If, instead,
17 .... P×P; 18 P×Kt, is decisive (18 ....
P×B; 19 R—R8 ch, K×R; 20 P×R, forcing

mate, or 18 .... R—Kt2; 19Q—R3, etc.).
Again, if 17 .... R—Kt2; 18 P—R6, and
Black has no defence.

18 B×P
An interesting line is 18 Q—Kt4, P×B;
19 P×Kt, R—Kt2; 20 Q—R5, K—B1;
21 Q—R8 ch, R—Kt1; 22 P—Kt7 ch,
K—B2; 23 P×KP, and White's frontal
attack now develops on three files.

18 ......   P×P
Here 18 .... Q—Q1; affords Black better
chances of resistance.

19 P×Kt   P×Kt
Now 19 .... Q—Q1; would come too
late: 20 P×R db ch, K×P; 21 R—R7 ch,
K—K1; 22 R—R8 ch, B—B1; 23 B—R6,
K—K2; 24 R—R7 ch, K—K1; 25 Q—Kt6
mate. On the other hand, if 19 ....
R—Kt2; 20 Q—R3, is conclusive.

20 P×R db ch
Under stress of time, White discards a
quicker win, as follows: 20 R—R8 ch,
K×R (if 20 .... K—Kt2; 21 P×R dis ch,
and the Queen mates at Kt8); 21 Q—R3 ch,
B—R5 (otherwise, if 21 .... K—Kt1;
22 P×R ch, K×P; 23 Q—R5 ch, K—Kt2;
24 B—R6 ch, etc.); 22 Q×B ch, K—Kt1;
23 P×R ch, K×P; 24 Q—B6 ch, K—K1;
25 P×P, Q—Q1; 26 Q—Kt6 ch, K—Q2;
27 R×P ch, P×R; 28 P—K6 ch, K—K2;
29 Q—B7 mate.

20 ......   K×P
21 Q×P   K—K1
Forced, as otherwise 22 R—R8, cuts off
the King, who would clearly be in a mating
net.

22 R—R8 ch   K—Q2
Now the black King looks very snug with
two Bishops against Rook and some pawns.
But both his QR and QB are in chancery.

23 R×P ch
Alexander in his element.

23 ......   K—B2
If instead, 23 .... P×R; 24 P—K6 ch,
K×P; 25 Q—R3 ch, K—B2; 26 Q—R5 ch,
K—K3; 27 Q—Kt6 ch, B—B3 (if 27 ....
K—Q2; 28 Q—B5 mate); 28 Q—Kt4 ch,
K—K2; 29 R—R7 ch, K—B1; 30 B—R6 ch,
etc.

24 R—Q1
Simplest is 24 B—K3, Q—Kt5; 25 R—Q3,
etc., with an easily won ending, thanks to the
K side pawns. The text-move, however,

keeps up the pressure against Black's congested position.

24	Q × P
25 B—K3	

More ambitious than 25 P—KKt3.

25	Q—B4

After 25 .... Q × P; the diversion 26 R—Kt1, followed by R—Kt7, is decisive, e.g. 26 .... Q—K5; 27 R—Kt7, K—Kt1; 28 R × B, Kt × R; 29 Q—B5, Q—B3; 30 Q × Kt, etc., or else 26 .... Q—Q4; 27 R—Kt7, K—Kt1; 28 B—Kt6, Q—Q2; 29 R(Kt7)—Kt8, etc.

26 P—KKt4	Q—Kt3

If 26 .... Q × KP; 27 Q × Q, Kt × Q; 28 B—B4, B—Q3; 29 K—Kt1, and the KKtP marches in. Or 26 .... Q × KtP; 27 R—R7, K—Kt1; 28 R × B, Kt × R; 29 Q—B5, Kt—B4; 30 R—Q8, and Black gets mated in broad daylight.

27 B—B5	Q—Kt4 ch

Or 27 .... B × B; 28 Q × B, Q—Kt4 ch; 29 K—Kt1, Q × KP; 30 R—R7 ch, K—Kt1; 31 Q × Q, Kt × Q; 32 P—Kt5, and Black can restrain this passed pawn only at the cost of a piece.

28 Q—K3	P—Kt4

If 28 .... Q × KtP; 29 R—R7, wins a piece.

29 B—Kt6 ch	K—Kt1

If 29 .... K—Kt2; 30 R—R7, K—Kt1; 31 K—Kt1, with the threat of 32 B—B7 ch.

30 K—Kt1	Q—Kt2

An exchange of Queens would have prolonged the agony. Now comes a delightful finish.

31 R—Q7	B—B4

For if 31 .... Q × R; 32 B—B7 ch, K—Kt2; 33 Q—Kt6 mate.

32 B—B7 ch	K—Kt2
33 Q × B	Resigns

Thus ended a great game, which held the onlookers spellbound and decided the tournament.

38

L. EVANS	C. PILNICK

(New York, 1947)

The very young American from college shows in the following game that his early attempts already bear the hallmark of the master.

1 P—K4	P—K3
2 P—Q4	P—Q4
3 Kt—QB3	

Here a *blockading strategy* by 3 P—K5, also has supporters. A fine illustration of its possibilities is furnished by the following miniature game, Milner-Barry–Trott, *Ilford,* 1951: 3 P—K5 (this advance, much favoured by Steinitz and Nimzowitsch, is said by the theory to be premature, but in actual practice it has scored many triumphs), 3 .... P—QB4; 4 P—QB3 (theoretically sound, of course, as strengthening the centre. In his later years, however, Nimzowitsch gave preference to the more aggressive and tricky 4 Q—Kt4), 4 .... Kt—QB3; 5 Kt—B3, Q—Kt3; 6 B—Q3 (more forcible than 6 B—K2), 6 .... KKt—K2 (a careless move, which gives Milner-Barry an opportunity to exercise his exceptional gift for attack. Black should play 6 .... P × P); 7 P × P (the point now is that Black's Queen will lose many moves after 7 .... Q × BP; 8 B—K3, or get into serious difficulties in the line actually played), 7 .... Q—B2; 8 Kt—R3, Kt × P, 9 QKt—Kt5, Kt × B ch; 10 Q × Kt, Q × BP; 11 B—K3, P—Q5; 12 B × P, Q—B3; 13 Kt—K5, Q × P (Black's Queen is saved, but his King is in a trap); 14 Kt—Q6 ch, K—Q1; 15 B—Kt6 ch, Black resigns. Delightful! (15 .... P × B; 16 Kt × BP db ch, K—K1; 17 Q—Q8 mate, or 16 .... K—B2; 17 Q—Q6 mate).

3	Kt—KB3
4 B—Kt5	

He decides on the pin in preference to simplification: 4 P × P (*Svenonius*), or the central advance 4 P—K5, KKt—Q2.

4	B—K2
5 B × Kt	

This line, preferred by the German masters, Anderssen and Richter, is not without venom.

5	B × B
6 P—K5	

Steadier is first 6 Kt—B3.

6	B—K2
7 Q—Kt4	Castles
8 Castles	

Less hurried, but equally bold is 8 B—Q3, as illustrated in a game Paoli–Stalda from the *Italian Championship, Venice,* 1950: 8 B—Q3, P—QB4 (playable also is, first, 8 .... P—KB4; 9 Q—R3, although here too White's attack remains very dangerous); 9 P × P, Kt—B3; 10 Kt—B3 (accelerating his action, White discards the usual

10 P—B4, which gives Black just the necessary time to build up an active defence by 10 .... P—B4; 11 Q—R3, P—QKt3; 12 Castles, B×P, etc.), 10 .... P—B3; 11 Q—R5, P—KKt3; 12 B×P, P×B; 13 Q×P ch, K—R1; 14 P—KR4, B×P; 15 Q—R6 ch, K—Kt1; 16 R—R3, Q—Kt3; 17 Q—Kt6 ch, K—R1; 18 Q—R5 ch, Black resigns.

8 ...... P—QB4

The position demands 8 .... P—KB4; e.g. 9 Q—R3, P—QKt3; 10 P—B4, P—B4; 11 Kt—B3, P—QB5; 12 R—Kt1, P—QKt4; and the game is evening out.

9 P—KR4

White's treatment of the opening shows no lack of courage, and the play hereafter leaves the paths of theory. More conformable is 9 P×P.

9	P×P
10 QKt—K2	Kt—B3
11 P—KB4	Q—R4
12 K—Kt1	P—Q6

The idea of this move is to force 13 P×P (13 R×P, Q—K8 ch), after which this Rook cannot readily go over to the K side *via* Q3. If, instead 12 .... B—B4; 13 Kt—B1, and White's attack prevails.

13 P×P	B—Q2
14 R—R3	QR—B1
15 R—Kt3	P—KKt3
16 P—Q4	P—QKt4
17 P—R5	Kt—Kt5
18 P—R3	Kt—B3
19 P×P	BP×P
20 Kt—QB3	

Played with consummate skill; White deliberately jeopardises his King's field for the sole purpose of enabling his KB to occupy the right diagonal.

| 20 ...... | P—Kt5 |
| 21 B—Q3 | B—K1 |

The crisis. Black's KKt3 appears to be sufficiently protected and White's game seems to be compromised.

22 Kt—B3

There emerges the miracle of the sacrifice.

22 ...... P×P

Here 22 .... P×Kt; leads to much the same finish.

| 23 Q×KP ch | B—B2 |
| 24 B×P | |

A magnificent conception! If now

Position after 21 .... B—K1

24 .... B×Q; 25 B×P db ch, K—R1 (25 .... K—B2; 26 B—Kt6 ch, K—Kt2; 27 B—K8 dis ch, etc.); 26 R—R1, P—R7 ch; 27 K—R1, R×P; 28 B—B5 dis ch, B—R5; 29 Kt×B, with mate to follow.

24 ...... P×P

25 B×P db ch

Not 25 B×B db ch, K—R1; and White would have missed his way.

25	K—R1
26 Q—R6	Q—R8 ch
27 K—B2	P—Kt8(Q) ch

Or 27 .... Kt—Kt5 ch; 28 K—Q2, and Black is at the end of his resources.

| 28 R×Q | Kt—Kt5 ch |
| 29 K—Q1 | Resigns |

An inspiring finish! A remarkable feature of contemporary chess is the great number of very young players who show outstanding promise all over the world.

No one would guess that the winner of this game, playing against a ranking player of the U.S.A., was only 15 at the time.

39

NEUMAN   EILEEN TRANMER
(*Lancashire*)   (*Middlesex*)

(British Counties' Championship, Manchester, 1950)

Since the sad and premature death of Mrs. Stevenson-Menchik, the number of ladies capable of holding their own against players of the opposite sex has steadily increased.

1 P—K4 P—K3

2 P—Q4	P—Q4
3 Kt—QB3	Kt—KB3
4 B—Kt5	B—Kt5

This *counter-pin*, introduced by the American McCutcheon, still gives experts everywhere much food for thought.

5 P—K5

Much less energetic are the following continuations: 5 P×P, 5 Kt—K2, and 5 B—Q3. The last-named was played in a curious little game from the *U.S.A. Open Championship*, 1951, between Coles and Westbrook: 5 B—Q3, P×P (playable also is, at once 5 .... P—B4; 6 Kt—B3, Kt—B3); 6 B×P, P—B4; 7 Kt—K2 (7 P×P, Q—R4), 7 .... P×P; 8 Kt×P, Q—R4; 9 B×Kt, B×Kt ch; 10 P×B, Q×P ch; 11 Q—Q2 (inspired by the motif of the "Immortal Game," Anderssen–Kieseritzky, *London*, 1851), 11 .... Q×R ch; 12 K—K2, Q—Kt7 (Black realises that the capture of the second Rook would be suicidal because of 13 Kt×P, and he therefore tries to maintain his Queen on the long black diagonal, so as to reply to 13 Kt×P by 13 .... Q×B); 13 R—QKt1 (a *deflecting sacrifice*), 13 .... Q×R; 14 Kt×P, B—Q2; 15 Kt×P ch, K—B1; 16 Kt—K6 ch, P×Kt (or 16 .... K—K1; 17 Kt—B7 ch, etc.); 17 Q—Q6 ch, K—Kt1; 18 Q—Kt3 ch, and mate in two.

5	P—KR3
6 B—Q2	

The routine retreat.

6	B×Kt
7 P×B	Kt—K5
8 B—Q3	

A critical moment. The most dynamic continuation is known to be 8 Q—Kt4, P—KKt3 (if 8 .... K—B1, giving up any idea of castling, White continues 9 P—KR4, P—QB4; 10 R—R3, Q—R4; 11 B—Q3, Kt×B; 12 R—Kt3, P—KKt3; 13 K×Kt, etc., with multiple chances); 9 B—B1 (the idea of this fine retreat is due to Duras. Inferior is 9 P—KR4, P—QB4; 10 B—Q3, Kt×B; 11 K×Kt, Kt—B3; 12 R—R3, P×P; 13 P×P, Q—Kt3; 14 Kt—B3, B—Q2, and Black has the better game: Dr. Euwe–Castaldi, *Venice*, 1948), 9 .... Kt×QBP (if 9 .... P—QB4; White has the subtle continuation, 10 B—Q3, P×P; 11 Kt—K2, etc.: Bronstein–Goldenov, *Kiev*, 1944); 10 B—Q3, P—QB4; 11 P×P, Kt—B3; 12 Kt—B3, Q—R4; 13 Castles, Q—R5 (more prudent than 13 .... Q×BP; 14 Q—R4, and White's attack is stronger than ever: Smyslov–Donner, *Venice*, 1950); 14 Q×Q, Kt×Q; 15 B—K3, and White's

positional advantage takes a definite shape: Barden–Donner, *University Match, England v. Holland*, 1951.

8	Kt×B
9 Q×Kt	P—QB4

The real play begins here, and is a good illustration of what Black's strategy should be in the "French". Black's K side is safe, and with this move Black starts an attempt to undermine White's centre and to obtain counter-play on the Q side.

10 P×P

White gives in too soon. However, 10 Kt—B3, would delay his intended thrust, P—KB4, and Black then obtains additional chances on the Q side after 10 .... Kt—B3; 11 Castles KR, Q—R4; etc. Again, after 10 P—KB4, Kt—B3; 11 B—Kt5, Q—R4; 12 B×Kt ch, P×B; 13 Kt—B3, B—R3; Black's game is preferable.

10	Q—B2

White's weak points bring retribution.

11 Q—K3	Castles
12 Kt—K2	Kt—Q2
13 P—KB4	Kt×BP
14 Castles KR	B—Q2
15 R—B3	

We should prefer 15 P—Kt4, retaining some initiative on his wing.

15	QR—B1
16 R—R3	P—B4
17 Q—Q4	R—B2
18 P—B4	P×P
19 B×P(B4)	B—K1
20 Q—K3	P—QKt4

While White is reduced to marking time, Black energetically exploits her advantage on her wing.

21 B—Kt3	R—K2
22 Kt—Q4	K—R2
23 Q—K2	Q—Kt3

Black's objects have been achieved. Her K side is still secure, but she has a definite pull on the opposing wing.

24 K—R1	Kt—K5
25 R—Q3	P—QR4
26 P—QR3	B—B2

Freeing the KR for operations on the Q side, where Black's onslaught is steadily increasing in momentum.

27 Q—K3	Q—B4
28 R—KB1	P—R5
29 B—R2	Kt—B6

30 B—Kt1   R(K2)—B2
31 Q—B1
White defends his possessions by artificial means.

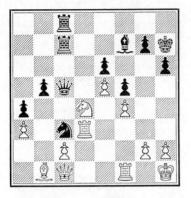

31 ......   P—Kt5
The break-through. Black's conduct of the attack displays a masterly touch. If 32 P×P, Q×KtP; followed by ....·. R—QKt1; and the Bishop is trapped.

32 R(B1)—B3   Q—R4
Black works with the precision of a watch maker.

33 Q—Kt2   P×P
34 Q—R1   Q—Kt5
35 B—R2
White is demoralised. But he is equally lost after 35 R—B1, Q—Kt7; 36 Q×Q, P×Q; followed by the advance of the QRP.

35 ......   Kt×B
36 Q×Kt   Q—K8 ch
                    Resigns
After playing over this game, Mme. de Silans remarked: "I can see that women are even more dangerous than men."

40
STANNARD   NIKOLENKO
(West Australian Championship, 1950)

Lovers of chess cannot help rejoicing in the fact that chess flourishes and is played expertly in the farthest parts of the globe.

1 P—K4   P—K3
2 P—Q4   P—Q4
3 Kt—QB3   B—Kt5

The idea of this early pin was first favoured by Winawer, then by Maróczy and Nimzowitsch. Finally Alekhine and Botvinnik elaborated its details so that it began to be considered almost a refutation of White's third move.

Thus theory is in a constant state of flux.

4 P—K5
From a number of possible replies, White selects the most incisive. Less stable is 4 P—QR3, which is illustrated in a *correspondence game*, Dr. Törber–Menke, 1950, as follows: 4 P—QR3, B×Kt ch; 5 P×B, Kt—KB3 (less troublesome for Black is 5 .... Kt—K2; 6 P—K5, P—QB4, etc., or even 5 .... P×P; 6 Q—Kt4, Kt—KB3; 7 Q×KtP, R—Kt1; 8 Q—R6, P—B4, etc., with equality); 6 P—K5 (this delayed blockade is even more troublesome), 6 .... KKt—Q2; 7 P—QR4 (providing a powerful subsidiary diagonal for the QB), 7 .... P—QB4; 8 Q—Kt4, K—B1 (it is clear that 8 .... Castles would lose the exchange, while 8 .... P—KKt3 would dangerously weaken the King's field); 9 P—R4, Q—B2; 10 KR—R3, P×P (seeking counter-play, Black reckons only with the artless continuation 11 P×P, Kt×P; 12 P×Kt, Q×P ch; followed by .... Q×R; but matters turn out differently); 11 B—R3 ch, K—Kt1; 12 Q×P ch, a hammer-blow which leads to a mate in four.

4 ......   P—QB4
The normal reaction, but 4 .... Kt—K2; also is worth considering.

5 P—QR3   B×Kt ch
6 P×B   Kt—K2
7 Kt—B3
He prefers the quiet mobilisation of his forces to uncertain enterprises, such as 7 Q—Kt4 (7 .... Kt—B4; 8 B—Q3, P—KR4; 9 Q—B4, Q—R5; 10 B×Kt, Q×Q; 11 B×Q, P×B; equalising), or 7 P—QR4 (7 .... QKt—B3; 8 Kt—B3, Q—R4; 9 B—Q2, P—B5; with even chances).

7 ......   QKt—B3
Black also prefers noncommittal moves to defining his intention by 7 .... Q—R4, or 7 .... B—Q2. •

8 B—Q3
Or 8 P—QR4, Q—R4; 9 B—Q2 (9 Q—Q2, P×P; 10 P×P, Q×Q ch; 11 B×Q, Kt—B4; with equality), 9 .... P—B5; and now Lilienthal's idea: 10 P—Kt3, B—Q2; 11 B—R3, increases White's dynamic possibilities.

8 ......   P—B5
More forcible is 8 .... Q—R4; e.g.
9 Castles, Q × BP; 10 B—Q2, Q—Kt7;
11 R—Kt1, with a draw by repetition of
moves, or 9 B—Q2, P—B5; 10 B—K2, and
Black has established strong points on the
Q side.

9 B—K2   B—Q2
10 B—Q2   Q—B2
Here again 10 .... Q—R4; is more active.
The black Queen stays quietly at home,
leaving her King to face a difficult problem.
If he castles KR, White's forces are better
placed for attack on the K side than are
Black's for defence. .... Castles QR; on
the other hand, is very risky, in view of the
open QKt file.

11 Q—B1
White's play has been deliberate, waiting
for Black's decision to castle on one side or
the other, and he is indeed well prepared for
either contingency.

11 ......   Castles QR
12 P—QR4   P—KR3
More energetic is 12 .... P—B4; with
chances of counter-action on the K side.
If 13 P × P e. p., P × P; Black also has an
open file, and if 13 B—Kt5, P—KR3; he
threatens an advance by his K side pawns.

13 R—R2   K—Kt1
14 Q—R1   Q—R4
He stops the advance of the hostile
QRP, and at the same time, makes up for the
inaccuracy of his tenth move.

15 Castles   Kt—B1
16 R—Kt1   Kt—Kt3
17 B—QB1
A random thought: there is in chess what
might be called the topography of the game.
Many a contest recalls manœuvres in
mountainous country; others jungle war-
fare. Here we are forcibly reminded of a
fight in the bush, such as could occur,
precisely, in Australia. Going one step
further, we might assume that the physical
geography of a country (its contours,
climate, irrigation, etc.), has a considerable
influence, not only on the way of life of its
inhabitants, but on their manner of thinking.

17 ......   Kt—K2
18 B—R3
Refuting his opponent's threats; Black
must change his plans.

18 ......   Kt—B3
19 B—Q6 ch   K—B1

20 B—Kt4   Q—R3
21 B—B5
A busy Bishop. Various dangerous
threats are impending, e.g. 22 P—R5,
Kt—R1; 23 R—Kt6, Kt × R (or 23 ....
P × R; 24 P × P, Q—Kt4; 25 R × Kt ch,
Kt—Kt1; 26 R × Kt ch, followed by mate in
two); 24 P × Kt, Q—Kt4; 25 P × P, Kt × RP;
26 R—R5, Q—B3 (if 26 .... B—B3; then,
first 27 B × Kt, and then R × Q, and Black
would have no equivalent for his Queen);
27 R × Kt, K—B2; 28 B—Q6 ch, and wins.

21 ......   Kt—R1
22 P—R5   QR—K1
The black King should have been given
more breathing space by 22 .... QR—Kt1.

23 B—Q6
A psychological moment: White proceeds
methodically in preference to embarking on
the combination shown above, commencing
with 23 R—Kt6.

23 ......   Kt—B2
24 Kt—Q2
Calling up the reserves.

24 ......   Kt—Q1
Black has been to great pains to obtain a
little freedom, but ...

25 Kt—Kt3

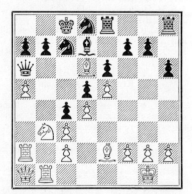

here is a brilliant conception, whether
Black take the Knight or not, e.g.: 25 ....
Q—B3; 26 Kt—B5, Kt—Kt4; 27 R × Kt,
Q × R; 28 R—Kt2, Q—B3; 29 R—Kt6, and
Black is without resource. In taking the
Knight, Black obtains Rook and two pieces
for the Queen, but he cannot save the game.

25 ......   P × Kt
26 B × Q   P × R

27	B×P ch	Kt×B
28	Q×P	Kt×B
29	P×Kt	Kt—Kt4
30	Q—Kt3	K—Kt2
31	P—QB4	

Leaving behind the last zone of the bush, after which the fight in the open will be of short duration.

31	......	P×P
32	Q×P	R—QB1
33	R×Kt ch	B×R
34	Q×B ch	K—R1
35	P—R6	Resigns

An exciting struggle. If now 35 .... R—QKt1; 36 Q—B6 ch, etc.

41

PLECI ENDZELINS
(*Argentine*) (*Latvia*)
(Olympiad, Buenos Aires, 1939)

The following game, which was called the pearl of the Olympiad, is a breath-taking struggle not only for the players, but for those also who play it over as they watch the White forces penetrating the enemy lines in the manner of a motorised column.

1	P—K4	P—K3
2	P—Q4	P—Q4
3	Kt—QB3	P×P

The *Polish Variation*, tried out by Rubinstein, attempts to eliminate the tension in the centre. A similar idea, applied a move later, is 3 .... Kt—KB3; 4 B—Kt5, P×P; and must be credited to Burn. That it is not without danger is shown in a Moyse–Sweby, *correspondence*, 1950; game 5 B×Kt, P×B (more solid is 5 .... Q×B; 6 Kt×P, Q—Q1; and Black's position would be difficult to overthrow); 6 Kt×P, P—KB4; 7 Kt—Kt3, B—Kt2 (better is 7 .... P—B4; 8 Kt—B3, Kt—B3); 8 Kt—B3, P—B4; 9 Kt—R5, B×P; 10 P—B3 (more precise is 10 B—Kt5 ch, K—K2; 11 P—B3, B—B3; 12 Q—R4, etc., as played in a game Milner-Barry–Louma, *London*, 1947), 10 .... B—B3; 11 B—Kt5 ch, K—K2; 12 Q—R4, R—Kt1; 13 R—Q1, Q—B2; 14 Kt×B. Simple and decisive. Black resigns, for, if 14 .... K×Kt; 15 Q—R4 ch, K—Kt2; 16 Q—Kt5 ch, K—R1; 17 Q—B6 ch, his game breaks up.

| 4 | Kt×P | Kt—Q2 |

After 4 .... Kt—KB3; 5 Kt×Kt ch, P×Kt; 6 Kt—B3, P—Kt3; 7 B—KB4, B—QKt2; 8 B—Kt5 ch, P—B3; 9 B—Q3,

B—Q3; 10 B—Kt3, etc., and White stands considerably better.

| 5 | KKt—B3 | P—QB4 |

The actual order of moves was: 1 P—K4, P—K3; 2 P—Q4, P—Q4; 3 Kt—Q2, P—QB4; 4 KKt—B3, P×P; 5 Kt×P, Kt—Q2.

Against 5 .... KKt—B3; White's best line is 6 Kt×Kt ch, Kt×Kt; 7 B—Q3, B—K2 (or 7 .... P—QKt3; 8 Q—K2, B—Kt2; 9 B—Kt5, B—K2; 10 R—Q1, Castles; 11 Castles, and White's prospects remain slightly superior); 8 Q—K2, Castles; 9 Castles, and Black is still in danger.

| 6 | P×P | Kt×P |
| 7 | Q×Q ch | K×Q |

One might think that Black, by the early exchange of Queens, has surmounted the difficulties of the opening, when, in fact, they have only begun.

| 8 | B—Kt5 ch | P—B3 |

Of course, not 8 .... B—K2; 9 Kt×Kt.

| 9 | Castles ch | K—K1 |

Nolens volens, the black King must continue his travels.

10 B—Kt5 ch
White throws all his forces into the fray.

| 10 | ...... | K—B2 |

And now the black King is in relative security, while two of White's pieces are *en prise*.

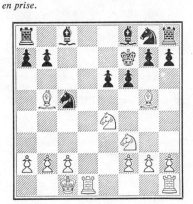

11 R—Q8
"*À la* Morphy" or, as some spectators remarked, "*à la* Pleci."

| 11 | ...... | B—K2 |

Black realises that all of his opponent's proffered sacrifices are entirely sound.

Let us examine:
(a) 11 .... P × B; 12 Kt—K5 ch, K—K2;
13 R—K8 mate.
(b) 11 .... Kt × Kt; 12 Kt—K5 ch,
K—K2 (or 12 .... P × Kt; 13 B—K8 mate);
13 R—K8 ch, K—Q3; 14 Kt—B7 ch, K—B4;
15 Kt × R, K × B; 16 R × KB, and White has
finally won the exchange, while still maintaining his terrible Rook on the eighth rank.

12 Kt—K5 ch
The dizzy dance of the white Knights
continues.

12 ...... P × Kt
13 Kt—Q6 ch K—Kt3
Black's King attempts to escape from this
inferno, leaving victims by the way. Clearly
not 13 .... B × Kt; 14 B—K8 ch, K—B1;
15 B—Kt6 (or 15 B—R5) mate.

14 B × B Kt × B
15 R × R P—QR3
The beginning of another act in the drama.
Although White has emerged with the
advantage of the exchange, Black puts up a
desperate resistance.

16 B—K2 P—K5
17 P—KB4 P—Kt4
Hoping to free his position by 18 ....
B—Kt2.

18 R—K8 K—B3
Forced.

19 R—B8 ch
Occupying the KB file with the gain of a
tempo, in keeping with White's strategy
throughout this game.

19 ...... K—Kt3
20 P—KR4 B—Kt2
If 20 .... P—R3; 21 P—R5 ch, K—R2;
22 R—K8, etc., and if 20 .... P—KR4;
21 P—KKt4.

21 P—R5 ch Resigns.
Just in time, for there follows 21 ....
K—R3; 22 Kt—B7 mate.

42

BRONSTEIN   SZABÓ
(Saltsjöbaden, 1948)

*As is nearly always the case when the two
leaders meet towards the end of a tournament
and the first place depends on the outcome of
their encounter, the following game is not
only in the highest degree combative, but also
is of great theoretical value.*

1 P—K4 P—K3
2 P—Q4 P—Q4
3 Kt—Q2
This ancient continuation has become
very popular since 1939, in the main because
the Winawer pin after 3 Kt—QB3, B—Kt5;
has proved uncomfortable for White.

3 ...... Kt—QB3
An imaginative reply, much practised by
the Argentine master, Guimard. Stubborn
contests result from 3 .... Kt—KB3
(4 P—K5, KKt—Q2; 5 B—Q3, P—QB4;
6 P—QB3, Kt—QB3; 7 Kt—K2, etc.).
Playable is 3 .... P—KB4; but less tractable
is 3 .... P × P; 4 Kt × P, leading to the
Polish Variation (see preceding game).
The most simple and sensible is 3 ....
P—QB4; with the continuation, 4 KP × P,
KP × P; 5 B—Kt5 ch, B—Q2; 6 Q—K2 ch,
Q—K2; tending to equality.

4 KKt—B3 Kt—B3
5 P—K5 Kt—Q2
6 Kt—Kt3
A rational continuation.

6 ...... P—B3
Instead of this routine move, the quiet
6 .... B—K2; can also be played.

7 B—QKt5
Too limp would be 7 P × P, because of
7 .... Q × P; 8 B—KKt5, Q—B2; 9 B—R4,
P—K4; 10 P × P, KKt × P; 11 Kt × Kt,
Kt × Kt; and, if anything, Black stands a
little better. But, 7 B—KB4, consolidating
White's position, can well be played, e.g.
Menke–Dr. Herberg, *correspondence*, 1950:
7 B—KB4, P—QR3 (there is no time for this
preventive manœuvre, and he should play
7 .... P × P; 8 P × P, B—K2); 8 P—B3,
Kt—R2 (an ugly move, intended to make
possible a belated advance of the QBP, but
it leads to trouble); 9 B—Q3, P—QB4;
10 Kt—Kt5, P × Kt (guarding his KP by
10 .... Kt—Kt1; would be equally bad);
11 Q—R5 ch, K—K2; 12 B × P ch, Kt—B3;
13 B × Kt ch, Black resigns. If 13 ....
P × B; 14 P × P ch, K × P; 15 Q—R4 ch,
winning the Queen. A refreshing skirmish.

7 ...... P—QR3
Or 7 .... B—K2; 8 B—KB4, Castles;
9 P × P, P × P; 10 Castles, Kt—Kt3;
11 R—K1, B—Q3; 12 B—Kt3, and White
maintains a slight pull.

8 B × Kt P × B

9 Castles   P—QB4

An active defence. If 9 .... P—QR4; 10 B—B4, P—R5; 11 QKt—Q2, and White achieves an harmonious development of his forces.

10 P—B4

With this counter-thrust, he upsets all his adversary's plans. Lifeless would be 10 KP × P, Q × P; 11 R—K1, P—B5; 12 Kt—B5 (if 12 Kt—Kt5, Kt—Kt1), 12 .... B × Kt; 13 P × B, Castles; and Black's chances are on the up-grade.

10 ......   QP × P

After 10 .... P—B3; could follow: 11 KP × P (good also is 11 B—Q2), 11 .... KtP × P; 12 Q—K2, K—B2; 13 R—K1, Kt—Kt3; 14 Kt × P, B × Kt; 15 P × B, Kt × P; 16 P—QKt3, Kt—R4; 17 Kt—K5 ch, and White is on the way to success.

11 Kt—R5

A fine manœuvre which threatens to "mate" the adverse Queen.

11 ......   Kt—Kt3

Preferable is 11 .... Kt—Kt1.

12 KP × P   Q × BP

Or 12 .... KtP × P; 13 R—K1, Q—Q4; 14 Kt—K5, and White penetrates the enemy lines.

13 P × P

Black's position is deteriorating. White's venturesome pawn cannot be captured because of 14 B—Kt5, followed by Q—Q8 ch, and Q × R.

13 ......   Q—B4

Now White cannot well reply with 14 P × Kt, because of 14 .... Q × QKt. Two worthy opponents!

14 B—Kt5   Q × P

Inadequate is 14 .... B—Q2; because of 15 P × Kt, Q × QKt; 16 P—Kt7 (a quicksilver pawn), 16 .... R—QKt1; 17 R—K1, R × P; 18 Kt—K5, Q—R5; 19 Q—R5 ch, and wins.

Had Black foreseen the pending trouble, he would have chosen, as the lesser evil, 14 .... Kt—Q4; 15 Q—R4 ch, B—Q2; 16 P—B6, B—B1; 17 Q × P, and although Black has now shed an important pawn, he would avoid more serious losses.

15 Q—Q8 ch   K—B2

At this point Bronstein reflected for a long time and found a move of extraordinary vigour.

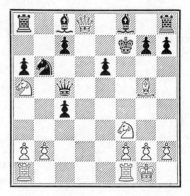

16 QR—Q1

This move comprises the potential threat of R—Q4—B4 ch, but its main purpose is to prevent Black from freeing his game by .... B—Q2. From a technical point of view the text-move continues the thorough exploitation of the Q file, which Black's tenth move has allowed to be opened.

16 ......   B—Kt2

Quite bad would be 16 .... Q × Kt; e.g. 17 Q × P ch, K—Kt3 (not 17 .... K—Kt1; 18 Kt—K5, B—Q2; 19 R × B, R—B1; 20 R × P ch, B × R; 21 Q—B7 mate); 18 Kt—K5 ch, K × B; 19 P—B4 ch, K—R3; 20 R—B3, Q—B4 ch; 21 K—R1, Q × Q; 22 R—R3 mate. With the text-move, Black voluntarily gives up a piece. He could have tried 16 .... P—R3.

17 Kt × B   R × Q
18 Kt × Q   R—Q4

Black's misfortune is that he cannot play 18 .... R × R on account of 19 Kt—K5 ch, K—Kt1; 20 R × R, B × Kt; 21 R—Q8 ch, B—B1; 22 B—K7, and he still loses a piece in a hopeless position.

19 Kt—K4

The rest is a long drawn-out agony: 19 .... B—Q3; 20 Kt—B3, R—R4; 21 B—B1, P—R3; 22 KR—K1, Kt—R5; 23 Kt × Kt, R × Kt; 24 P—QR3, P—B6; 25 P—QKt3, R—R4; 26 R—Q3, R—QB4; 27 B—K3, R—QR4; 28 R × P, R × P; 29 B B5, R—R4; 30 P—QKt4, R—R5; 31 Q × Q, R—Q1; 33 K—Kt2, R—R7; 34 B × B, P × B; 35 R—B7 ch, K—B3; 36 Kt—Q4, R—K1; 37 P—Kt6, P—K4; 38 P—Kt7, and Black resigns.

13. CARO-KANN DEFENCE

43

ALEKHINE   ELISKASES
(*France*)   (*Germany*)
(Olympiad, Buenos Aires, 1939)

*Alekhine's play was ever passionately
ambitious, as is shown in the masterly game
that follows.*

1 P—K4	P—QB3
2 P—Q4	P—Q4
3 P×P	P×P
4 P—QB4	

The *Panov Attack*, which came to the fore
in the game Réti–Duras, *Vienna*, 1908,
creates many difficulties for Black.

Another continuation, 4 B—Q3, belies its
apparent simplicity. Nevertheless, Black
can here solve the problem of the opening
fairly satisfactorily after 4 .... QKt—B3;
5 P—QB3, Kt—B3; 6 B—KB4, B—Kt5;
7 Q—Kt3, Kt—QR4; 8 Q—R4 ch, B—Q2;
9 Q—B2, Q—Kt3; 10 Kt—Q2, P—K3;
11 KKt—B3, B—Kt4; 12 Castles KR, B×B;
13 Q×B, etc., with equality.

4	Kt—KB3

The game Capablanca–Czerniak, played
in the same Olympiad, went as follows:
4 .... QKt—B3; 5 Kt—B3, B—Kt5;
6 P×P, Q×P; 7 B—K2, P—K3; 8 Castles,
Kt—B3; 9 Kt—B3, Q—QR4; 10 P—KR3,
B—R4; 11 P—R3, and White gains space.

5 Kt—QB3	P—K3
6 Kt—B3	B—K2
7 P×P	

Now 7 P—B5, would be inferior, because
of 7 .... Castles; 8 P—QKt4, Kt—K5;
9 Q—B2, P—B4; etc. Nor is 7 B—KKt5,
convincing, again on account of 7 ....
Castles; which is why Alekhine himself
seeks simplification.

7	Kt×P
8 B—Kt5 ch	B—Q2

Too submissive. More tenacious is
8 .... Kt—B3, e.g. 9 Kt—K5, B—Q2;
10 B×Kt, P×B; etc., with a good game.

9 B×B ch	Kt×B
10 Kt×Kt	P×Kt
11 Q—Kt3	

Exchanges have cleared up the situation,
and White has secured the initiative.

11	Kt—Kt3

The only way to protect both the attacked
pawns, but White's opposing Knight
occupies a far more favourable post.

12 Castles	Castles
13 B—B4	B—Q3
14 B×B	Q×B
15 KR—K1	QR—B1
16 QR—B1	P—KR3
17 Kt—K5	R—B2
18 P—Kt3	KR—B1
19 R×R	R×R

He guards the QKtP and hopes to obtain
a theoretical equilibrium.

20 Q—Kt5	Kt—Q2
21 Kt×Kt	R×Kt

Or 21 .... Q×Kt; 22 R—K8 ch, K—R2;
23 Q—Q3 ch, P—Kt3; 24 Q—K3, etc.,
with considerable difficulties for Black.

22 R—K8 ch	K—R2
23 P—KR4	

With much-reduced material White still
aims high.

23	P—R3
24 Q—K2	R—Q1
25 R—K7	R—Q2
26 R—K5	P—KKt3
27 P—R5	

One can but admire the crystal-clear
strategy which enables White to disrupt the
enemy lines.

27	Q—KB3
28 Q—K3	R—Q3 (see diag.)

Black hopes to be able to play the equalising .... R—K3. If 28 .... P—QKt4;
29 P×P ch, Q×P (29 .... P×P;
30 R—K6); 30 Q—KB3, and Black's game
deteriorates rapidly.

29 Q—Kt3	R—Kt3

Or 29 .... P—QKt4; 30 R×P, R—K3;
31 Q—Q1, etc.

30 P×P ch	Q×P

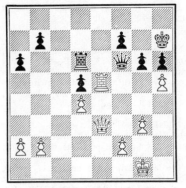

Position after 28 .... R—Q3

31 Q×P   R×P

Black defends himself with the greatest tenacity.

32 R—B5

At last White's two pieces succeed in invading the hostile entrenchments.

32 ......   R—Kt4

Trying, at the cost of a pawn, to save the situation in a Rook's ending. If 32 .... K—Kt1; 33 P—R4, White tightens his stranglehold.

33 R×P ch   K—Kt1
34 R—B6 dis ch   R×Q
35 R×Q ch   K—R2
36 R—Kt6   R×P
37 R×KtP ch   K—Kt1
38 R—Kt6   R—QR5

His only chance.

39 R×KRP   R×P
40 K—Kt2

As a result of his minutely calculated manœuvres, Alekhine has an extra pawn to show, and his two united pawns ensure his victory.

40 ......   P—R4
41 R—R6   P—R5
42 R—R7

Accomplished technique.

42 ......   P—R6
43 P Kt4   K—D1
44 P—Kt5   K—Kt1
45 K—Kt3   R—R8
46 K—Kt4   R—Kt8 ch
47 K—B5   R—Kt7
48 P—B4   P—R7
49 K—B6   Resigns

44

FUDERER   DONNER
(Beverwijk, 1952)

Short as it is, the following game displays many strategic ideas.

1 P—K4   P—QB3
2 P—Q4

Is this immediate occupation of the centre really necessary? Nowadays much attention is given to the "modern treatment," 2 Kt—QB3, P—Q4; 3 Kt—B3, when Black's best line is 3 .... P×P; 4 Kt×P, B—Kt5; 5 P—KR3, B×Kt; 6 Q×B, P—K3; etc., with a fairly stable position.

2 ......   P—Q4
3 Kt—QB3

For those who think the *Exchange Variation*, 3 P×P, too simplifying, or the *Blockade Variation*, 3 P—K5, too dogmatic, the *classical continuation* in the text is indicated. There are, however, other possibilities, as, for instance, the fanciful 3 P—KB3.

The following game from a German tournament, Rellstab–Edith Keller, *Duisburg*, 1948, shows that it is not without guile: 3 P—KB3, P×P (the best reply is 3 .... P—K3; transposing into the *French Defence* after 4 Kt—B3, Kt—B3; 5 P—K5, KKt—Q2); 4 P×P, P—K4; 5 Kt—KB3, P×P (careless. Preferable is 5 .... B—K3; 6 Kt—B3, B—QKt5; trying to check White's impetus); 6 B—QB4, B—Kt5 ch (Black goes on with her scheme and is now on the downward path. But if 6 .... B—K3; 7 B×B, P×B; 8 Castles, B—K2; 9 Kt×P, White has a manifest advantage); 7 P—B3, P×P; 8 B×P ch, K×B; 9 Q×Q, Kt—K2; 10 Q×R, P×P dis ch; 11 K—K2, P×R(Q) (Black is now a piece up, but Fate marches on); 12 Kt—Kt5 ch, K—Kt3; 13 Q—K8 ch, K—R3; 14 Kt—K6 dis ch, Black resigns (if 14 .... P—Kt4; 15 B×P mate).

3 ......   P×P
4 Kt×P   Kt—B3

A challenge.

Nimzowitsch's suggestion 4 .... Kt—Q2; also leaves Black worse off positionally after 5 KKt—B3, KKt—B3; 6 Kt×Kt ch (the traditional continuation is 6 Kt—Kt3, P—K3; 7 B—Q3, B—K2; 8 Q—K2, Castles; 9 Castles, P—B4; with good chances of equality), 6 .... Kt×Kt; 7 Kt—K5, P—KKt3; 8 B—K2, B—Kt2; 9 Castles, Castles; 10 B—B3, B—B4; 11 P—B3, Kt—Q4; 12 B—Q2, Q—B2; 13 R—K1, QR—Q1; 14 Q—B1, and White has the better game. The most likely to survive is the good old line, 4 .... B—B4; 5 Kt—Kt3,

B—Kt3; e.g. 6 Kt—B3, Kt—Q2; 7 P—KR4, P—KR3; 8 B—Q3, B×B; 9 Q×B, Q—B2; and Black holds his own.

5 Kt×Kt ch   KP×Kt
Against Nimzowitsch's "No. 2 recipe," 5 .... KtP×Kt; the energetic continuation 6 P—QB3, B—B4; 7 Kt—K2, P—K3; 8 Kt—Kt3, B—Kt3; 9 P—KR4, P—KR3; 10 P—R5, B—R2; 11 B—QB4, Kt—Q2; 12 P—R4, reveals some weaknesses in Black's game.

6 B—QB4   B—Q3
If 6 .... B—K3; 7 Q—K2, Q—K2; White has a striking preponderance on the K file.

7 Kt—K2
An important moment.
The consequences of 7 Q—K2 ch, B—K2; 8 Kt—B3, B—Kt5; 9 P—B3, Kt—Q2, etc., are not enticing. If (instead of 8 Kt—B3), 8 Q—R5, P—KKt3; 9 Q—Q1, Castles; 10 Kt—B3, B—Kt5; Black also holds his own. More subtle is at once 7 Q—R5, as in a game, Keres–Mikenas, *Buenos Aires*, 1939: 7 .... Castles; 8 Kt—K2, P—KKt3; 9 Q—B3, R—K1; 10 B—KR6, B—KB4; 11 Castles QR, and White's K side attack progresses.
In the light of these experiences, White prefers first to complete his development.

7 ......   Castles
8 Castles   Q—B2
Unlike his opponent, Black shows a tendency to counter-attack without first attending to his development. However, both 8 .... B—K3; and 8 .... B—KKt5; are not without awkward points. Best, therefore, is 8 .... R—K1; so that .... B—K3; and .... Kt—Q2; can be played without harm.

9 Kt—Kt3   Kt—Q2
10 Q—R5
This *sortie*, which neither attacks nor weakens anything, has a psychological meaning.

10 ......   P—QB4
Full of confidence in the strength of his King's field, and as yet entirely unscathed, Donner embarks on a doubtful enterprise on the Q side. Black hopes to be able to play .... P—QKt3; and to solve the problem of his QB, but he will not succeed.
He could have tried 10 .... B—B5; in order to ease the situation.

11 B—Q3   P—KKt3
The defences begin to fritter away, but

if 11 .... P—KR3; he would collapse at once after 12 B×P, etc.

12 Q—R6   R—K1
Necessity: the beautiful threat 13 Kt—R5, can now be met by 13 .... B—B1. Clearly insufficient would be 12 .... B×Kt; on account of 13 BP×B, with the threat R—B4 —KR4. And if 12 .... P—B4; 13 Kt×P, P×Kt; 14 B×P, and wins.

13 P×P   Kt×P
Neglecting this Knight's defensive functions (guarding the pawn at KB3), Black sinks into the abyss.
The lesser evil would be 13 .... B×P, even though White's pressure then persists after, e.g., 14 B—KB4, B—Q3; 15 QR—K1, Kt—K4; 16 Kt—R5, or 13 .... Q×P; 14 Kt—K4, Q—B2; 15 Kt×B, Q×Kt; 16 B—KB4, Q—B1; 17 QR—K1, Q×Q; 18 B×Q, etc. More coolheaded is first 13 .... B—B1; 14 Q—R4, Q×P, although Black's position remains disjointed.

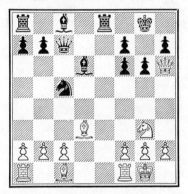

14 Kt—R5
The trumpets of Jericho.

14 ......   P×Kt
For now, if 14 .... B—B1; 15 Kt×P ch, followed by mate at KR7. But after the text move Black cannot escape being mated in a few moves.

15 B×P ch   K—R1
16 B—Kt6 dis ch   K—Kt1
17 Q—R7 ch   K—B1
18 B—R6 ch
The dormant Bishop springs to life.

18 ......   Resigns
Just in time to avoid mate in two. It is most remarkable that a King's field, guarded by *four pawns*, could so thoroughly be demolished in so short a time.

14. SICILIAN DEFENCE

45

BOLESLAVSKY   L. STEINER
(Saltsjöbaden, 1948)

Champions of to-day use system in their genius and genius in their systems.

1 P—K4	P—QB4
2 Kt—KB3	Kt—QB3
3 P—Q4	P×P
4 Kt×P	Kt—B3
5 QKt—B3	P—Q3
6 B—K2	

The normal formation.

6 ......   P—K3

The restricted but unyielding contours of the *Scheveningen Formation* find to-day numerous adherents.

7 Castles	P—QR3
8 B—K3	Q—B2
9 P—B4	

This innovation of Boleslavsky's is more energetic than the preparatory 9 K—R1 played in the famous game Maroczy–Dr. Euwe, *Scheveningen, 1923.*

9 ......   Kt—QR4

A crisis. Impatiently Black strives to secure the initiative on the Q side, instead of first completing his K side development.
After 9 .... B—K2; a coherent sequel could be: 10 Q—K1, Castles; 11 Q—Kt3, B—Q2; 12 B—B3, QR—B1; 13 QR—Q1, K—R1; and, in spite of the pressure which White exercises in the centre and on the K side, it will not be easy for him to break through.

10 K—R1

At the right moment, Boleslavsky adopts Maroczy's manœuvre, as shown above. 10 P—B5, here would be shiftless and White's impetus would be halted by 10 .... P—K4. A mistake would be 10 P—B5, Kt—B5; 11 B×Kt, Q×B; 12 P×P, P×P; 13 R×Kt, etc.

10 ......   B—K2
11 Q—K1

A clever manœuvre.

11 ......   Kt—B5

He hastens to drive the QB to its original square, before White's QR can get into play.

12 B—B1   P—QKt4

Black follows an active policy on the Q side. The continuation in a game Alexander–Szabó, *Hilversum*, 1947, was more superficial: 12 .... Castles; 13 P—QKt3, Kt—QR4; 14 B—Q3, Kt—Q2; 15 B—Kt2, B—B3; 16 Kt—B3, Kt—B4; 17 P—K5, and once again this central break-through turns out to White's advantage.

13 P—QKt3	Kt—Kt3
14 B—B3	B—Kt2

Not 14 .... P—Kt5; 15 P—K5.

15 P—QR3

An important move.

15 ......   QKt—Q2

Here and on the next move Black wastes time on an indefinite plan which adds nothing to the dynamism of his game. More direct therefore would be 15 .... Castles KR; and eventually .... P—Q4.

16 B—Kt2	Kt—B4
17 P—QKt4	QKt—Q2
18 P—K5	

A thematic break-through. Black, who hoped to carry out unhindered the manœuvre .... Kt—Kt3—B5; will be bowled over.

18 ......   P×P

If, at once, 18 .... KKt—Kt1; 19 P×P, B×P; 20 Kt(B3)×P, P×Kt; 21 Kt×KtP, Q—Kt3; 22 Kt×B ch, Q×Kt; 23 B×B, and wins.

19 P×P   Kt—KKt1

A sad retreat! Neither 19 .... Kt×P; 20 B×B, Q×B; 21 Q×Kt, nor 19 .... Kt—Q4; 20 Kt×Kt, P×Kt; 21 P—K6, etc., nor, finally, 19 .... B×B; 20 P×Kt, B×BP; 21 Kt×B, R—QB1; 22 Kt—Q5, etc., can be entertained by Black.

20 Q—Kt3

Although it cannot be claimed that the manœuvre Q—K1—Kt3 is Boleslavsky's invention, he deserves admiration for the energy with which he applied this stratagem in a number of games.

20 ......   B—KB1

Another melancholy withdrawal, but if 20 .... K—B1; 21 Kt×P ch, and wins, and if 20 .... P—Kt3; 21 B×B, Q×B; 22 Q—B4, etc., with a definite advantage to White.

21 QR—K1   Kt—R3

If 21 .... Kt—Kt3 (to be able to castle without losing the KBP); 22 B×B, Q×B; 23 Kt—K4, Castles; 24 Kt×KP, P×Kt; 25 R×B, etc.

22 B×B   Q×B
23 B—B1   P—Kt3
24 B×Kt   B×B
25 Q—R3   B—Kt4

After 25 .... B—Kt2; the combination which occurs in the game would be equally effective.

26 Kt—K4   B—K2

Black's last eight moves must have been a nightmare to him, but he now hopes to have consolidated his position to some extent.

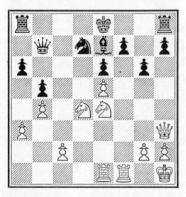

27 R×P
A spectacular sacrifice.

27 ......   Q—Q4

No one enjoys dying. Hopeless is 27 .... K×R; 28 Q×KP ch, K—B1 (28 .... K—K1; 29 Kt—Q6 ch); 29 R—B1 ch, etc. And if 27 .... Kt×P; 28 Kt—Q6 ch, prettily wins the Queen.

28 R×B ch
The carnage continues.

28 ......   K×R
29 Q—R4 ch   K—B2

Or 29 .... K—B1; 30 R—B1 ch, K—Kt1 (30 .... K—Kt2; 31 Q—K7 ch, K—R3; 32 R—B3, Q×P; 33 R—R3 ch, Q—R4; 34 R×Q ch, followed by 35 Q—Kt5 mate); 31 Q—K7, R—KB1; 32 R×R ch, Kt×R; 33 Kt—B6 mate.

30 Kt—Q6 ch

As shown in the preceding note, 30 R—B1 ch clinches matters.

30 ......   K—Kt2

Or 30 .... K—Kt1; 31 Q—K7, R—KB1; 32 Kt×KP, Q×P; 33 Q×R ch, Kt×Q; 34 R×Q, etc.

31 Q—K7 ch   K—R3
32 R—K3   Resigns

A brilliant game.

46

B. H. WOOD   WINTER
(London, 1948)

Contemporary British style, energetic and logical, is well illustrated in the following game.

1 P—K4   P—QB4
2 Kt—KB3   Kt—QB3
3 P—Q4   P×P
4 Kt×P   Kt—B3
5 QKt—B3   P—Q3
6 B—K2   P—KKt3

The dread *Dragon Variation* has lost much of its terrors.

7 B—K3   B—Kt2
8 Q—Q2

Without delay he makes for his goal, a contest with castling on opposite wings. Alternative continuations are 8 P—B3, 8 P—KR3, 8 P—B4, 8 Kt—Kt3, or, finally, 8 Castles.

8 ......   Castles

Doubtful is the transaction 8 .... KKt—Kt5; 9 B×Kt, B×B; because of 10 P—B4.

9 Castles QR

Voilà! If, first, 9 P—B3, then the liberating thrust 9 .... P—Q4; becomes possible.

9 ......   B—Q2

Black underestimates his adversary's prospects, thinking that he can complete his counter-preparations at leisure.

A more active policy is required, such as

9 .... Kt×Kt; 10 B×Kt, Q—R4;
11 K—Kt1, P—K4; 12 B—K3, B—K3;
13 Kt—Q5, Q×Q; 14 Kt×Kt ch, B×Kt;
15 R×Q, B—K2; 16 P—QB4, KR—B1;
17 P—QKt3, P—Kt3; with tendency to
equalisation.

10 P—B3	P—QR3
11 P—KKt4	P—QKt4
12 P—KR4	Kt×Kt
13 B×Kt	P—Kt5
14 Kt—Q5	Kt×Kt
15 B×B	K×B
16 P×Kt	

The exchanges have cleared the field, but
the black King has lost his defending
Bishop.

| 16 ...... | B—Kt4 |

A semblance of counter-play.

| 17 P—R5 | B×B |
| 18 P×P | |

White's fury is let loose: he threatens
Black with extinction by 19 R×P ch.

| 18 ...... | BP×P |

Or 18 .... RP×P; 19 Q—R6 ch, K—B3;
20 P—Kt5 ch, K—B4; 21 Q—R4, B×P;
22 KR—B1, and there is no escape for
Black's King.

| 19 Q—R6 ch | K—B3 |

Is this salvation?

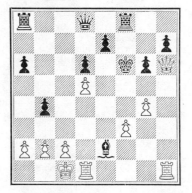

20 P—Kt5 ch

The *coup de grâce*, which, however, had
to be calculated to a nicety already on
White's eighteenth move.

| 20 ...... | K—B2 |

A bewildered King. If 20 .... K—K4;
21 KR—K1, R×P; 22 R×B ch, K—B4;
23 Q×P, etc. Or 20 .... K—B4; 21 Q—R4

(a "quiet" move, which threatens mate in
two); 21 .... B×P; 22 KR—B1, K—K4;
23 Q—Q4 ch, K—B4; 24 R×B ch, K×P;
25 R—Kt1 ch, K—R3; 26 R—R3 mate.

21 Q×RP ch	K—K1
22 Q×KtP ch	K—Q2
23 Q—K6 ch	K—K1
24 Q×B	

Simple and convincing; White remains
two strong pawns ahead.

Black resigns.

47

SZABÓ   LUNDIN

(Groningen, 1946)

*The following game received the first
Brilliancy Prize, mainly because Black's
inspiration was guided by a pitiless logic
derived from the general conception of the
contest.*

1 P—K4	P—QB4
2 Kt—KB3	Kt—QB3
3 P—Q4	P×P
4 Kt×P	Kt—B3

If 4 .... P—KKt3; 5 P—QB4.

| 5 QKt—B3 | P—Q3 |
| 6 B—KKt5 | |

The famous *Pomeranian* or *Richter
Attack*, introduced by the German master
Kurt Richter, which can serve, at the
same time, as an *Anti-Dragon* recipe where White
prefers to avoid the *Dragon Defence*.

| 6 ...... | P—K3 |

The best reply, reverting to the formation
of the *Scheveningen Defence*.

7 Q—Q2

The *Rauser Variation*. A possible improvement is the *Keres Continuation* 7 Q—Q3.

The original idea of the *Richter Attack*, a
gambit continuation, has been abandoned,
because, after 7 Kt×Kt, P×Kt; 8 P—K5,
P×P; 9 Q—B3, R—QKt1; 10 R—Q1,
B—Q2; 11 B—QB4, B—K2; 12 B×Kt,
P×B; 13 Q—Kt3, K—B1; 14 Castles,
Q—B2; etc., there is little in it for White.

| 7 ...... | P—QR3 |

More subtle than, at once, 7 .... B—K2;
e.g. 8 Castles, Castles; 9 Kt—Kt3, P—QR3;
10 B×Kt, P×B; 11 P—B4, and White has
command of the situation.

| 8 Castles | B—Q2 |

Another finesse of contemporary analysis: Black makes some useful waiting moves, reserving the option, eventually, of recapturing at his KB3 with Queen instead of with Bishop or pawn. An appropriate measure, superior to an immediate 8 .... B—K2; is here 8 .... P—R3.

9 P—B4
The key-move in many variations of the *Richter Attack*, but, in view of his opponent's expert treatment of the defence, a purely positional scheme, such as 9 P—B3, P—R3; 10 B—K3, etc., deserves consideration.

9 ...... P—R3
Challenging the pinning Bishop at the right moment.

10 B—R4
Even less promising than this retreat is the exchange 10 B × Kt, Q × B.

10 ...... B—K2
Careless would be 10 .... Kt × P; because of the fine reply 11 Q—K1.

11 B—K2   Q—B2
Methodically, Black prepares his action against the enemy King, daringly castled on the open QB file.
Too sudden would be 11 .... Q—R4; 12 Kt—Kt3, etc., as well as 11 .... Kt × Kt; 12 Q × Kt, Q—R4; 13 P—K5, etc.

12 B—B2
For his part White seems unable to cope with the situation which demands energetic measures. The retreat in the text is intended to eliminate the threat 12 .... Kt × P; 13 QKt × Kt, B × B; 14 Kt × Kt, B × Kt; 15 Kt × P ch, K—B1; etc. But a simpler way is 12 Kt—B3, which at the same time paves the way for a possible thrust P—K5.

12 ......   QR—B1
13 Kt—Kt3
If permitted to do so, White would like to play Kt—R4—Kt6, but Black, having marshalled all his forces on the Q side, now decides on direct action.

13 ......   P—QKt4
14 B—B3   Kt—QR4
15 Kt × Kt   Q × Kt (R4)
16 K—Kt1   P—Kt5
17 Kt—K2   P—K4
The infantry at work.

18 Kt—B1

If 18 P—B5, P—Q4; e.g.: 19 P × P, P—K5; 20 P—Q6, P × B; 21 P × B, P × Kt; 22 Q × KP, Q × P; etc., with a winning balance for Black.

18 ......   Castles
19 Kt—Q3   R—B5
Defending the QKtP and attacking the KP, not to mention the potential doubling of Rooks on the QB file.

20 P—QR3
He feels he has to "do something" in preference to merely defensive measures: e.g. 20 KR—K1, KR—B1; 21 R—QB1, B—B3; 22 P—QKt3, R—B6; and Black is firmly established within the enemy lines.
The hour of crisis has arrived.

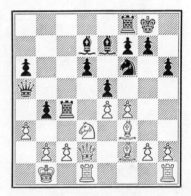

20 ......   Q—B2
A logical sequence of events. Black turns the *loss* of a pawn into a well-grounded *sacrifice* as a prelude to further *sacrifices*.

21 Kt × KtP   P—QR4
22 P—QKt3
Or 22 Kt—Q3, R—B1; 23 R—QB1, Kt × P; and Black has the last word.

22 ......   P × Kt
23 P × R   R—Kt1
As a result of White's feverish manoeuvres, the QKt file has definitely become the main theatre of operations.

24 Q—Q3
Or 24 RP × P, P—Q4; 25 P—B3, P—Q5; 26 KBP × P, P × P; and White's defences quickly collapse.

24 ......   B—K3
25 B—K2   Q—Kt2
26 RP × P   Kt × P
Not 26 .... Q × P ch; 27 Q—Kt3.

27 B—K1	P—Q4
28 P—B3	QP×P
29 Q—B2	

If 29 Q—B3, Black continues his assault with 29 .... R—R1; 30 K—Kt2, B—Q4; 31 Q—K3, Q—R3; with a forced mate.

29	B—KB4
30 K—B1	Kt—Kt6
31 B×Kt	B×Q
32 K×B	P×P
33 B—B3	Q—B1
34 B—B2	Q—B4 ch
35 K—Kt2	B×P

A blaze of glory!

36 P×B	R×P ch
37 K—B3	R—Kt6 ch
38 K—Q2	Q—K4
Resigns	

Black's threats of mate starting with R—Kt7 ch, or R—Q6 ch, are too strong.

48

RICO   NAJDORF
(*Spain*)   (*Argentina*)

(Radio Match, 1949)

Every opening is subject to the laws of fashion. The Dragon *formation, which held the stage from 1904 onward, gave way about 1923 to the* Scheveningen System. *Since 1946 another system, much more baroque, and, in appearance, anti-positional, was introduced into master practice by Opocensky* (London) *and Boleslavsky* (Groningen).

This new system comprises the preposterous-looking advance .... P—K4; *well in keeping with the spirit of the times, which largely relies on refinements. This game gives the opportunity to follow the modern treatment of this old opening.*

1 P—K4	P—QB4
2 Kt—KB3	P—Q3

More elastic than 2 .... Kt—QB3; as Black reserves the option of developing this Knight at Q2 if required.

3 P—Q4	P×P
4 Kt×P	Kt—KB3
5 Kt QB3	P—QR3

Another refinement: instead of deciding at once on one of the available systems 5 .... P—KKt3 (*Dragon*); 5 .... P—K3 (*Scheveningen*); or 5 .... P—K4; Black interpolates the text-move which can prove useful in all of these variants. Besides, if, at once, 5 .... P—K4; the white Knight is not compelled to move to KB3 (obstructing the KBP) nor to KKt3 (a decentralising manœuvre), but White can, much more favourably, play 6 KKt—K2, with a very good game.

6 B—K2	P—K4

Anti-positional as this thrust may appear, as his Q3 will for a long time remain weak, it brings life into Black's play in the centre. A game, Schlechter–Dr. Lasker, ninth game of the *match, Berlin,* 1910, can be regarded as the forerunner of this variation: 1 P—K4, P—QB4; 2 Kt—KB3, Kt—QB3; 3 P—Q4, P×P; 4 Kt×P, Kt—B3; 5 QKt—B3, P—K4.

7 Kt—Kt3	

More concentric is the return to B3, e.g. 7 Kt—B3, P—R3 (or 7 .... B—K2; 8 B—Kt5, QKt—Q2; 9 Q—Q2, Castles; 10 Castles KR, etc., with a continued pressure by White); 8 B—K3, B—K3; 9 Castles, QKt—Q2 (or 9 .... B—K2; 10 Q—Q2, Castles; 11 P—KR3, Kt—B3; 12 QR—Q1, or 9 .... Kt—B3; 10 Kt—Q5); 10 P—KR3, P—QKt4; 11 P—R3, R—B1; 12 Kt—Q2, Kt—Kt3; 13 P—B4, and White succeeds in clearing up the situation.

7	B—K3

Preparing for .... P—Q4. Prudent players play here 7 .... B—K2; so as to reply to 8 B—Kt5, with 8 .... Kt×P.

A violent counter-thrust is 7 .... P—QKt4; which succeeded fully in the following game, McCormick–Evans, *U.S.A. Championship,* 1951: 8 Castles, B—Kt2; 9 B—Kt5, QKt—Q2; 10 P—B4, P—R3; 11 P×P, P×P; 12 B—R4, B—K2; 13 B—Q3, P—Kt5; 14 Kt—K2, Kt×P; 15 Kt—Kt3, Q—Kt3 ch; and White resigns.

8 Castles	

If 8 B—Kt5, Black strengthens his game with 8 .... QKt—Q2; 9 Castles, B—K2. A static continuation is 8 B—B3.

8	QKt—Q2

In a game Boleslavsky–Ståhlberg, *Budapest,* 1950, Black played, impatiently, 8 .... B—K2; and after 9 P—B4, P×P; 10 B×BP, Castles; 11 K—R1, Kt—B3; 12 B—Q3, Q—Kt3; 13 K—K2, KR—K1; 14 QR—K1, QR—B1; 15 B—K3, Q—B2; 16 Kt—Q4, a draw was agreed.

9 P—B4	

A purely positional treatment here is 9 B—K3, B—K2; 10 P—B3, e.g. the game, Smyslov–Najdorf, *Budapest*, 1950: 10 .... Kt—Kt3; 11 B—B2, Q—Q2; 12 P—QR4, Kt—B5; 13 B×Kt, B×B; 14 R—K1, Castles KR; 15 Kt—Q2 (aiming at Q5 *via* KB1 and K3), 15 .... B—K3; 16 Kt—B1, etc.

9 ......   Q—B2

Played with circumspection. Another method of securing the flight-square QB5 for the QB is 9 .... P—QKt4.

10 P—B5

Tempting, but positionally wrong. After the advance in the text, ... P—Q4; by Black will be still more effective.

10 ......   B—B5
11 B—Q3

This is altogether too defensive. It is true that after 11 B×B, Q×B; 12 Kt—Q2, Q—Q5 ch; 13 K—R1, Kt—B4; White is in danger of losing a pawn, but he could play 11 Kt—Q2, B×B; 12 Q×B, etc., or 11 .... P—Q4; 12 Kt×P, B×Kt; 13 P×B, Kt×P; 14 Kt—K4, with fair chances.

11 ......   P—QKt4
12 B—K3   B—K2
13 Q—K2   R—QB1
14 QR—B1   Castles
15 Kt—Q2

Simpler is 15 B×B.

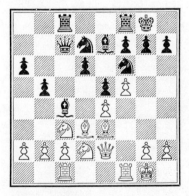

15 ......   P—Q4

He has achieved his object under favourable conditions. White must exchange either the pawns or Bishops, and Black will be first to benefit from the open Q file.

16 B×B   QP×B

17 P—QR3   P—Kt5

This move required fine positional judgment. He deliberately breaks up his united pawns merely to give himself increased space on the Q side and a distant passed pawn.

18 P×P   B×P
19 P—Kt4

A new struggle breaks out.

19 ......   B×Kt
20 P×B   Q—B3
21 Q—Kt2   Kt—B4
22 B×Kt   Q×B ch
23 K—R1   KR—Q1
24 Q—K2

After 24 P—Kt5, Black is under no necessity to sacrifice the exchange for two pawns (by 24 .... R×Kt; 25 Q×R, Kt×P; 26 Q—Kt2, Kt×BP; etc.) for he can continue .... Kt—R4—B5.

24 ......   P—R3
25 R—R1   Q—Q3

If, at once, 25 .... Q—B3; 26 R—R5. That is why Black adopts strong-arm measures.

26 KR—Q1

A passive defence. After 26 Kt×P, the sequel could be 26 .... Q—B4; 27 R—R4, Q—B3; 28 KR—R1, Kt×KP; and Black has achieved his object.

26 ......   Q—B3
27 K—Kt2

Now the threat, 27 .... R×Kt; 28 R×R, Kt×KP; is not serious, as there is no longer a double check, e.g. 29 R×P, Q×R; 30 Q×Kt.

27 ......   R—Q3
28 P—R3   QR—Q1
29 K—B3   Q—Q2

There is nothing to be done against the accumulated power of Black's major pieces.

30 K—K3   Kt—K1

The beginning of a fateful Knight's tour.

31 R—R5   Kt—B2
32 R×KP   Kt—Kt4
33 R—Q5   R×R
34 P×R   Kt×P
35 Q—B3   Kt×R ch
Resigns

Black's play, so full of subtle finessing, is eminently logical.

49

ALEXANDER   BOGOLJUBOW
(Cheltenham, 1951)

Some players know how to conduct an attack. Of these, a few—Alexander among them—know that they know.

1 P—K4	P—QB4
2 Kt—KB3	P—Q3
3 P—Q4	P × P
4 Kt × P	Kt—KB3
5 Kt—QB3	

Against 5 P—KB3, Black can react energetically in the centre with 5 .... P—K4.

5	P—QR3
6 P—KKt3	P—K4

A more astute manœuvre here is 6 .... B—Kt5; e.g. (a) 7 P—B3, B—Q2; 8 B—Kt2, Kt—B3; and, thanks to the artificial closure of the long white diagonal, Black has greater freedom of action; (b) 7 Q—Q3, Q—B1; 8 P—KR3, B—Q2; and Black again is able to develop his game satisfactorily.

Doubtful at this stage is the *Dragon Formation*: 6 .... P—KKt3; 7 B—Kt2, B—Kt2; 8 P—KR3, Kt—B3; 9 B—K3, etc.

Too forcing is the lateral counteraction: 6 .... P—QKt4; 7 B—Kt2, B—Kt2; 8 Castles, etc. On the whole, the most suitable formation here is the *Scheveningen*: 6 .... Kt—B3; 7 B—Kt2, B—Q2; 8 Castles, P—K3 (here it is! The restricted centre is quite solid); 9 P—KR3, B—K2; etc., with equality.

7 KKt—K2
The best square for the Knight.

7	B—K2
8 B—Kt2	B—K3
9 Castles	QKt—Q2
10 P—KR3	R—QB1
11 P—QR4	

Played with fine positional understanding. In trying for .... P—Q4; Black would normally play his QKt to QKt3, whence it can now be driven back by P—R5. In addition, the counter-demonstration .... P—QKt4; is henceforth prevented.

11	Castles

Played too nonchalantly. Now or never Black should have hastened to play 11 .... Kt—Kt3; for after 12 P—R5, he has 12 .... Kt—B5; attacking the RP, and the Knight is in play. If White plays, first, 12 P—Kt3, then 12 .... P—Q4; e.g. 13 P × P, QKt × QP; etc., or 13 P—R5, P—Q5.

It follows that White's best reply to 11 .... Kt—Kt3; is 12 P—B4, in order to gain the initiative as quickly as possible.

12 B—K3	Kt—Kt3

Too late! More promising is 12 .... Q—R4.

13 P—Kt3
Preventing the Knight's emancipation shown above. As now Black is no longer able to play 13 .... P—Q4 (14 B × Kt, Q × B; 15 Kt × P, and he loses a vital pawn); he is henceforth reduced to aimless manœuvring.

13	Q—B2
14 P—R5	Kt—R1

No better would be 14 .... QKt—Q2; 15 P—B4, Kt—Kt1; 16 P—B5, B—Q2; 17 B—Kt6, Q—B3; 18 P—KKt4, with a hopeless position for Black.

15 P—B4
The key-move, assisted by White's seventh move.

15	P × P
16 P × P	KR—K1
17 B—Q4	

Judicious timing. If 17 P—B5, at once, there follows 17 .... B—Q2; 18 Kt—B4, B—B3; 19 B—Q4, Kt—Q2; 20 Q—Kt4, Kt—K4; and Black has a defence.

17	Q—Q1
18 P—B5	B—Q2
19 Q—Q3	B—B3
20 Q—Kt3	B—B1

If 20 .... Kt—R4; 21 Q—B3, with loss of time for Black.

21 Kt—B4	Kt—B2

Black realises that he has some reserve cavalry. Fatal would be 21 .... Kt × P; 22 Kt × Kt, B × Kt; 23 B × P, B × B; 24 Kt—R5.

22 QKt—Q5	B × Kt
23 P × B	Kt—Kt4

Black makes a sustained effort to re-establish his position as best he can.

24 B—Kt6	Q—Q2
25 P—B4	Kt—B2
26 P—R4	Kt—K5
27 Q—Q3	Kt—B4
28 Q—QB3	Kt—R1
29 B × Kt	R × B
30 B—R3	

Excellent play. Beside the threat of a discovery by P—B6, the Bishop makes way for the QR after R—R2.

30 ......   Q—Q1

On 30 .... P—B3; White need not go in for precipitate action by 31 Kt—K6, QR—B1; 32 R—R2, Kt—B2 (a small counter-threat, 33 .... Kt×P); for he can play much more vigorously 31 R—R2, K—R1; 32 R—KKt2, QR—B1 (32 .... Kt—B2; 33 Kt—Q3); 33 Q—B3, etc., making straight for victory.

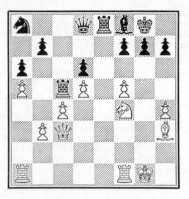

31 P—B6

The most remarkable move in a remarkable game. The move which the black Queen was intended to stop can be played after all: White allows the exchange of Queens, knowing that he still has a mating attack.

31 ......   Q×BP
32 Q×Q   P×Q
33 Kt—R5   R—K6
34 Kt×P ch   K—Kt2
35 R—R2   R×B
36 R—Kt2 ch   K—R3
37 R—B5   Resigns

A splendid finish.

50

H. PILNIK   KASHDAN
(New York, 1949)

Like the alchemist of old, for ever searching for the philosopher's stone, the analyst to-day never stops looking for stronger moves to prevent the defender from establishing equality. White's play in the following game has this quality.

1 P—K4   P—QB4
2 Kt—KB3   P—Q3
3 P—Q4   P×P
4 Kt×P   Kt—KB3

5 Kt—QB3   P—KKt3

Having avoided the *Richter Attack* by playing 2 .... P—Q3; in place of 2 .... Kt—QB3; Black thinks he can adopt the *Dragon Formation* under more favourable conditions. White's energetic next move calls him back to reality.

6 P—B4

With the immediate threat, 7 P—K5. Note that after the move 5 .... P—QR3; White can still play 6 P—B4.

6 ......   B—Kt2

He suspects nothing. Relatively best is 6 .... B—Kt5; 7 B—K2, B×B; 8 Q×B, B—Kt2; 9 B—K3, although White maintains his pressure.

7 P—K5   P×P
8 P×P   Kt—Kt5

Where to take refuge? All the five available squares are uninviting. For instance, after 8 .... Kt—Q4; the continuation in a game Shapiro-Somov, *Red Army Championship, Leningrad, 1950*, was: 9 B—Kt5 ch, K—B1; 10 Castles (a magnificent conception), 10 .... B×P; 11 Kt×Kt, Q×Kt; 12 Kt—B5, Q—B4 ch (not 12 .... Q×Q; 13 B—R6 ch, K—Kt1; 14 Kt×P mate, nor 12 .... Q×B; 13 Q—Q8 ch, Q—K1; 14 B—R6 ch); 13 B—K3, Q—B2; 14 B—R6 ch, K—Kt1; 15 Kt×P ch, Q×Kt; 16 R×P (a *crescendo* of brilliance), 16 .... K×R; 17 Q—Q5 ch, Q—K3; 18 R—B1 ch, B—B3; 19 R×B ch, K×R; 20 Q—Q4 ch, K—K2 (20 .... Q—K4; 21 B—Kt7 ch); 21 B—Kt5 ch, K—B2; 22 B—QB4, R—K1 (on 22 .... Q×B; there follows miraculously 23 Q—B6 ch, K—Kt1; 24 B—R6, Q—B4 ch; 25 K—R1, and Black cannot meet the two mating threats at KKt7 and KB8); 23 Q—B6 ch, K—Kt1; 24 B—KR6, Black resigns. One of the most brilliant games of all time!

9 B—Kt5 ch   Kt—B3

If 9 .... K—B1; 10 Kt—K6 ch, or 9 .... B—Q2; 10 Q×Kt.

10 Kt×Kt   Q×Q ch
11 Kt×Q

Also good is 11 K×Q, Kt—B7 ch; 12 K—K2, Kt×R; 13 Kt—Q4 dis ch, followed by 14 B—KB4, and White has two minor pieces for his Rook.

11 ......   P—QR3
12 B—R4   B—Q2

Black tries to recover his piece and hopes to escape from this hot affray with only the loss of a pawn.

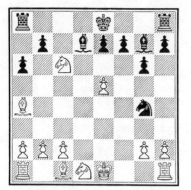

13 P—KR3
The Argentine master's ingenuity is proverbial.

13 ......   Kt—R3
If 13 .... Kt×KP; 14 Kt×Kt, Black loses a piece.

14 Kt×P
An acrobatic Knight.

14 ......   B×B
For a moment Black looks like recovering his pawn.

15 Kt—Q5
With each move White produces a new threat.

15 ......   R—Q1
16 P—B4   Kt—B4
Clearly not 16 .... B×P; 17 B×Kt. However, he could have tried 16 .... B×Kt; 17 K×B, P—QKt4.

17 B—Kt5   R—Q2
18 Kt(Q1)—B3
Introducing the threat, 19 Kt—Kt6.

18 ......   B—QB3
19 Castles QR   P—KR4
20 Kt—B7 ch
Things are getting serious for Black; he will lose a piece after all.

20 ......   K—B1
If 20 .... R×Kt; 21 R—Q8 mate.

21 R×R   B×R
22 R—Q1   B×P
There is no saving clause. If 22 .... B—K1; 23 R—Q8, P—B3; 24 R×B ch, K—B2; 25 P—K6 mate.

23 R×B   P—R5
Black's position is beyond hope.

24 Kt—K4   Kt—Q5
25 R—Q8 ch   K—Kt2
26 Kt—K8 ch   K—R2
27 Kt(K4)—B6 ch B×Kt
28 Kt×B ch   Resigns

51

ROSSOLIMO   O'KELLY
                   DE GALWAY
(Oldenburg, 1949)

The following game is full of subtle devices, and is enjoyable for players and critics alike.

1 P—K4   P—QB4
2 Kt—KB3   Kt—QB3
3 B—Kt5
This development of the KB in the *Sicilian* is not to everybody's taste. It nevertheless contains some irksome features.

Adopted, in their time, by Wyvill, Max Lange and Winawer, and, among moderns, by Nimzowitsch, W. Henneberger and Tartakower, it has been brought to the fore by Rossolimo's virtuosity.

3 ......   P—KKt3
Not bad. 3 .... Q—B2; and 3 .... P—QR3; have also been tried. 3 .... P—K3; was played in a game, Rossolimo-Kottnauer, *Bad Gastein*, 1948, and led to a fearsome finish: 3 .... P—K3; 4 Castles, Kt—B3; 5 R—K1, P—Q4; 6 P×P, Kt×P; 7 Kt—K5, Q—B2; 8 .Q—B3, B—Q3 (a blind spot); 9 Kt×Kt, P×Kt; 10 Q×Kt, B×P ch; 11 K—R1, Castles; 12 Q—R5, Black resigns.

4 Castles   B—Kt2
5 P—B3
Playable also is 5 Kt—B3, or 5 R—K1.

5 ......   P—K3
A questionable move, leaving a dangerous hole at his Q3. Generally speaking, Black should play .... P—Q3; with a *King's Fianchetto* or .... P—K3; with a *Queen's Fianchetto*. At this stage 5 .... Q—Kt3; can be recommended.

6 P—Q4   P×P
7 P×P   Q—Kt3
But now the position is different, and he should play 7 .... P—QR3.

8 Kt—R3   Kt×P
9 Kt—B4
Refuting the capture of the QP, for if now 9 .... Q×B; 10 Kt—Q6 ch, wins the

Queen. Black's weak Q3 has become a serious embarrassment.

9	Kt×Kt ch
10 Q×Kt	Q—B2
11 B—B4	P—K4

He has nothing better. If 11 .... Q—Q1; 12 Kt—Q6 ch, with a hopeless game for Black.

| 12 Kt×P | B×Kt |
| 13 QR—B1 | Q—Kt1 |

Black misses a chance of much tougher resistance by 13 .... Q—Q3; 14 KR—Q1, Q—KB3; 15 R×B ch, R×R; 16 B×P ch, K—B1 (not 16 .... K—Q1; 17 B—R4 dis ch, ˡ -B2; 18 Q—B3 ch, and wins); 17 Q—R3 ch, K—Kt2; 18 B×B, Q×B; 19 B×R, Q×KP; 20 Q×P, Q—B7; 21 Q—Q4 ch, with a won ending.

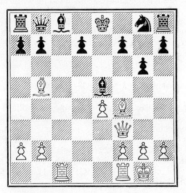

14 R×B ch	Q×R
15 B×B	P—B3
16 B×P	Kt×B
17 Q×Kt	R—B1
18 Q—K5 ch	

More precise is 18 Q—K6 ch, K—Q1; 19 R—Q1, and Black can resign.

| 18 ...... | K—Q1 |

No better is 18 .... K—B2; 19 R—Q1.

19 Q—Kt5 ch	K—K1
20 R—B1	Q—Q1
21 Q—K5 ch	Q—K2
22 B×P ch	K—B2
23 B—K6 ch	K—K1
24 R—B7	Resigns

An attractive game, in spite of sins of omission on both sides.

52

CROWN   KOTOV
(Anglo-Russian Match, London, 1947)

Skill in manœuvring is not all that is required; the art of sacrifice is a necessary adjunct, as can be seen in the following game.

| 1 P—K4 | P—QB4 |
| 2 Kt—QB3 | |

With 2 Kt—KB3, the text-move is the classical continuation against the Sicilian.

| 2 ...... | Kt—QB3 |
| 3 P—KKt3 | |

The close treatment, in which White does not seek to open the Q file by P—Q4. This old continuation, practised by L. Paulsen, and then by Tchigorin and Mieses, is held by the moderns not to give White full value for "the move." Nevertheless, it is one of those variations which theoretically should set Black no arduous problems, but which are frequently successful in actual play. White has chances of a King's side attack against any but the best play.

3	P—KKt3
4 B—Kt2	B—Kt2
5 P—Q3	P—K3

Black's real difficulty is that he must play .... P—K3; which does not harmonise very well with .... P—KKt3. Unpromising is 5 .... Kt—B3; 6 KKt—K2, P—Q3; 7 Castles, Castles; 8 P—KR3, B—Q2; 9 B—K3, Kt—K1; 10 P—B4, Kt—Q5; 11 P—KKt4, and White's attack is already taking definite shape.

| 6 B—K3 | P—Kt3 |

Here 6 .... P—Q3; is preferable, leaving an outlet for the Queen at QR4. Note that 6 .... Kt—Q5; is premature because of Smyslov's move, 7 QKt—K2. This is why White has waited so long before developing his KKt.

| 7 KKt—K2 | Kt—B3 |

A difficult decision. After 7 .... KKt—K2; White can start operations in the centre with 8 P—Q4, which, after the text-move, would be countered by 8 .... Kt—KKt5. On the other hand, White can, at the right time, play P—K5, opening the long white diagonal.

| 8 P—KR3 | B—QR3 |

This move is two-edged. If White carries out the obvious threat, 9 P—K5, Black has good attacking chances after 9 P—K5, Kt×P; 10 B×R, Q×B. But if White

refuses to be drawn, the Bishop is out of
play.

9 Q—Q2	P—Q4
10 P×P	Kt×P
11 B—Kt5	Q—Q2
12 Kt×Kt	P×Kt
13 B—R6	

White could have played this move earlier
without losing a *tempo*. As it happens,
Black is now tempted to capture the QKtP,
a notoriously risky adventure. He should
have castled KR.

13	B×KtP
14 R—QKt1	B—K4
15 Castles	P—Q5
16 KR—K1	Castles

Black is compelled to seek safety for his
King on the Q side, an extremely rare
occurrence in the Sicilian.

17 Kt—B4	KR—K1

Black is in a quandary whether to capture
the Knight, leaving his King's field exposed
to a double Bishop's battery, or allow the
white Knight to reach Q5. After the event,
one would say that he made the wrong choice.

18 Kt—Q5	Q—Q3

He has no option in view of the threats,
19 B—Kt5, winning the exchange, and
19 R×P, (19 .... P×R; 20 Kt×P ch,
winning the Queen).

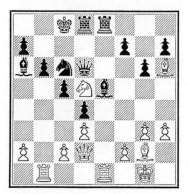

19 Kt×P ch

A *positional sacrifice* which requires
courage as well as keen judgment. The
ramifications of such a sacrifice are almost
beyond analysis in play over the board and
under a time limit. It proves, however,
entirely sound.

19	P×Kt
20 R×P	QB—Kt2
21 KR—Kt1	R—K2
22 Q—B1	R(Q1)—Q2

This looks like an oversight, but in fact
no manœuvring would enable him, without
loss, to double his Rooks for the defence of
his QB, e.g. two moves previously: 21 ....
R—Q2; 22 Q—B1, R—B2; 23 Q—R3,
R—Q1; and now it looks as if he has time
safely to double his Rooks, but 24 R×B,
R×R; 25 Q—R6, R—Q2; 26 B×Kt, and
wins.

23 B—B8	R—B2
24 Q—R3	

In not capturing at once, he gains an
important *tempo*.

24	Q—K3
25 B×R	Q×B
26 Q—R4	Kt—Q1
27 Q—Kt5	P—R4
28 P—QR4	P—R5
29 P×P	B—Q3

Intending .... Q—K4; a final bid for
salvation.

30 P—QR5	Q—Q2

He discards 30 .... Q—K4; which fails
after 31 R×QB (he must retain the vital
Bishop), 31 .... Kt×R; 32 P—R6, Kt—Q1;
33 Q—Kt8 ch, K—Q2; 34 P—R7, and wins
(34 .... Kt—B3; 35 B×Kt ch, R×B;
36 R—Kt7 ch, R—B2; 37 R×R ch, B×R;
38 Q—Kt5 ch, followed by P—R8(Q)).

31 P—R6	Q×Q
32 P×B ch	K—Kt1
33 R(Kt1)×Q	B—B5
34 R—R6	Kt×P
35 R(R6)—Kt6	Resigns

An impressive victory.

15. CENTRE COUNTER

53

MILNER-BARRY   van den BOSCH
(Anglo-Dutch Match, Utrecht, 1949)

The following struggle between two tacticians of the first order is, as can be expected, full of subtle and varied skirmishes, in which pawns on either side are left en prise with joyous abandon.

1 P—K4	P—Q4
2 P×P	Q×P
3 Kt—QB3	Q—QR4
4 P—QKt4	

An interesting gambit, which seeks to derive an immediate advantage from the black Queen's eccentric sortie. While not sound, it is a dangerous weapon in the hands of an imaginative opponent. The normal continuation is 4 P—Q4, which also denies the black Queen a peaceful life, e.g. Solmanis–Pirtskalava, *U.S.S.R. Championship*, 1949, 4 P—Q4, Kt—KB3; 5 B—K2 (more usual is 5 Kt—B3), 5 .... B—B4; 6 Kt—B3, Kt—B3 (the safest here is 6 .... P—B3, providing an outlet for the Queen); 7 B—Q2, Castles; 8 Kt—QKt5, Q—Kt3; 9 P—QR4, P—QR4 (the Queen is in dire straits, and instead of developing his game, Black will have to devote all his energy to saving her); 10 P—B4, Kt—QKt5; 11 B×Kt, P×B; 12 P—R5, Q—R3; 13 P—B5, Q—K3; 14 P—R6, P×P; 15 P—B6 (White's *pawn strategy* is very clever and worth a thorough examination), 15 .... Q—Q4; 16 Kt—Kt5 (neater would be 16 R×P, K—Kt1; 17 R—R8 ch, K×R; 18 Q—R1 ch, with mate to follow. But if 16 R×P, Kt—Q2; 17 R—R8 ch, Kt—Kt1; 18 Kt—R7 mate), 16 .... Q×KtP; 17 B—B3, Black resigns (17 .... Q×Kt; 18 R×P, etc.).

4 ......   Q—Kt3

Definitely inferior to accepting the gambit by 4 .... Q×KtP; 5 R—Kt1, Q—Q3; 6 Kt—B3, Kt—KB3; 7 P—Q4, P—QR3; 8 B—QB4, P—K3; 9 Castles, B—K2; etc. (Sir G. A. Thomas–du Mont, *Tunbridge Wells*, 1912). It is useful to know that the key-moves for the defence are in the *gambit accepted* .... P—QR3; and in the *gambit declined* .... P—QB3. Black's game can easily become untenable if these are neglected.

5 Kt—B3	Kt—KB3
6 B—B4	B—K3

This is the type of artificial manœuvre which, more often than not, runs counter to the immutable elements of a position.

7 Q—K2	B×B
8 Q×B	P—K3
9 Castles	QKt—Q2
10 R—Kt1	Q—B3
11 Q—K2	Kt—Q4
12 Kt×Kt	Q×Kt
13 P—B4	Q—KB4

Black was compelled to make six ineffective moves out of thirteen with his Queen, and, worse still, the Queen is still exposed and will make two more useless moves before the end—a condemnation of his opening strategy.

14 R—Kt3	B—K2
15 B—Kt2	B—B3
16 Kt—Q4	B×Kt
17 B×B	Castles KR
18 R—KB3	Q—B7

He has nothing better. If 18 .... Q—KR4 or Kt5; 19 B×KtP, and if then 19 .... K×B; 20 R—KKt3, wins the Queen.

19 R—KKt3	P—KKt3
20 P—B4	QR—K1
21 P—QR3	P—KB3
22 R—QB3	Q—R5
23 R—K3	P—K4
24 R—K1	

Position after 24 .... R—Q1

With unyielding energy, White maintains, and even increases his pressure. Fruitless would be to strive for immediate material gain: 24 P×P, Kt×P; 25 B×Kt, P×B; 26 R×R ch, K×R; 27 R×P, R×R; 28 Q×R Q—Q8 ch, and Black saves the situation.

24 ......   R—Q1

The crisis is at hand (see diag.).

25 B—B3

A ruthless retreat which threatens a sacrifice by 26 P×P, P×P; 27 R×P, Kt×R; 28 Q×Kt, and wins.

25 ......   P×P
26 R—K7   P—QB4

Here 26 .... Q—B3; prolongs, but does not save, the game (27 P—B5, etc.).

27 Q—K6 ch   K—R1
28 P—Kt5   Resigns

16. ALEKHINE'S DEFENCE

54

GOLOMBEK   H. BROWN
(Mandrake Tournament, London, 1949)

The following game illustrates Golombek's strong point—quiet and reasoned preparation for large-scale and brilliantly conceived plans.

1 P—K4	Kt—KB3
2 P—K5	Kt—Q4
3 Kt—QB3	

A perfectly sound developing move, which, however, should not set Black any difficult problem.

Two accepted continuations are:

(*a*) marked by solidity: 3 P—Q4, P—Q3; 4 Kt—KB3 (as is well known, the idea of Black's defence is to undermine the centre, after having tempted the white pawns to advance, while White's plan consists in maintaining his hold on K5), 4 .... B—Kt5; 5 B—K2, etc.

(*b*) marked by skirmishing: 3 P—QB4, Kt—Kt3; 4 P—B5 (the "main" line runs: 4 P—Q4, P—Q3; 5 P—B4, P×P; 6 BP×P, Kt—B3; 7 B—K3, B—B4; 8 Kt—QB3, P—K3; 9 Kt—B3, etc. White conducts operations on a wide front), 4 .... Kt—Q4.

Here is an amusing skirmish, Fuller–Derby, *Felixstowe*, 1949: 3 P—QB4, Kt—Kt3; 4 P—B5, Kt—Q4; 5 Kt—QB3, Kt×Kt; 6 QP×Kt, P—Q3; 7 Q—Kt3 (an original conception. If 7 B—QB4, P—Q4; 8 Q×P, Q×Q; 9 B×Q, P—K3; 10 B—K4, B×P; etc., with equality), 7 .... P×KP; 8 B—Kt5, B—K3; 9 Q×P, Kt—Q2 (not 9 .... B—Q4; 10 B—Kt5 ch); 10 Castles, Q—B1; 11 Q—B6, P—QR3 (he might have tried to free himself by 11 .... P—KR3); 12 Kt—B3, R—R2; 13 Kt×P, P—B3; 14 B—QB4 (a charming idea. If 14 .... P×B; 15 B×B, with unavoidable mate. But the main line could serve as a problem theme: 14 .... B×B; 15 R×Kt, B—Kt4; 16 R—Q8 db ch, K×R; 17 Kt—B7 mate), Black resigns.

3	Kt×Kt

Black can also play 3 .... P—K3; as played by Alekhine himself against Sämisch, *Budapest*, 1921.

4 KtP×Kt	P—Q4

More in the spirit of the defence is 4 ....

P—Q3; at once challenging White's advanced pawn.

5 P—KB4	

The usual continuation is 5 Kt—K2, P—K3; 6 P—Q4, P—QB4; etc. Against the text-move Black could have tried 5 .... P—Q5.

5	P—K3
6 Kt—B3	P—QB4
7 P—Q4	P—QKt3

With the idea of developing the QB at QR3, in order to induce White to exchange Bishops. The plan goes "agley" and, in the end, only spells loss of time. The unpretentious development 7 .... Kt—B3; is indicated.

8 B—Q3	B—R3
9 Castles	B×B
10 Q×B	P—B5

An unwise decision. Now the Q side is blocked and White can devote his whole attention to the K side.

11 Q—K2	P—Kt3
12 P—Kt4	P—KR4

The start of open hostilities.

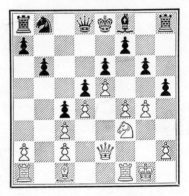

13 P—B5	

The prelude to a spectacular attack.

13	RP×P
14 P×KP	P×Kt
15 Q×KBP	

White has quickly reaped the benefit of his clever sacrifice and Black has no resource, e.g.:

(a) 15 .... Q—B2; 16 P×P ch, K—Q2; 17 Q×P ch, winning the QR, or 16 .... K—K2; 17 Q—B6 ch, winning the KR.

(b) More complicated is 15 .... Q—R5; against which the simplest continuation is 16 P×P ch, K—K2 (16 .... K—Q2; 17 Q×P ch, followed by B—B4); 17 B—R3 ch, K—K3; 18 Q—B6 ch, Q×Q; 19 R×Q ch, K—Q2; 20 P—K6 ch, K—Q1; 21 R×P, etc.

15	P—B4
16 P×P e.p.	B—Q3
17 B—Kt5	Q—B2
18 P—B7 ch	K—B1
19 Q—B6	B×P ch
20 K—R1	

The point of White's plan. He gives up the Queen in order to obtain two irresistible pawns on the seventh. A very attractive conception.

20	B—K4 dis ch
21 Q×R ch	B×Q
22 P—K7 ch	Resigns

17. NIMZOWITSCH'S DEFENCE

55

KERES   **MIKENAS**

(U.S.S.R. Championship, Tiflis, 1947)

The complications in the following game, arising from an overcrowded terrain, are surmounted by Keres with the ease which is the hallmark of genius.

1 P—K4	Kt—QB3
2 P—Q4	P—K4

Black could play 2 .... P—Q4; which is the original idea of this defence, e.g. 3 P—K5, B—B4; 4 P—QB3, P—B3.

If Black plays 2 .... P—Q3; he may not be able to enforce .... P—K4. Fine–Mikenas, *Hastings*, 1938, went as follows: 2 .... P—Q3; 3 Kt—KB3, B—Kt5; 4 B—QKt5, P—QR3; 5 B—R4, P—QKt4; 6 B—Kt3, Kt—B3; 7 P—B3, P—K3; 8 Q—K2, B—K2; 9 Castles, Castles; 10 QKt—Q2, B—R4; 11 P—QR4, and White has the better game.

Another system, akin to the *French Defence*, is: 2 .... P—K3; 3 Kt—QB3, B—Kt5; etc., or 3 Kt—KB3, P—Q4; etc.

3 P×P	Kt×P
4 Kt—QB3	

Or, at once, 4 P—KB4, when Black's best is 4 .... Kt—QB3.

4	B—B4
5 P—B4	Kt—Kt3

Here again 5 .... Kt—QB3; is preferable.

6 Kt—B3	P—Q3
7 B—B4	B—K3
8 Q—K2	

Paul Keres, who has not inaptly been called the modern Morphy, like his great prototype, seldom misses a chance of gaining a *tempo* in the opening. Here and on the next move the threat is Q—Kt5 ch (after 9 B×B), and Black is already reduced to time-wasting defensive moves.

8	B×B
9 Q×B	Q—Q2
10 P—B5	QKt—K2
11 B—Kt5	

White's play is admirable in its simplicity. After eleven moves, Black is already in difficulties without having made a palpable mistake. His problem is the development of his K side; and if he castles on the Q side, he will clearly be subjected to a swift and fierce attack.

11	P—KB3
12 B—B4	Kt—B3
13 Castles	Castles
14 P—KKt4	P—KKt4
15 B—Kt3	P—KR4
16 P—KR3	Q—R2

Intending 17 .... P×P; 18 P×P, Q×R; 19 R×Q, B—K6 ch; 20 K—Q1, R×R ch; and Black has quite a good game. Keres parries with the utmost precision.

17 R—R2	B—K6 ch
18 K—Kt1	P—R5
19 B—B2	B×B

If 19 .... B—B5; 20 R(R2)—R1, the K side is fixed, which has been White's object throughout, and he can start operations in earnest on the Q side.

20 R×B	R—Q2

He has to waste yet another *tempo*, as he cannot even now develop his KKt on account of 21 Q—K6 ch, winning a pawn.

21 Kt—Q4	

A powerful move. Black cannot allow Kt—K6, and so has to give up the only effective defender of his King's field. The main point, however, is that Black must lose another *tempo* and weaken the pawn formation in front of his King. Nevertheless, it is hard to believe that he will be forced to resign in another eight moves.

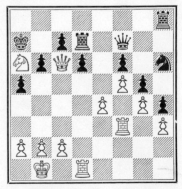

Position after 28 .... K—R2

21	......	Kt × Kt
22	Q × Kt	P—Kt3
23	Kt—Q5	Q—B2
24	Q—R4	K—Kt2
25	R—B3	Kt—R3

At last, but too late.

26 Kt—Kt4
Threatening mate in three.

26 ...... P—R4

27 Q—B6 ch   K—Kt1
If 27 .... K—R2; 28 R—R3, with the striking threat 29 R × P ch, P × R; 30 Q—R6 ch, K—Kt1; 31 Kt—B6 mate.

28 Kt—R6 ch   K—R2
The position merits a diagram. (*See* p. 90.)

29 Kt—B5   Resigns
Chess magic! If 29 .... KtP × Kt; 30 R—R3, K—Kt1; 31 R × RP, with mate to follow.

PART III

CLOSED GAMES

18. QUEEN'S GAMBIT ACCEPTED

56

STÅHLBERG   C. C. ALEXANDER

(Staunton Centenary Tournament,
Birmingham, 1951)

The technique of the attack—break-through in the centre, sacrifices on the wing—is well illustrated in the following game.

1 P—Q4	P—Q4
2 Kt—KB3	Kt—KB3
3 P—B4	P×P

Note the interpolation on both sides of Kt—KB3 in the modern version of the *Queen's Gambit*, mutually preventing P—K4, which used to be played in the old days.

4 P—K3
Simple and good, but the modern treatment, which breaks away from the classic principle not to move the Queen in the early phase of the game, is here 4 Q—R4 ch. Compare Game No. 94, Alekhine–Bogoljubow, in which this variant occurs, but in a different opening, the *Catalan*.

4	P—K3

Playable also is the *Swedish Variation*, 4 .... B—Kt5.

5 B×P	P—B4
6 Castles	Kt—B3
7 Q—K2	P—QR3
8 R—Q1	P—QKt4
9 B—Kt3	

If White fears the hostile pawn advance, he could play 9 P×P, Q—B2; 10 B—Q3, but he would thereby seriously reduce his pressure in the centre, which at present is his main asset.

9	P—B5

With this manœuvre Black succeeds in eliminating the hostile KB, but his pawn structure becomes inelastic. Appropriate would be 9 .... Q—Kt3.

10 B—B2	Kt—QKt5
11 Kt—B3	Kt×B
12 Q×Kt	B—Kt2
13 P—Q5	

A well-known break-through, which relies on the immediate support of the KP.

An unfortunate inversion of moves would be first 13 P—K4, because of 13 .... P—Kt5.

13	Q—B2

With the idea of blockading the centre by .... P—K4. Against 13 .... P×P; 14 P—K4, is a powerful reply.

14 P—K4
The point! Here 14 P×P, P×P; 15 P—K4, is answered by 15 .... P—Kt5.

14	P—K4
15 B—Kt5	Kt—Q2

Evading the threatened capture at KB3, followed by Kt—KR4—B5. At the same time Black intends himself to start a counter-action by Kt—B4—Q6.

16 QR—B1
A carefully conceived manœuvre by which White furthers his chances in a remarkable manner. In a game Reshevsky–Flohr, *Nottingham*, 1936, which ended in a draw, White at this point was chiefly concerned with the prevention of the manœuvre indicated above and played 16 B—K3.

16	B—Q3

Black sees that 16 .... Kt—B4; would be unavailing, for there would follow 17 Kt—K2, Q—Kt1; 18 B—K3, Kt—Q6; 19 R—R1, followed by P—QKt3, and Black's advanced detachment would cause trouble only to himself.

17 Kt—K2
Examining the position, we find that Black's K side is denuded, while White's pieces are well-placed for a direct attack.

17	Castles KR

A mistake which results in a serious loss of time. His proper course is 17 .... P—B3; 18 B—K3, K—B2; etc. This would enable the KR to reach in one move instead of two whatever file is the most effective.

18 Kt—Kt3	P—B3
19 B—K3	P—Kt3
20 P—KR4	

In this game Ståhlberg shows that he has all the qualities of a great player.

20 ......   QR—B1

Had Black realised even now the full scope of White's intention, he would have renounced all ideas of counter-action and played 20 .... K—B2.

21 P—R5   Kt—B4
22 Kt—R4   K—B2

The lost *tempo*! It is instructive to note how a seemingly unimportant finesse can tip the scales in a critical situation. The King, denuded of his defenders, tries to look after himself. If, instead, 22 .... Q—B2; White continues his attack equally decisively with 23 Q—K2.

23 Q—K2   R—KKt1
24 P×P ch   P×P

It would now seem that all Black's vulnerable points are adequately guarded, but here the miracle of the sacrifice comes on the scene.

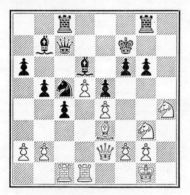

25 Kt(Kt3)—B5

Black must decline the offer, for if 25 .... P×Kt; 26 Q—R5 ch, K—B1; 27 Kt×P, with the terrible threat 28 B—R6 ch.

25 ......   B—B1
26 Kt×P   R×Kt

If 26 .... K×Kt; 27 Q—Kt4 ch, K—B2; 28 Q—R5 ch, R—Kt3; 29 Kt—R4, winning.

27 Q—R5   Q—Q2
28 B×Kt

Not 28 Kt—R4, Q—Kt5.

28 ......   R×B
29 R—B3   Resigns

The finish is simple, but impressive.

57

MUFFANG   DEVOS
(France)   *(Belgium)*

(Match, France v. Belgium, Paris, 1948)

"It is urgent to wait," a principle applied with great success in the following game.

1 P—Q4   .   P—Q4
2 P—QB4   P×P
3 Kt—KB3

The continuation 3 Kt—QB3, is not without guile, as can be seen in the following two miniature games:

Haberditz–Prohaska, *Austria*, 1948, 3 Kt—QB3, P—K3; 4 P—K4, Kt—KB3; 5 B×P, P—B4; 6 Kt—B3, P×P; 7 Kt×P, B—B4; 8 B—K3, Q—K2; 9 Castles, P—K4; 10 B—Kt5 ch, K—B1; 11 Kt—B5, Black resigns (11 .... B×Kt; 12 B×B, Q×B; 13 Q—Q8 ch, with mate to follow).

Tartakower–Füster, *Budapest*, 1948: 3 Kt—QB3, P—K4; 4 P—Q5, P—QB3; 5 P—K4, B—QKt5; 6 B×P, Kt—B3; 7 Q—Kt3, Q—Q3; 8 Kt—K2 (the reason for this pawn sacrifice becomes clear at a later stage), 8 .... Kt×KP; 9 P×P (at the right moment), 9 .... Castles; 10 Castles, B×Kt; 11 P×P (the decisive skirmish), 11 .... QB×P; 12 Q×QB, Kt—QB3 (12 .... Kt—B4; 13 Q—Q5); 13 P×B, Black resigns.

3 ......   Kt—KB3

Doubtful is the immediate *sortie* 3 .... B—Kt5 (because of 4 Kt—K5); but quite reasonable is the new *Swedish Variation*, 3 .... P—QR3; 4 P—K3, B—Kt5; 5 B×P, P—K3; 6 P—KR3, B—R4; etc.

4 P—K3   P—K3
5 B×P   P—B4
6 Castles   P—QR3
7 P—QR3

White has the choice between strictly preventive measures by 7 P—QR4 (e.g. 7 .... Kt—B3; 8 Q—K2, B—K2; 9 R—Q1, Q—B2; 10 Kt—B3, Castles; etc., with equality), and the line of least resistance by 7 Q—K2, Kt—B3; 8 R—Q1, P—QKt4; 9 B—Kt3, etc. (as in the preceding game, Ståhlberg–Alexander). White here decides on a middle course which allows Black's pawn storm, but limits its scope. At the same time, the unostentatious little move in the text reserves for White's KB an advantageous retreat and also provides for the development of the QB in *fianchetto*. We see how a move of modest appearance can have the widest repercussions!

7	B—K2
8 Q—K2	P—QKt4
9 B—R2	B—Kt2

The tempting 9 .... P—B5; would be wrong. White would at once react against this advance with 10 P—QKt3, and remain in command of the centre.

10 P×P	B×P
11 P—QKt4	B—R2

A hasty move. 11 .... B—Kt3; is essential.

12 B—Kt2	Castles

As can easily be seen, White is two *tempi* ahead.

13 QKt—Q2	Kt—K5

This move has several drawbacks: Black loses another *tempo* in his development besides leaving his King's field bare. He wants to prevent P—K4, but should play 13 .... QKt—Q2; 14 KR—Q1, Q—K2; 15 QR—B1, QR—B1; contesting the QB file, which the text-move allows White to capture.

14 KR—Q1	Q—K2
15 QR—B1	

Black is now in trouble. He can no longer play 15 .... QKt—B3 (16 Kt×Kt); nor 15 .... Kt—Q2 (16 R—B7). See note to Black's eleventh move.

15	Kt×Kt
16 Q×Kt	B—Kt3

Too late! But it would be too dangerous to open the KKt file for the white Rooks by 16 .... B×Kt; 17 P×B. On the other hand, if 16 .... Kt—B3; 17 R×Kt, B×R; 18 Q—B3, with a double threat at KKt7 and QB6.

17 Q—B3	P—B3

Black now feels the absence of a defending Knight at KB3.

18 Kt—Q4	B×Kt

Black must concede his adversary the advantage of the "two Bishops," lest he lose the weakened KP. For if 18 .... B—Q4; 19 Kt—B5, Q—KB2; 20 R×B, P×Kt; 21 B×P, winning the Queen.

19 Q×B	Kt—B3
20 Q—B5	KR—K1

If 20 .... Q×Q; 21 B×P ch, K—R1; 22 R×Q, and White has gained the vital pawn.

21 R—Q6	Kt—Q1
22 Q—Q4	B—B1

White's threat was 23 R—Q7. Black cannot play 22 .... B—Q4; because of 23 B×B, Q×R; 24 B×R. If 22 .... R—QB1; 23 R—B5.

The Black forces are now tied to the defence of the pinned KP, and unable to perform their normal functions. Such a position must sooner or later yield combinative opportunities for the attack.

23 P—KR4	K—R1
24 B—Kt1	R—QKt1

One threat was 25 R×Kt, R×R; 26 Q—K4, winning a piece.

25 Q—K4	P—B4

The black King's defences are crumbling. If 25 .... P—Kt3; 26 Q—KB4 (threatening both 27 B×P ch and 27 R×Kt, followed by Q×R), 26 .... P—K4; 27 R×BP, K—Kt2 (if 27 .... P×Q; 28 R—B8 mate); 28 B×KP, Q×B; 29 R—QB7 ch, Q×R; 30 Q×Q ch, K×R; 31 Q×R, with an easy win.

26 Q—K5	R—R1

To avoid 27 R×Kt, followed by Q×R, and also trying to preserve his material. If 26 .... B—Kt2; or 26 .... Kt—Kt2; 27 R×RP, or 26 .... Q—Kt2; 27 R—Kt6, or 26 .... Q—R2; 27 B—Q4.

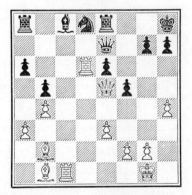

27 R—B7	Resigns

A magnificent stroke and not at all obvious. If 27 .... Q×QR; 28 R×Kt, and if 28 .... R×R; 29 Q×Q, or 28 .... Q×Q; 29 R×R mate, or 28 .... Q×R; 29 Q×P mate.

19. ALBIN COUNTER-GAMBIT

58

FLOHR   BENKÖ
(*Moscow*)   (*Budapest*)

(Moscow v. Budapest, 1949)

*Who shall secure the initiative? That is
the motif of the following game.*

1 P—Q4   P—Q4
2 P—QB4   P—K4

The *Albin Counter-gambit* remains the
fancy of adventurous spirits. Another such
opening is *Tchigorin's Defence*. 2 ....
Kt—QB3. Here is an example, Hrdy–
Haberditz, *Vienna*, 1951: 3 P—K3 (the more
energetic continuation, 3 Kt—KB3, B—Kt5;
4 Q—R4, prevents the emancipation of
Black's game by .... P—K4), 3 ....
P—K4; 4 P × KP, P—Q5 (bringing about a
sort of *Albin Deferred*. Or 4 .... P × P;
5 Q × Q ch, K × Q; 6 B × P, Kt × P; 7 B—K2,
etc., with equality); 5 P—QR3, B—KB4;
6 B—Q3 (instinctive but faulty. After
6 Kt—KB3, P × P; 7 Q × Q ch, R × Q;
8 B × P, KKt—K2; etc., the chances are
approximately even), 6 .... P × P (White
should realise his misconception and play
7 B—K2, or 7 B—B2); 7 B × B, P × P ch;
8 K—K2, Q × Q ch; White resigns.

3 QP × P   P—Q5
4 Kt—KB3

It is well-known that White cannot
refute the gambit by 4 P—K3, because of
4 .... B—Kt5 ch; 5 B—Q2, P × P; 6 B × B,
P × P ch; 7 K—K2, P × Kt(Kt) ch; and wins.

A violent continuation, 4 P—K4, was
successfully tried in a game Kortchnoj–
Shapkine, *Leningrad*, 1949.   4 P—K4,
Kt—QB3; 5 P—B4, P—KKt4; 6 P—KB5,
Kt × P; 7 Kt—KB3, Kt × Kt ch; 8 Q × Kt,
Q—B3; 9 B—Q3, B—Q3; 10 P—K5
(a great-hearted gift), 10 .... B × KP;
11 Kt—Q2, Q—K2; 12 Castles, P—KB3;
13 P—B5, Q × P (prudence dictates
13 .... Kt—R3; although, even then,
White secures a fine attack after
14 Q—R5 ch, Kt—B2; 15 Kt—K4, Castles;
16 P—KR4, etc.); 14 Kt—B4, K—Q1;
15 P—QKt4 (a masterly conception),
15 .... Q—B3; 16 Kt × B, P × Kt;
17 B × P ch, Kt—K2; 18 P—B6, Black
resigns.

4 ......   Kt—QB3
5 P—QR3

More usual is 5 QKt—Q2, with a choice
of continuations in 6 P—KKt3, or 6 P—KR3.
Flohr's treatment of the opening is interesting and supports the opinion, that "when the
opponent tries to assume the initiative, as,
for instance, by a counter-gambit that is not
quite sound, it is a wise policy not to attempt
immediate counter-measures." The weakness in the opponent's position carries the
germ of disaster, and, in due course, satisfactory moves will become increasingly
hard to find.

A scientific continuation here is
5 P—KKt3, as played in a game Muir—
Mitchell, *Atlanta*, 1939: 5 P—KKt3,
B—Kt5 (Kostic, the great expert in the
Albin Counter-gambit, prefers 5 ....
B—K3); 6 B—Kt2, B—Kt5 ch; 7 B—Q2,
Q—K2; 8 Castles, B × B; 9 QKt × B,
Castles; 10 Q—R4, K—Kt1; 11 P—QR3,
Kt × P; 12 Kt × Kt, Q × Kt; 13 Q—Kt4,
B—B1; 14 P—B5, Kt—B3; 15 Kt—B4,
Q—K2; 16 Kt—R5, Black resigns.

5 ......   B—Kt5
6 P—Kt4

More incisive than 6 QKt—Q2.

6 ......   P—QR4
7 P—Kt5   B × Kt
8 KP × B   Kt × P

He has recovered his pawn, but has lost
whatever attacking chances there are in a
normal *Albin*.

9 P—B4   Kt—Kt3
10 P—Kt3   B—B4

Examining the position, we note that the
white pawn formation is not in itself promising, but that, on the other hand, Black
lacks a QB and cannot undertake anything
against the "white" holes on White's K side.
Moreover, one black Knight is undeveloped
and the other has little scope.

11 B—KKt2   Q—K2 ch
12 K—B1

Excellent. If, instead, 12 Q—K2, Castles;
threatening .... P—Q6; and, after the
exchange of Queens, the black KKt is
developed and his QP becomes an asset.

12 ......   R—Kt1

Now 12 .... Castles; fails against 13 Q—B3.

13 R—R2	Q—Q3
14 Kt—Q2	Kt—B3
15 Kt—Kt3	Castles
16 Kt×B	

Much superior to 16 Kt × RP, after which 16 .... P—B3; would free Black's game.

16	Q×Kt
17 Q—Q3	P—B3
18 P—QR4	P×P

Black misses an opportunity of getting more of the play by 18 .... Kt—Q4; 19 B×Kt, P×B; 20 B—R3, Q×BP; 21 Q×Q, P×Q; 22 B×R, K×B. White has won the exchange, but accurate play will be needed to cope with the black pawn phalanx.

19 RP×P	KR—B1
20 R—B2	Q—Kt5

The fly enters the parlour. No doubt Black wishes to bring more forces to bear on the hostile QBP and hopes to make something of his own passed QRP. If now 21 Q×P, R—Q1; and White is in danger.

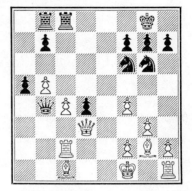

21 B—B3
A wily move, to all appearances intending to guard Q1.

21 ...... Kt—B1
He evidently suspects nothing and wishes to bring his Knight into play.

22 B—R3	Q—R5
23 R—B1	Resigns

The Queen is trapped!

20. QUEEN'S GAMBIT DECLINED

59

RABAR   BAJEC

(Jugoslav Championship, Sarajevo, 1951)

The strategy based on the idea of attack on strong rather than weak points in the opponent's formation succeeds in the following game.

1 P—Q4	P—Q4
2 P—QB4	P—K3
3 Kt—QB3	Kt—KB3
4 B—Kt5	

The actual order of the moves was: 1 P—QB4, Kt—KB3; 2 P—Q4, P—K3; 3 Kt—QB3, P—Q4; 4 B—Kt5, etc.

4 ......   B—K2

A quiet reply. The counter-pin 4 .... B—Kt5; so effective in the *French Defence*, is not to be recommended. Here is a game from an inter-club match, Makarczyk–Szymanski, *Lodz*, 1952: 4 .... B—Kt5; 5 Q—Kt3, P—B4; 6 P×BP, Kt—B3; 7 P—K3, P—Q5; 8 Castles, B×P; 9 Kt—B3, P—K4 (bringing on the crisis. He should castle); 10 Kt×KP, Kt×Kt; 11 P×P, B×P; 12 Kt—Kt5, B×P ch (or 12 .... Kt—B3; 13 Kt×B, Kt×Kt; 14 Q—K3 ch, B—K3; 15 R×Kt, and with a good extra pawn, White has advantageously recovered his piece); 13 Q×B, QKt—Q2; 14 Q—R3, Black resigns. The threats, 15 R—K1 ch, or 15 Kt—Q6 ch, or after 14 .... Q—K2; 15 Kt—B7 ch, are deadly.

5 P—K3	Castles
6 R—B1	

An opening finesse: after the immediate 6 Kt—B3, Black can effect "Lasker's unpin" 6 .... Kt—K5; whereas now there follows 7 B×B, Q×B; 8 P×P, Kt×Kt; 9 R×Kt, P×P; 10 B—Q3, and the control of the semi-open QB file ensures for White a permanent advantage.

6	QKt—Q2
7 Kt—B3	P—B3

The *normal position* in the *orthodox* variation of the *Queen's Gambit Declined*.

8 B—Q3	P×P
9 B×P	Kt—Q4

This is "Capablanca's unpin," based,

logically, on the loss of a *tempo* by the opposing KB.

10 B×B	Q×B
11 Castles	

The *Rubinstein Attack*.

11	Kt×Kt
12 R×Kt	P—K4
13 B—Kt3	

A good reinforcing move, in place of the main variation 13 Kt×P, Kt×Kt; 14 P×Kt, Q×P; 15 P—B4, when Black can hold his own. Alternative moves are 13 Q—B2, or, even more astutely, 13 Q—Kt1, concentrating his forces on the Q side.

13	R—K1
14 Q—Kt1	

An ultra-positional manœuvre; the Queen makes way for the KR, preparing at the same time for the well-known minority attack: P—QKt4—Kt5. More incisive is Rubinstein's continuation: 14 Kt×P, Kt×Kt; 15 P×Kt, Q×P; 16 P—B4.

14 ......   P×P

Boldly, Black decides on an open fight, relying mainly on establishing a solid rampart at his K3.

Against 14 .... P—K5; an interesting continuation was played in a correspondence game in *Sweden*, 1950: 15 Kt—Q2, Kt—B3; 16 R—B5, Q—B2; 17 KR—B1, B—Q2; (17 .... B—Kt5; 18 P—Q5) 18 B—B2, P—QKt3; 19 R—B3, Kt—Q4; 20 R—B4, P—KB4; 21 B—Kt3 (threat 22 R×P), 21 .... Q—Q3; 22 R(B4)—B2, P—QKt4; 23 B×Kt, P×B; 24 P—KKt3, and White, having neutralised the K side, has kept up his pressure on the opposite wing.

15 P×P   Kt—B1

Black prepares to block the open K file.

16 R—K1	B—K3
17 R(B3)—K3	KR—Q1

A crisis. Black sees himself compelled to divert one of the four defenders from the key-point K3, since, after the more natural 17 .... QR—Q1; there follows 18 P—Q5, P×P; 19 B—R4, Kt—Q2; 20 Kt—K5, and White wins at least the exchange.

Nevertheless, Black could have saved himself much trouble with 17 .... Q—B3; e.g. 18 P—Q5, P×P; 19 B×P, R—K2; etc.

18 Q—B5
A nice turn! Black did not take into account that White possesses a weapon in the vertical pin of the Bishop.

18 ...... Q—B2
Black's forces are in disarray. Unattractive is 18 .... B×Q; 19 R×Q, etc. But the lesser evil is 18 .... Q—B3; for after 19 Q×Q, P×Q; Black would have some compensation for the deterioration of his pawn structure in the vulnerability of White's QP.

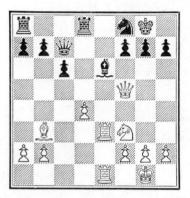

19 R×B
Mind over matter.

19 ...... P×R
Or 19 .... Kt×R; 20 R×Kt, P×R; 21 B×P ch, K—R1; 22 Kt—Kt5, P—KKt3; 23 Q—B6 ch, Q—Kt2; 24 Kt—B7 ch, K—Kt1; 25 Kt×R dis ch, and White has a decisive advantage in material (two pieces and a pawn for a Rook).

20 R×P
A *complementary sacrifice*, which Black prefers to decline, to avoid the line shown above.

20 ...... K—R1
21 Kt—Kt5 R×P
Attempting an active defence. If 21 .... R—Q2; 22 R—K4, threatening 23 Kt—B7 ch, Black must give back the exchange, without stopping White's attack.

22 Kt—B7 ch K—Kt1
23 Kt—Q8
Continued brilliance. This closure of the

eighth rank encroaches on the domain of the problemist. Much less precise is 23 Kt—Q6, Kt×R.

23 ...... Kt×R
There is no saving the day. If 23 .... R—Q8 ch; 24 R—K1 dis ch, R—Q4; 25 R—K8, Q—Q3; 26 Q—B7 ch, K—R1; 27 Q×Kt ch, followed by mate.

24 B×Kt ch K—R1
25 Q—B8 mate
Q.E.D.
An elegant finish.

60

RESHEVSKY   GUIMARD
(New York, 1951)

In the following game Reshevsky is rather dogmatic in exchanging pawns in the centre, while no particular consideration incites him to do so. His reasoning is as follows:
1. *Sooner or later Black will have to play* .... *P—QR3; and* .... *P—QB3; which will create holes in his position.*
2. *My "secret weapon" will then be the famed "minority attack."*
3. *It follows that the early simplification in the centre is sought by me only in order to become the more active, even violent, on the flanks.*

1 P—Q4 Kt—KB3
2 P—QB4 P—K3
3 Kt—QB3 P—Q4
4 P×P P×P
The "simplified" scheme of things is far from being "simple."

5 B—Kt5 P—B3
6 Q—B2
More subtle is first 6 P—K3, or 6 Kt—B3.

6 ...... B—K2
An important juncture. Capablanca's advice not to allow the pinning Bishop to act on two diagonals at the same time could be acted on here by 6 .... P—KR3. This move also contains a painful trap. If after 6 .... P—KR3; White imagines that he can punish his adversary with 7 B×Kt, Q×B; 8 Kt×P, Q×P; 9 Kt—B7 ch, he will himself have caught a Tartar after 9 .... K—Q1; 10 R—Q1, B—Kt5 ch; and Black wins.

7 Kt—B3 QKt—Q2
8 P—K3 Kt—R4

Black thinks that now or never is the time to relieve the tension, for after 8 .... Castles; 9 B—Q3, unpinning would become much more difficult.

9 P—KR4
White unexpectedly adds to the dynamic strength of his game. There is nothing in 9 B×B, Q×B, e.g. 10 B—Q3, Kt—B5; 11 Castles KR, Kt×B; 12 Q×Kt, Castles; etc., or, as was played in a game, Bolbochan –Euwe, *Utrecht*, 1950: 10 Castles, Kt—Kt3; 11 B—Q3, B—Kt5; followed by castling on the Q side.

9 ......   P—B3
After 9 .... P—KR3; 10 P—KKt4, P×B; 11 P×P, B×P; 12 P×Kt, and White's game remains dynamically superior.

10 P—KKt4
Total war! Observe what can be the outcome of a modest exchange variation.

10 ......   Kt—B1
This interim measure prevents White from enlarging the scope of his operations by opening the KR file. If at once 10 .... P×B; 11 P×P, KKt—B3 (or 11 .... B×P; 12 R×Kt); 12 P×Kt, Kt×P; 13 P—Kt5, and in this warm affray White wins a good pawn.

11 P×Kt   P×B
12 P×P   B×P
13 Kt—K5   B—B3
He hopes, for example, after 14 B—Q3, to be able to play 14 .... Q—B2; e.g. 15 QKt×P, Q—R4 ch; 16 Kt—B3, B×Kt; 17 P×B, Q×KP; after which Black has recovered his pawn while reducing the material on either side.

14 Castles   Q—K2
As the more active post at B2 is no longer available, because of 15 QKt×P, the black Queen must occupy a less vigilant position.

15 P—B4   B—K3
With much trouble, Black has brought out his pieces and prepares to obtain an acceptable game by castling.

16 P—K4
The central *break-through*. After all, pawn play constitutes the finest and most artistic feature of the art of chess.

16 ......   P×P
He is still unable to put his King in safety by castling, e.g. 16 .... Castles; 17 P×P,

Position after 15 .... B—K3

B×P; 18 Kt×B, R×Kt; 19 B—B4 (not 19 Kt×P, P×Kt; 20 Q×P ch, because of 20 .... Q—B2), 19 .... R—R4 (19 .... R—Q3; 20 Kt—B7); 20 Kt—B7, R—Kt1; 21 Kt—Q6 ch, winning the exchange.

17 P—Q5
Reshevsky handles his forces in a manner masterly—not to say magical! In one action he opens up wide avenues of attack for Bishop and Rooks.

17 ......   B×Kt
If 17 .... P×P; 18 B—Kt5 ch, Kt—Q2; 19 Kt×Kt, QB×Kt; 20 Kt×QP, and Black's game is swamped. That is why he decides to eliminate the advanced Knight.

18 BP×B   B—Kt5
19 B—K2   B×B
20 Q×B   Kt—Q2
If 20 .... Q×P; 21 P×P, P×P; 22 Kt×P, K—K2; 23 Q—K3, and the black King cannot escape.

21 Q×P   Castles KR
At last Black has somehow succeeded in castling. But in the meantime the battle for the centre has already turned in White's favour.

22 P—K6   P×P
23 Kt×P   Q—Kt4 ch
24 K—Kt1   Kt—B4
If 24 .... Kt—B3; 25 Kt×Kt ch, Q×Kt; 26 R—Q7, and White has the whip-hand.

25 Q—QB4   QR—B1
26 P—K7   KR—K1
27 Kt—B6 db ch   Resigns

61

FINE   EUWE
(Avro, 1938)

The following game illustrates the difficulties which may arise when White—in contradistinction to the happenings in the preceding game—toys too much with his gambit pawn, and allows the pseudo-gambit to turn into a real gambit.

1	P—Q4	Kt—KB3
2	P—QB4	P—K3
3	Kt—KB3	P—Q4
4	B—Kt5	B—Kt5 ch
5	Kt—B3	P×P

Black's last two moves, which can also be played in inverted order, constitute the famous *Vienna Variation*, elaborated in 1933 by experts in that city, headed by Grünfeld. It is full of pitfalls.

6 P—K4

White must at once react in the centre, for neither 6 P—K3, P—Kt4; 7 P—QR4, P—B3, etc., nor 6 Q—R4 ch, Kt—B3; 7 P—K4, B—Q2; etc., is satisfactory.

6 ...... P—B4

Accepting the challenge. In one of the original examples of this variation, Grünfeld and Dr. Kaufmann *v.* Kmoch and H. Wolf, *Vienna,* 1933, Black prefers to smooth out complications by 6 .... P—KR3; 7 B×Kt, Q×B; 8 B×P, P—B4; etc.

7 P—K5

The original main line, which after much analysis and practical play has now become a secondary one. The improvement, 7 B×P, is shown in the next game.

7 ...... P×P
8 Q—R4 ch

A venturesome Queen. After 8 P×Kt, P×P; 9 B—R4, Kt—B3; Black recovers his piece without injury.

8 ...... Kt—B3
9 Castles B—Q2

A dexterous defence. If 9 .... P—KR3; 10 P×Kt, P×B; 11 P×P, R—KKt1; 12 Kt×P, etc., or 9 .... B×Kt; 10 P×B, B—Q2; 11 P×Kt, KtP×P; 12 B—R6, etc., and in neither case does Black secure the respite necessary to counteract his opponent's impetus.

10 Kt—K4 B—K2

Masterly play on both sides. White, with consummate virtuosity, has brought his reserve cavalry towards the front, while Black adds fuel to the fire by sacrificing a piece, in preference to the less propitious 10 .... P—KR3.

| 11 | P×Kt | P×P |
| 12 | B—R4 | R—QB1 |

Shrewd play. Black masses his artillery before sending his cavalry into the fray. Weak would be 12 .... Kt—Kt5; 13 Q×Kt, B×Q; 14 Kt×P ch, K—B1; 15 R×P, and thus the loss of the Queen has become a winning sacrifice (Fine–Grünfeld, *Amsterdam,* 1936). Playable, however, is, at once, 12 .... Kt—R4; 13 Q—B2, P—K4; etc., or, more insistently, 12 .... Kt—K4; 13 Q—B2, Kt×Kt; 14 P×Kt, P—K4; and the black pawn phalanx is menacing.

13 K—Kt1

If 13 B×KBP, B×B; 14 Kt—Q6 ch, K—B1; 15 Kt×R, Q×Kt; 16 Q×BP, P—K4; and Black's pressure is too strong.

13 ...... Kt—R4

An interesting suggestion by Pachman is here 13 .... P—Kt4; 14 Q×KtP, P—B6.

| 14 | Q—B2 | P—K4 |
| 15 | Kt×QP | |

A hand-to-hand fight. White's counter-sacrifice indicates that he is losing his grip. Better first 15 B—Kt3, with the latent threat Kt×KP.

15	......	P×Kt
16	R×P	Q—Kt3
17	Q—B3	

Too slow. Best is 17 R—Q6, the correct reply being 17 .... R—B3 (evidently not 17 .... B×R; 18 Kt×P ch, and wins). An ingenious expedient, well adapted to the situation, is 17 R×B, K×R; 18 B—K2, with, however, an uncertain issue.

| 17 | ...... | B—KB4 |
| 18 | P—KKt4 | B—Kt3 |

Not 18 .... B×P; 19 Kt×P ch, B×Kt; 20 B×B, R—KKt1 (20 .... Q×B; 21 R—K4 ch); 21 R×B, R×R; 22 B—R3, R—Kt3; 23 R—K1 ch, K—B1; 24 B—K7ch, K—Kt1; 25 B×R, and White remains a piece ahead.

19 P—B4

White will not succeed in cutting off the QB by 20 P—B5. His best chance here is 19 B—Q3, Castles; 20 B—QB2, and Black's advantage is not overwhelming.

19	......	B—QB4
20	R×P	Kt×R
21	P—B5	

If 21 Q×Kt, Castles; 22 P—B5, B—K6; winning.

| 21 ...... | B—Q5 |
| 22 Q—QKt3 | |

If 22 Kt×P ch, B×Kt; 23 B×B, Q×B; White cannot take the Queen (24 Q×Q, Kt—Q7 ch; followed by mate).

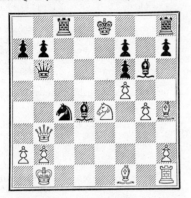

| 22 ...... | Q—B3 |

A deadly blow. Simple as it looks, it needed finding (and preparing!).

| 23 B—Kt2 | Q×Kt ch |

The point of the point.

24 B×Q	Kt—Q7 ch
25 K—R1	Kt×Q ch
26 P×Kt	Castles
27 P×B	RP×P
28 K—Kt1	KR—K1
29 B—Q3	R—K6
30 R—Q1	B—K4
Resigns	

62

STÅHLBERG   SEFC
(Trencianske–Teplice, 1949)

There follows a game which leaves an æsthetic and lasting impression.

1 P—Q4	Kt—KB3
2 P—QB4	P—K3
3 Kt—KB3	P—Q4
4 B—Kt5	B—Kt5 ch
5 Kt—B3	P×P
6 P—K4	P—B4
7 B×P	

This possibility of recovering the gambit pawn is based on a subtle point which will become manifest five moves later.

| 7 ...... | P×P |
| 8 Kt×P | Q—R4 |

He chases shadows, urged by the double threat to QB and QKt. The great connoisseur Ragozin prefers 8 .... Q—K2.

| 9 B×Kt | B×Kt ch |

If 9 .... P×B; 10 Castles, B—Q2; 11 R—B1, Kt—B3; 12 P—QR3, B×Kt; 13 R×B, etc., turns out in White's favour.

| 10 P×B | Q×P ch |

Inconsistent is 10 .... P×B; 11 Castles, etc.

| 11 K—B1 | |

A miraculous point! If 11 Q—Q2, Q×Q ch; 12 K×Q, P×B; equalising.

| 11 ...... | Q×B ch |
| 12 K—Kt1 | |

Here, Black's impetus comes to a stop. As he is threatened by 13 R—B1, followed by R×B ch, he has no time to capture a piece.

| 12 ...... | Kt—Q2 |

Proposed by Spielmann after the failure of both 12 .... Castles; 13 Q—Kt4, P—KKt3; 14 Q—B4, Kt—Q2; 15 P—K5, etc., and 12 .... B—Q2; 13 R—B1, Q—R3; 14 Kt×P, etc.

| 13 B×P | R—KKt1 |
| 14 R—B1 | |

Much less convincing is the immediate 14 B—R6, because of the counter-threat, 14 .... Kt—K4; and 15 .... Q×Kt; e.g. the game, Subaric–Dr. Trifunovic, *Jugoslav Championship*, 1946: 14 B—R6, Kt—K4; 15 B—K3, Kt—Kt5; 16 B—B1, B—Q2; 17 P—KR3, Kt—K4; 18 B—K3, B—R5; 19 Q—QB1 (he should play 19 Q—R5), 19 .... Q×Kt; White resigns (20 B×Q, Kt—B6 ch; and the Bishop mates).

| 14 ...... | Q—R3 |

If 14 .... Q×P; 15 Kt—Kt5.

| 15 B—R6 | Kt—B3 |

Here 15 .... Kt—K4; 16 Q—R5, Q—R4; 17 B—B4, Kt—B3; 18 Kt—Kt5, wins. But 15 .... P—K4; 16 Kt—B5, Q—KKt3; enables Black to hold his own.

| 16 P—K5 | Kt—Q4 |

If 16 .... Kt—Kt5; 17 B—B4, Q×P; 18 Kt—K2 (parrying the threat at KB2 and maintaining his own threat to capture the Knight by 19 P—R3).

17 P—KR4

This pawn is destined to do great deeds.

17 ......   B—Q2
18 Q—B2   R—Kt3

Intending to parry the threat 19 Q×P. If 18 .... R—QB1; 19 Q×P, R×R ch; 20 B×R, etc.

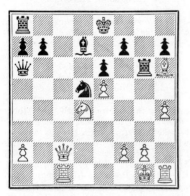

19 P—R5

Black has not "seen" this startling rejoinder. After 19 .... R×B; 20 Q—Q2, wins the exchange.

19 ......   R—Kt5
20 Q×P   K—K2
21 R—R4

Again brilliant! If 21 .... R×R; 22 B—Kt5 ch, with mate to follow.

21 ......   KR—Kt1

If 21 .... QR—KKt1; 22 R×R, R×R; 23 Q—R8, threatening 24 Q—B8 mate, and if then 23 .... B—K1; 24 R—B8, Q—R5; 25 Q—B8 ch, and mate next move.

22 B—Kt7   Q—R6
23 B—B6 ch

White strikes unremittingly. If now 23 .... Kt×B; 24 P×Kt ch, K×P; 25 R—B4 ch, K—K4; 26 Kt—B3 ch, Q×Kt (forced); 27 R×Q, and wins quickly. A breathless as well as instructive King-hunt.

23 ......   K—B1
24 R—B7

More brilliance! If 24 .... Kt×R; 25 P—R6, and there is no reply to

26 Q×R ch, K×Q; 27 P—R7 ch, and the pawn queens unhindered and mates.

24 ......   Kt×B
25 P×Kt   Q—Q3

Hoping to drive off the intruding Rook (26 R×P, would be a blunder because of 26 .... Q—Q4). But now comes a final combination of great beauty.

26 P—R6   Resigns

There is no defence against 27 Q—Kt7 ch, R×Q; 28 RP×R ch, and the KR mates. A gem of modern chess.

63

VERA MENCHIK   TERESA MORA
(Women's Championship, Buenos Aires, 1939)

We see in the next game an illustration of the principle that the opening of lines benefits only the player with the superior development.

1 P—Q4   P—Q4
2 P—QB4   P—K3
3 Kt—QB3   Kt—KB3
4 Kt—B3   QKt—Q2
5 P—K3   B—K2
6 B—Q3   P×P
7 B×BP   P—B4

The game assumes the character of a *Gambit Accepted*, but with a more artificial development of Black's QKt at Q2 instead of at QB3.

8 Castles   P—QR3
9 P—QR4

Boldly preventing Black's counter-action by .... P—QKt4. The weakening of White's own QKt4 is not to be feared as there is no black Knight available for the manœuvre Kt—QB3—Kt5; and eventually Q4.

9 ......   P×P
10 P×P

An isolated pawn, but one in the centre.

10 ......   Kt—Kt3

Blocking White's Q5, but it would be better to centralise by 10 .... Castles; followed by .... R—K1; .... Kt—B1; .... B—Q2; etc.

11 B—Kt3	Castles
12 Q—K2	B—Q2
13 Kt—K5	R—B1

In order to go on with .... B—B3; without fear of weakening the pawns.

14 B—Kt5

Ex ossibus ultor.

14 ......   B—B3

Now the Bishop is fully developed, but the critical square, Black's K3, is thereby weakened. Black hopes to hold up White's attack momentarily by the threat to the QP, and to simplify the position by 15 QR—Q1, B—Q4.

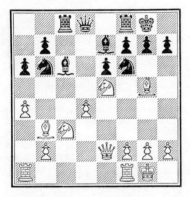

15 KR—K1

A masterly decision: White does not fear the loss of a pawn, as the sequel would be 15 .... Q×P; 16 QR—Q1 (not 16 Kt×P, R×Kt; 17 Q×KP, R—B1; 18 Q×KB, Q—KKt5), 16 .... Q—QKt5; 17 B—R2, and White dominates all the avenues.

15 ......   B—Q4

Still trying—unwisely—to simplify the position.

16 Kt×B	QKt×Kt

Less damaging is 16 .... KKt×Kt.

17 QR—Q1	P—R3

Speeding up defeat. "Whom the god would destroy, he first makes mad."

18 QB×Kt	P×B
19 Kt×P	

A fairly well-known sacrifice, but the precision with which White's major pieces have been posted on the critical K file is to be admired.

19	R×Kt
20 Q×KP	Resigns

64

GLIGORIC	BERNSTEIN
(Belgrade)	*(Paris)*

(Belgrade *v.* Paris, 1950)

The following game is particularly remarkable for the ingenuity which secures for White the victory against a doughty opponent.

1 P—Q4	P—Q4
2 P—QB4	P—K3
3 Kt—QB3	Kt—KB3

The *Tarrasch Defence*, 3 .... P—QB4; called by the Doctor himself the "Modern Defence," no longer has much attraction for the modern spirit. Here is a brevity which illustrates this defence, Casas–Piazzini, *Argentine Championship*, 1950: 3 .... P—QB4; 4 BP×P, KP×P; 5 Kt—B3, Kt—QB3; 6 P—KKt3 (the famous *Rubin-stein-Schlechter System*, which masters the idea of this defence), 6 .... Kt—B3; 7 B—Kt2, B—K2; 8 Castles, Castles; 9 P×P, P—Q5 (if 9 .... B×P; there can follow 10 Kt—QR4, B—K2; 11 B—K3, conquering the strategic square Q4); 10 Kt—QR4, B—B4; 11 B—B4, B—K5; 12 R—B1, Q—Q4; 13 Kt—K1, B×B; 14 Kt×B, Kt—K5; 15 P—QR3, Kt×QBP; 16 Kt×Kt, B×Kt; 17 P—K4, Black resigns. He loses a piece. A piquant turn.

4 Kt—B3	P—B4

The *Semi-Tarrasch Defence*, by which Black hopes to obtain a more fluid game than with waiting moves such as 4 .... B—K2; 4 .... QKt—Q2; or 4 .... P—B3.

5 BP×P	Kt×P

Recommended by Nimzowitsch. After 5 .... KP×P; White has the choice of two systems: the *Rubinstein-Schlechter*, 6 P—KKt3, Kt—B3; 7 B—Kt2, etc., and *Marshall's plan*, 6 B—Kt5, B—K3; 7 P—K4, etc.

6 P—K3

Typical of the modern style. Both 6 P—KKt3, and 6 P—K4, which are often played, commit White to a definite line of play.

6	Kt—QB3
7 B—Q3	

A quiet but strong continuation. More
"rowdy" is the course followed in a game,
Botvinnik–Alekhine, *Avro*, 1938: 7 B—B4
(threat, 8 B×Kt, P×B; 9 P×P), 7 ....
P×P (best here is 7 .... Kt—B3; transposing into a *Queen's Gambit*); 8 P×P, B—K2;
9 Castles, Castles; 10 R—K1. White has
now the better game. Like the preceding
move, this is again noncommittal and gives
the opponent a chance to go wrong—

7 ......   Q—R4

which he promptly does. This early attempt
to gain material by a Queen's pin is fundamentally unsound and will cost Black many
precious *tempi*. It is true White will have
an isolated QP, but this will be more than
counterbalanced by a greatly superior
development.

A quiet continuation could be 7 ....
B—K2; 8 Castles, Castles; etc., but it does
not conform with the enterprising temperament of Dr. Bernstein, who has the secret
of eternal youth.

8 Q—Kt3   P×P
9 P×P   Q—Kt3
10 Q—Q1   Q—R4

Avoiding a well-known trap: 10 ....
Kt×P; 11 KKt×Kt, Q×Kt; 12 B—Kt5 ch,
winning the Queen; but Black is wrong
in reverting to this artless and inoperative
pin. If 10 .... KKt—Kt5; 11 B—Kt1 (not
11 B—K2, Kt×QP; 12 Kt×Kt, Q×Kt;
13 Q×Q, Kt—B7 ch; followed by ....
Kt×Q). Better than the text-move is
10 .... B—Kt5.

11 Castles

An obvious sacrifice which has been seen
before. Black should refrain from taking
the pawn and play 11 .... B—K2; with a
laborious defence.

11 ......   Kt×Kt
12 P×Kt   Q×BP
13 R—Kt1   B—K2

Again Black avoids the trap of taking the
QP and tries desperately to make good his
development.

14 Kt—K5

Energetic play, offering a second pawn.
As so often, when there is no really satisfactory continuation, the defender decides
that he might as well take what he can and
be that much to the good.

14 ......   Q×P

Even less promising is 14 .... Kt×Kt;
15 P×Kt, Q×P.

15 Kt×Kt   P×Kt
16 B—K3   Q—Q3

A critical moment. Black hopes that
the text-move will prevent B—KB4, but on
the contrary he loses a valuable *tempo*, which
White will gain in enforcing this effective
manœuvre. Better is 16 .... Q—Q2.

17 Q—B2

White prepares his attack with consummate virtuosity. The threat is 18 B—KB4,
Q×QB; 19 Q×P ch, and wins.

17 ......   Q—B2

If 17 .... P—K4; 18 P—B4, with increased space for manœuvring. Better is
once more 17 .... Q—Q1; for if 18 Q×P ch,
B—Q2; with a slight easing of the position.

18 B—KB4   Q—Q1

Confusion. He should try 18 ....
B—Q3.

19 KR—Q1

Of course White does not oblige his
opponent by blindly rushing at the pawn
offered, 19 Q×P ch, B—Q2; and Black will
recover his balance.

19 ......   P—KB4

Black has no move. If 19 .... Castles;
20 B×P ch.

20 B—K4   B—Q2

Black hopes for a respite by retiring the
Bishop; if 21 B—B3, Q—B1 (preventing
the irruption, 22 R—Kt7); Black avoids the
worst for the time being.

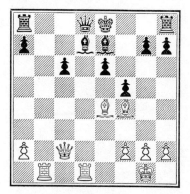

21 R × B

White plays superlative chess in taking advantage of his opportunity. A "dual" sufficiently convincing, however, is 21 B × QBP, R—QB1; 22 R × B, etc.

21 ......   Q × R

A beautiful death would be 21 .... K × R; 22 Q × P mate.

22 B × QBP   Q × B

Here Black overlooks that he has the right to resign. This oversight gives his opponent the opportunity to finish off the game with devastating competence.

23 Q × Q ch	K—B2
24 R—K1	B—B3
25 Q × P ch	K—Kt3
26 P—Kt4	P × P
27 Q × P ch	K—B2
28 Q—R5 ch	P—Kt3
29 Q—Q5 ch	Resigns

21. SLAV DEFENCE

65

G. WOOD YANOFSKY
(Hastings, 1946-7)

Drawn games are sometimes more scintillating than any conclusive contest.

1 P—Q4	P—Q4
2 P—QB4	P—QB3
3 Kt—KB3	Kt—B3
4 Kt—B3	P×P

The *Slav Accepted*, a highly modern variation, leading to many interesting complications. Black now wants to play 5 .... P—QKt4.

5 P—QR4
Prevention or dislocation? The choice made by White—prevention—is to be commended, for the alternative 5 P—K3, P—QKt4; 6 P—QR4, P—Kt5; fails to give White sufficient initiative, e.g. 7 Kt—R2, P—K3; 8 B×P, QKt—Q2; 9 Castles, B—Q3 (inferior is 9 .... B—Kt2; 10 Q—K2, P—B4; 11 R—Q1, etc.); 10 R—K1, Q—K2; 11 P—K4, P—K4; etc., with equality.

| 5 ...... | B—B4 |
| 6 P—K3 | |

An alternative is 6 Kt—K5 (*Dr. Krause's Attack*), which was frequently adopted in both matches, Alekhine–Euwe, 1935 and 1937. The best continuation is 6 .... QKt—Q2; 7 Kt×P(B4), Q—B2; 8 P—KKt3, and White, unable to force P—K4, has to develop his KB at Kt2, with an equal game.

| 6 ...... | P—K3 |

Here Black can play 6 .... B—Q6; eliminating White's KB, and 6 .... QKt—Q2. The move selected is considered the best.

A rich theme for the analyst is 6 .... Kt—R3; a move due to the well-known Canadian theoretician, G. Maréchal, with the plausible continuation, 7 B×P, Kt—QKt5; 8 Castles, P—K3; 9 Q—K2. Here, according to Maréchal's analysis, 9 .... QKt—Q4; 10 Kt—K5, P—KR3; 11 P—B3, B—QKt5; 12 B—Q2, B—R2; 13 P—K4, Kt—Kt3; 14 B—K3, Q—B2; 15 B—Q3, Castles KR; and Black holds his own.

| 7 B×P | B—QKt5 |

Intercepting White's pressure in the centre, a manœuvre due to the inventive spirit of Canal (1919).

| 8 Castles | Castles |
| 9 Q—K2 | B—Kt5 |

If 9 .... Kt—K5; 10 B—Q3. Unpromising too are the attempts 9 .... P—B4; 10 Kt—R2, and 9 .... B—Kt3; 10 Kt—K5, followed by Kt×B.

10 R—Q1	Q—K2
11 P—K4	QKt—Q2
12 P—K5	

There is nothing in the interlude, 12 Kt—R2, B—QR4; 13 P—Kt4, B—B2; with improved chance for Black. But not 13 .... B×P; because of 14 Kt×B, Q×Kt; 15 B—R3, winning the exchange.

| 12 ...... | Kt—Q4 |
| 13 Kt—K4 | P—KR3 |

A clear-cut measure. Too restless is 13 .... P—B3; as played in a game Capablanca–Fine, *Semmering-Baden*, 1937.

| 14 P—R3 | B—KR4 |
| 15 Kt—Kt3 | |

No better is 15 P—Kt4, B—Kt3.

| 15 ...... | B—Kt3 |
| 16 B—Q3 | |

An excellent move which keeps the ball rolling and deprives Black of his best defensive piece.

| 16 ...... | B×B |
| 17 R×B | |

Far stronger than 17 Q×B, and played with a view to a subsequent sacrifice of the exchange.

| 17 ...... | P—QB4 |

A good move for Black is now hard to find. He apparently underestimated White's latent threats.

| 18 P×P | Kt×BP |

Very tempting, but 18 .... B×P; is better, leaving more forces available for the defence.

19 R×Kt

A very original, brilliant and sound sacrifice.

19	P×R
20 Kt—B5	Q—B2
21 Kt(B3)—R4	K—R2
22 Kt×KtP	

Bravo!

22 ......   Q—Kt3

He cannot take the Knight, e.g. 22 .... K×Kt; 23 Kt—B5 ch, K—R2; 24 B×P, Q—Kt3; 25 B×R, R×B; 26 Q—R5 ch, K—Kt1; 27 Kt—K7 ch, K—Kt2; 28 Kt×P, Q—R4; 29 Q—Kt5 ch, K—R1; 30 Kt—B6, and mate follows.

23 Kt(Kt7)—B5   Kt—Kt6

In desperation he tries to get as much material as he can.

| 24 B×P | Kt×R |
| 25 B×R | |

A pity! After the nervous strain of a complicated combination, White seeks relief in a "safe" continuation, when he could have brought about a brilliant finish with either 25 B—K3, or 25 B—Kt5, winning in all variations.

As it is he has nothing better than a perpetual check.

25 ......   B×B
26 Q—R5 ch

Draw by perpetual check.
A thrilling contest.

66

ABRAHAMS   CANAL
(Bad Gastein, 1948)

Attacking technique consists not so much in colourful sacrifices (they come in at the end) as in subtle and patient manœuvres, frequently on the opposite wing.

1 Kt—KB3	P—Q4
2 P—QB4	P—QB3
3 P—Q4	Kt—B3
4 Kt—B3	P×P
5 P—QR4	B—B4
6 Kt—R4	B—Q2

Not a sound retreat, as it unnecessarily blocks the QKt, which takes no further part in the game. Unsatisfactory also is 6 .... B—Kt3 (7 Kt×B, RP×Kt; 8 P—K3, followed by B×P); and equally so 6 .... P—K3; for example, 7 Kt×B, P×Kt; 8 P—K3, QKt—Q2; 9 B×P, Kt—Kt3; 10 B—Kt3, B—Q3; 11 Q—B3, Q—Q2; 12 P—R3, Kt—B1; 13 P—R5, and White's forces have much greater scope.

The accepted continuation is 6 .... B—B1; and it then is best for White to retrace his steps with 7 Kt—B3.

7 P—KKt3	Q—R4
8 B—Q2	P—K3
9 P—K4	Q—Kt3

Black's sixth and seventh moves have already given him an awkward game.

10 Kt—B3	B—Kt5
11 P—K5	Kt—Q4
12 B×P	Castles
13 P—R5	

An excellent move both tactically and strategically. The pawn lames Black's Q side, and if 13 .... B×P; there follows 14 R×B, Q×R; 15 Kt×Kt, and White has two pieces for the Rook.

13	Q—B2
14 Castles	Kt×Kt
15 P×Kt	

A positional sacrifice of a pawn (in place of 15 B×Kt, etc.). The point is that the Bishop is diverted from the future battle-field and the Queen is tied to its defence.

| 15 ...... | B×RP |
| 16 Kt—Kt5 | |

The hunt is on. The Lancashire stalwart joyously leaps into the fray.

16 ......   B—K1

The more obvious 16 .... P—KR3; does not ease his position after 17 Kt—K4, followed by 18 Q—Kt4.

17 Q—R5   P—KR3
Black thinks that the Knight will have to retire to KB3, which would slow down White's attack.

18 Kt—K4
Threatening to win quickly by 19 Kt—B6 ch, and without fear of the loss of a piece which the text-move implies.

18 ......   P—KB4

A desperate measure which, while it does not solve the problem of his exposed King's field, at least wins a piece.

19 B×P ch   K—R1
20 Q—R4   P×Kt
21 B×P   B—B2
22 B—B5   B—R4
Despair!

23 B×P ch
A convincing sacrifice. If now 23 ....
Q×B; 24 Q×B ch, K—Kt1; 25 B—K6 ch, R—B2; 26 R×B, etc.

23 ......   K×B
24 Q—Kt5 ch   K—B2
25 P—K6 ch   K—K1
26 Q×B ch   K—K2
27 Q—R4 ch   R—B3
If 27 .... K—Q3; there is also a very elegant win after 28 P—K7, Q×P (28 ....
R—K1; 29 Q—B6 ch, etc.); 29 Q—B4 ch, K—Q4; 30 R×B ch, etc.

28 Q—Kt5   Resigns
There is no reply to 29 Q—Kt7 ch.
A very fine performance.

22. SEMI-SLAV DEFENCE

67

TAIMANOV   LISSITSIN

(U.S.S.R. Championship, Leningrad, 1949)

The winner in the following game, born in 1927, gained in early youth not only a supreme mastery in Chess, but also outstanding success as a concert pianist.

It is well-known that chess and music go well together, and many are those who have achieved unusual proficiency in both. An outstanding example is Philidor who became a front-rank master in both arts.

1 P—Q4	P—Q4
2 P—QB4	P—QB3
3 Kt—KB3	P—K3
4 Q—B2	

Uncharted territory. The more usual continuations in the *Semi-Slav Defence* are 4 P—K3, or 4 Kt—B3 (and if 4 .... P×P; 5 P—QR4). The text-move has a number of advantages; White commands an important diagonal and retains the option to play either Rook to the QB file.

4 ......   Kt—Q2

Premature. A better way to realise his intentions is: 4 .... B—Q3; 5 P—KKt3, P—KB4; 6 B—Kt2, Kt—B3; 7 Castles, Castles; 8 QKt—Q2, Q—K1; 9 P—Kt3, Q—R4; 10 B—Kt2, and only now 10 .... QKt—Q2.

5 P—KKt3	B—Q3
6 B—Kt2	P—KB4

An interesting conflict between two systems, the *Stonewall* for Black, the *Catalan* for White. Black's problem, which will increase in urgency, is the development of his QB.

7 Castles	KKt—B3
8 P×P	BP×P

Owing to his unfortunate fourth move, Black cannot recapture with the KP, and he must concede to his adversary the big advantage of the command of the QB file.

9 Kt—B3   P—QR3

A necessary precaution. If 9 .... Castles; 10 QKt—Kt5, B—K2; 11 Kt—B7, winning the exchange, or 10 .... B—Kt1;

11 B—B4, B×B; 12 P×B, Kt—Kt3; 13 Kt—B7, R—Kt1; 14 Kt—KKt5, Q—Q3; 15 Q—B5, and White has the better game.

10 B—B4	B×B
11 P×B	Castles

He could have tried to cut the Gordian knot with 11 .... P—QKt4.

12 Kt—QR4   Kt—Kt3

The first result of the black Bishop's retarded development: White threatens 13 KR—B1, with full control of the QB file. On the other hand the text-move enables White to occupy the vital squares QB5 and K5, dominating the whole field.

13 Kt—B5	Q—Q3
14 Kt—K5	R—Kt1
15 P—QR4	Kt—R1

In the hope of getting the Knight into play via B2, but events will it otherwise.

16 P—R5	B—Q2
17 KR—B1	B—Kt4
18 P—K3	KR—B1
19 R—R3	R—B2
20 R—B3	Q—K2

The threat was: if 20 .... QR—QB1; 21 Kt×KtP, R×R; 22 P×R, Q—B2; 23 Kt—B5, and White not only is a pawn to the good, but Black's KP is *en prise*.

21 B—B1	B×B
22 K×B	QR—QB1
23 Q—Kt3	

Again threatening 24 Kt×KtP. The counter-attempt, 23 .... Kt—K5; is answered 24 Kt×Kt, BP×Kt; 25 Q×KtP, R×Q; 26 R×R ch, Q—B1; 27 R×Q ch, K×R; 28 R—B8 ch, and wins.

23 ......   Kt—K1 (see diag.)

Black is mistaken in thinking that he still can make a fight for the open file. He should have been content with the elastic retreat 23 .... R—K1.

24 Kt×KtP

The long threatened blow falls. It is the beginning of a monumental combination.

24	R×Kt
25 Q×R	Q×Q
26 R×R	K—B1

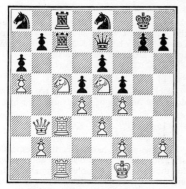

Position after 23 .... Kt—K1

If 26 .... Kt—B2; 27 R(B1)×Kt, Q×R(B2); 28 R×Kt mate.

27 R—Kt8
The key to this beautiful manœuvre; if 27 .... Q×R; 28 Kt—Q7 ch, and wins. The rest plays itself.

27 ......   Q—K2
If 27 .... Q—R2; 28 R×Kt ch, K×R; 29 R—B8 ch, K—K2; 30 Kt—B6 ch, followed by Kt×Q.

28 R×Kt	P—Kt3
29 R(B1)—B8	K—Kt2
30 R×Kt	Q—QB2
31 R(K8)—QB8	Q—Kt2
32 QR—Kt8	Q—R2
33 R—KR8	Q—K2
34 QR—Kt8 ch	K—R3
35 R×KtP ch	

The final chord.

35	K—R4.
36 R—Kt3	K—R5
37 Kt—B3 ch	K—R4
38 R(R8)—KKt8	Resigns

A fascinating game.

68

BRONSTEIN   KOTOV
(Budapest, 1950)

"Played à la Morphy." *What greater praise can be given, and how well it applies to the winner's style in the following game.*

| 1 P—Q4 | P—Q4 |
| 2 P—QB4 | P—K3 |

| 3 Kt—QB3 | P—QB3 |

Tchigorin's legacy.

4 P—K4
This dynamic continuation was adopted in several games by Pillsbury and Marshall. It was tried in a deferred form in a *correspondence game*, Munich-Augsburg, 1941, as follows: 4 Kt—B3, Kt—Q2; 5 P—K4, P×KP; 6 Kt×P, KKt—B3; 7 B—Q3, Kt×Kt; 8 B×Kt, Kt—B3; 9 B—B2, P—B4; 10 Castles, P×P; 11 B—Kt5, P—Q6; 12 B—R4 ch, B—Q2; 13 Kt—K5, Black resigns.

| 4 ...... | P×KP |
| 5 Kt×P | B—Kt5 ch |

A check too tempting to omit. Nevertheless, development by opposition, 5 .... Kt—B3; is worth considering.

6 B—Q2
Unequivocal and consistent, for, on 6 Kt—B3, Black has a favourable development by 6 .... P—QB4.

6 ......   Q×P
He takes up the challenge. In a previous game between the same opponents Kotov played 6 .... B×B ch; and drew. No doubt, on the present occasion, he relied on some new ideas in accepting the sacrifice. In any event, after 6 .... B×B ch; 7 Q×B, Kt—B3; 8 Kt×Kt ch, Q×Kt; 9 Kt—B3, Castles; 10 B—K2, White has an advantage in space, due to the fact that Black can, at present, play neither .... P—QB4; nor .... P—K4; to free his game.

| 7 B×B | Q×Kt ch |
| 8 B—K2 | |

Here, Canal prefers 8 Kt—K2.

8 ......   Kt—QR3
A tense moment. Practically suicidal is 8 .... Q×KtP, e.g. 9 B—KB3, Q—Kt4; 10 Kt—K2, Kt—K2; 11 R—KKt1, Q—B3; 12 Kt—Kt3, Kt—B4; 13 Kt—K4, Q—Q1; 14 R×P, with a winning position.
Thus it is seen that Black is beset by two problems: the open black diagonal, controlled by White's QB, and the vulnerability of the black Queen. Instead of the text-move, 8 .... Kt—Q2; is positionally more correct in spite of the ominous 9 Q—Q6, e.g. 9 .... P—QB4; 10 B—B3, Kt—K2; and Black is not without resources.
Subsequent analysis has shown the merit of the ingenious counter-measure, 8 .... P—QB4.

9 B—B3

An elegant idea is 9 B—B8, Q×KtP;
10 Q—Q6.

9 ......   Kt—K2

Up to this move the game is identical with
Flohr–Szily and Bronstein–Szily, both from
the *Moscow-Budapest Match*, 1949. Here,
in both cases, Szily played 9 .... P—B3;
but, whereas Flohr continued 10 Kt—B3,
and drew with difficulty, Bronstein played
10 Q—Q6, and scored a convincing win.

10 B×P

An intriguing manœuvre, for White does
not intend to capture the Rook. On 10 ....
Q×KtP; the continuation is 11 B—B6,
Q×R; 12 Q—Q6, Castles (there is nothing
better); 13 Q—Kt3 ch, Kt—Kt3; 14 B—KB3,
and the Queen is lost.

10 ......   R—KKt1
11 B—B3

Possible is the interlude 11 B—B6,
R—Kt3; 12 B—B3.

11 ......   Q×KtP

"Now or never," thinks Black, but his
opponent's clever reply proves that it is not
a case of "now or never," but rather one of
"later." Later analysis by Judovitch pro-
poses here the counter-sacrifice, 11 ....
Kt—Q4; 12 P×Kt, and only *now* 12 ....
Q×KtP, having considerably reduced
White's pressure on the Q file.

12 Q—Q2

Not 12 B—B3, Q×Kt ch; 13 R×Q,
R×R ch; winning a piece.

12 ......   Q×R

Here again Black could reasonably try
12 .... Kt—Q4.

13 Castles   Kt—Q4

Too late, but he has no option.

14 Kt—B3

White is not now compelled to capture
the Kt, which would shut off his base of
action (14 P×Kt, R×Kt) but he can continue his attack in *crescendo* style.

14 ......   Q×R ch

Black must at all hazards try to slow
down the impetus of his adversary's efforts.

15 B×Q   Kt×B
16 Q×Kt

A new phase begins in this desperate
struggle. Black has two Rooks and a pawn
for the Queen. It denotes judgment of the
highest order to decide several moves ahead
that this position can be won for White.
The reason is of a fleeting kind: the disconnected state of the Black forces. But to
carry out successful operations by forceful
play and exact timing is akin to solving a
difficult problem or ending.

16 ......   K—K2

To prevent 17 Q—B6.

17 Kt—K5   B—Q2

The Queen is astonishingly effective along
the third rank, e.g. if, instead of the text-
move 17 .... P—B3; 18 Q—R3, R—Kt2;
19 Q—R6, and wins.

18 Q—R3 ch   P—B4

Or 18 .... K—K1; 19 Q—Q6, R—Q1;
20 B—R5, R—KB1; 21 Kt—Kt4, and wins.

19 Q—KB3

Attacking two vital pawns.

19	QR—Q1
20 Q×P ch	K—Q3
21 Q—B4	QR—KB1
22 Kt—B7 db ch	K—K2
23 B—R5	B—B3
24 Q—Q6 ch	K—B3
25 Kt—R6	R—Kt8 ch
26 K—Q2	K—Kt2
27 Kt—Kt4	

Now the Black's Rooks are disconnected
again and the threats against his King are
mounting up.

27	R×Kt
28 Q—K7 ch	K—R3
29 B×R	R×P ch
30 K—K3	R—B8
31 P—KR4	K—Kt3
32 B—R5 ch	Resigns

An object lesson in subtle attacking play.

Meran Variation

69

KOTTNAUER   KOTOV
(Prague-Moscow, 1946)

The famous Meran Variation, *of which
we present three brilliant examples, has been
adopted in many remarkable games since its
first appearance at the Meran Tournament of
1924. As the defence has scored many a
victory, the variation still has a strong appeal
for enterprising spirits.*

*The following game is of special interest
because of a new aspect of the well-known
sacrifice at KR7.*

1 P—Q4	P—Q4
2 P—QB4	P—QB3
3 Kt—KB3	Kt—B3
4 Kt—B3	P—K3
5 P—K3	QKt—Q2
6 B—Q3	P×P

A cold war has started. Less stubborn
are *Semi-Slav defences* properly speaking:
6 .... B—Q3; or 6 .... B—K2; or 6 ....
B—Kt5. A war of attrition results from
6 .... B—K2; 7 Castles, Castles; 8 P—QKt3.
Unconvincing is 8 P—K4, P×KP; 9 Kt×P,
P—QKt3; whereby Black solves the problem
of his QB.

7 B×BP	P—QKt4
8 B—Q3	P—QR3
9 P—K4	

The main line of the *Meran Variation.*
Less dynamic are the continuations,
9 Castles, 9 Q—K2, and 9 P—QR4.

9	P—B4
10 P—K5	P×P

White gets the upper hand after both
10 .... Kt—Q4; 11 Kt—Kt5, P×P;
12 Kt×Kt, P×Kt; 13 Castles, Kt—B4;
14 P—B4, etc., and 10 .... Kt—Kt5;
11 B—K4 (not 11 Kt—Kt5, P×P;
12 Kt×BP, Q—R5, etc., and the tables are
turned!), 11 .... R—R2; 12 B—B6, threatening 13 P—Q5.

11 Kt×KtP
Blumenfeld's discovery.

11 ......   P×Kt

This continuation, discredited for a time,
has regained popularity. If 11 .... Kt×P;
12 Kt×Kt, P×Kt; 13 Q—B3, etc. If
11 .... Kt—Kt5; 12 Q—R4, B—Kt2;
13 QKt×P, and White maintains his
pressure.

12 P×Kt	Q—Kt3
13 P×P	

It is important to break up Black's K side
before castling. If 13 Castles, P×P;
14 B—K4, B—QKt2; 15 B×B, Q×B;
16 Kt×P, R—KKt1; Black has consolidated his position, or 13 Q—K2, B—Kt5 ch;
14 B—Q2, B×B ch; 15 Q×B, Kt×P; etc.,
and Black has the advantage.

13	B×P
14 Q—K2	

The text-move threatens 15 B×KtP, and
particularly 15 Q—K4. For 14 Castles, see
the following game.

14 ......   Castles

Clearly not 14 .... Kt—B4; 15 B×P ch,
but, according to Grigorieff, counter-action
is to be recommended by 14 .... P—Kt5;
15 Castles, R—R4; 16 B—KB4, Kt—B4;
17 B—K5, Kt×B; 18 B×B, R—Kt1; with
considerable counter-play.

15 Castles

A will-o'-the-wisp would be 15 Q—K4,
P—B4; 16 Q×R, B—QR3; confiscating the
Queen.

A wrong turning, too, would be 15 B×P,
P—K4.

15 ......   Kt—B4

This looks like the right move, parrying
both the threats mentioned above. Unfortunately the move allows a decisive sacrifice
by White.

However, Black's position is delicate. If,
for example, 15 .... P—B4; 16 B—KB4,
blockading Black's weakened KP, or 15 ....
B—Kt2; 16 B×P, etc. Best is a resolute
counter-action, beginning with 15 ....
P—K4.

16 B×P ch

Incredible, but true. Such a catastrophe is made possible by the absence of a defensive Knight at Black's KB3, or, at least, of a Knight in reserve at his Q2, which could have hastened to the rescue. Wrong would be 16 B×P, P—Q6; 17 B×P, Kt×B; 18 Q×Kt, B—QR3; etc., and Black has the advantage.

16 ......   K×B

Declining the gift loses rapidly after 16 .... K—R1; 17 Kt—Kt5, P—K4; 18 Q—R5, B—KR3; 19 Kt×P ch, R×Kt; 20 B—Kt6, etc.

17 Kt—Kt5 ch   K—Kt3
18 Q—Kt4   P—B4
19 Q—Kt3   K—B3

Not 19 .... Q—Kt1; 20 B—B4, nor 19 .... P—B5; 20 Q—Kt4, and White's attack persists. 19 .... R—B2; was played in Kottnauer–Pachman, *Moscow*, 1947, with no better result for Black. This double success by Kottnauer with the *Meran Variation* created quite a stir in the chess world at the time.

20 B—B4   K—K2
21 QR—B1

The main threat is 22 R×Kt, followed by R—B1, and R—B7 ch.

21 ......   R—R2
22 KR—K1

The frontal assault in full swing.

22 ......   B—Q2
23 P—Kt4   Kt—R3
24 Kt×P

The beginning of the end.

24 ......   B×Kt
25 Q×B ch   R—B2
26 B—Kt5 ch   K—Q2
27 Q—R8   Q—Kt1

He tries desperately to prevent 28 Q—B8 ch.

28 Q×P ch   Resigns

The loser, a player of great enterprise and imagination, sometimes runs undue risks, and then he has to pay the due penalty.

70

BOTVINNIK   DR. EUWE
(Moscow, 1948)

When asked to which factor he attributed his victory in the World Championship Tournament, Botvinnik replied modestly that he made fewer mistakes than the other competitors. He could justly have asserted that, of them all, he created more numerous profound conceptions.

1 P—Q4   P—Q4
2 Kt—KB3   Kt—KB3
3 P—B4   P—K3
4 Kt—B3   P—B3
5 P—K3   QKt—Q2
6 B—Q3

There are here several *Anti-Meran* possibilities, such as 6 Kt—K5 (Rubinstein), or 6 Q—B2, or 6 P—QR3, or even 6 P—QKt3, but none of these gives White any appreciable advantage.

6 ......   P×P
7 B×BP   P—QKt4
8 B—Q3   P—QR3
9 P—K4   P—B4
10 P—K5   P×P
11 Kt×KtP   P×Kt
12 P×Kt   Q—Kt3
13 P×P   B×P
14 Castles

Here and in the sequel, Botvinnik concentrates all his efforts on one plan, and one plan only: blockade of the strategic square K5. The text-move strictly adheres to this plan, as it enables him to employ the KR as quickly as possible on the K file.

14 ......   Kt—B4

While Black now can eliminate the dangerous KB, the text-move reduces his control of the critical square in question. If, however, 14 .... Castles; White can play 15 Q—K2, but he could also frankly embark on an attack by 15 Kt—Kt5, P—R3; 16 Kt—R7, R—K1; 17 Q—B3, B—Kt2; 18 Q—Kt3, with manifold complications.

15 B—KB4

Simple and very strong. Playable too is 15 R—K1, B—Kt2; 16 B—KB4, etc.

If White wastes a move to conserve the Bishop by 15 B—Kt1, Black has a fine game after 15 .... B—Kt2. At *Ostrava*, 1946, Tikovsky fell into a trap against Foltys with 16 Kt×P, which loses after 16 .... R—Q1; 17 B—K3, P—K4.

15 ......   B—Kt2

Here or on the next move, ... Castles KR; would be met by B×P ch, and Kt—Kt5 ch.

16 R—K1

Not at once 16 B—K5, B×B; 17 Kt×B, Kt×B; 18 Q×Kt, R—KKt1; when Black assumes the initiative.

16 ......   R—Q1

An unhappy idea. It would be better to ease the situation by exchanges: 16 .... Kt×B; 17 Q×Kt, B×Kt; 18 Q×B, Castles KR; etc.

17 R—QB1   R—Q4
18 B—K5   B×B

It is now too late to castle, since 18 .... Castles; 19 Kt—Kt5, wins for White.

19 R×B   R×R
20 Kt×R   Kt×B

Apparently the only way to avoid loss in material, for if 20 .... R—Kt1; 21 B—B1, Kt—Q2; 22 Kt×Kt, K×Kt; 23 Q—R5, R—Kt2; 24 B×P ch, and wins.

21 Q×Kt   P—B3

Not yet 21 .... Castles; 22 Q—Kt3 ch, K—R1; 23 R—B7, etc. Should Black succeed in restraining or exchanging the hostile pieces, he would save the day.

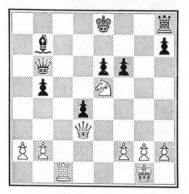

22 Q—KKt3

A beautifully neat sacrifice which wins by obtaining complete control of the seventh rank.

22 ......   P×Kt
23 Q—Kt7   R—B1
24 R—B7   Q×R

There is no other way of preventing mate. The rest is merely a matter of technique, and Botvinnik plays it in the most accurate manner.

25 Q×Q   B—Q4
26 Q×KP   P—Q6
27 Q—K3   B—B5
28 P—QKt3   R—B2
29 P—B3   R—Q2
30 Q—Q2

Not 30 P×B, P—Q7.

30 ......   P—K4
31 P×B   P×P
32 K—B2   K—B2
33 K—K3   K—K3
34 Q—Kt4   R—QB2
35 K—Q2   R—B3
36 P—QR4   Resigns

One of the World Champion's finest performances.

71

Mme. CHAUDÉ
DE SILANS   POMAR
(Sitges, 1949)

The following beautiful game will give many opportunities for those who like to praise, as also for those who prefer looking for "spots in the sun."

1 P—Q4   Kt—KB3
2 P—QB4   P—K3
3 Kt—QB3   P—Q4
4 Kt—B3   P—B3
5 P—K3   QKt—Q2

The following line carries out the *Meran* idea, while speeding the thematic advance of the QBP: 5 .... P—QR3; 6 B—Q3, P×P; 7 B×BP, P—QKt4; followed by 8 .... P—B4.

6 B—Q3   P×P
7 B×BP   P—QKt4
8 B—Q3   P—QR3

An ingenious idea introduced by R. G. Wade, *Venice*, 1950, is 8 .... B—Kt2; deferring a decision to play .... P—QR3; or .... P—Kt5; until after White has decided on a definite plan.

9 P—K4   P—B4
10 P—Q5

An idea conceived by Czechoslovakian players; this attempt to break-through in the centre (instead of the regulation 10 P—K5) is not easy to meet.

10 ......   P—B5

If 10 .... P×P; 11 P—K5, Kt—Kt5; 12 B—Kt5, P—B3; 13 P×P, P×P; 14 B—KB4, etc., with good attacking chances for this pawn. For this reason, in a game, Foltys–Dr. Trifunovic, *Prague*, 1946, Black preferred closing the centre by 10 .... P—K4. But, after 11 Castles, P—Kt3 (better is 11 .... B—Q3); 12 P—QKt3, B—KKt2; 13 P—QR4, P—Kt5; 14 Kt—Kt1, Castles; 15 R—R2, etc., and White has an easier game.

If 10 .... Kt—Kt3; 11 B—Kt5, P—B5; 12 B—B2, Q—B2; 13 Castles, B—K2; 14 R—K1, P—K4; 15 P—QR4, P—Kt5; 16 P—R5, QKt—Q2; 17 Kt—K2, there are certain weaknesses in Black's camp.

| 11 B—B2 | P—Kt5 |

This counter-thrust is less promising than it looks. 11 .... Kt—B4; shows more cohesion.

12 P×P	P×P
13 Kt—K2	Q—Kt3
14 QKt—Q4	

White increases the pressure in the centre in preference to 14 Castles, B—Kt2; 15 Kt—Kt3, R—Q1; or 14 B—K3, B—B4.

| 14 ...... | B—Kt2 |

He attacks the KP in order to gain time to get his QR into play. Nevertheless, 14 .... B—B4; 15 Castles, Castles; etc., is more adequate.

| 15 P—K5 | Kt—Kt5 |
| 16 P—KR3 | |

A magnificent conception.

16	KKt×KP
17 Kt×Kt	Kt×Kt
18 Q—R5 ch	Kt—B2
19 B—R4 ch	

The bilateral action of White's Queen and KB is highly artistic, and is in the best Alekhine tradition.

| 19 ...... | K—K2 |
| 20 B—K3 | |

And here a third diagonal K3—QKt6 comes to life. Threatened by 21 Kt—B5 ch, followed by B×Q, Black tries to build up his defences on the K side.

20	P—Kt3
21 Q—R4 ch	P—Kt4
22 Q—Kt3	

Clearly refusing to give up her best forces by 22 B×P ch, Kt×B; 23 Q×Kt ch, K—B2; etc.

| 22 ...... | K—B3 (see diag.) |

The King is to defend himself. If 22 .... Q—R4; 23 B—B6.

23 Kt—B6

Initiating a sacrificial combination of great energy. After the plausible 23 Kt—B3, Black has a defence in 23 .... Q—R4; 24 B—Q4 ch, P—K4; 25 B×P ch, Kt×B; 26 Q×P ch, K—K3; 27 Kt—Q4 ch, K—B2; 28 Q—B5 ch, K—Kt2; 29 Kt—K6 ch, K—Kt1; etc., and the position is unclear.

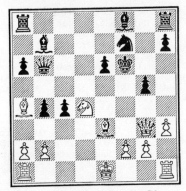

Position after 22 .... K—B3

| 23 ...... | B—B4 |
| 24 B×P ch | |

The lightning strikes.

| 24 ...... | Kt×B |
| 25 Q—B4 ch | K—Kt2 |

If 25 .... K—Kt3; 26 Kt—K5 ch, leads to mate.

| 26 Q×Kt ch | K—B1 |

And again if 26 .... K—B2; 27 Kt—K5 ch.

| 27 Q—B6 ch | K—Kt1 |
| 28 Q×P ch | |

Being short of time the French Lady Champion misses a quick and elegant win: 28 Kt—K5, R—KB1; 29 Q—Kt5 mate, or 28 .... B×P ch; 29 K—B1, etc., or, finally, 28 .... Q—B2; 29 B—Q7, etc.

| 28 ...... | K—Kt2 |

If 28 .... K—B1; 29 Q—B6 ch, K—Kt1; 30 Kt—K7 ch, winning the Queen.

| 29 Castles QR | B×Kt |

If 29 .... B—QB1; 30 Q—K5 ch, and the fact that the black Rooks are disconnected must lead to an immediate *débâcle*.

| 30 B×B | QR—Q1 |

Black *almost* saves the situation.

31	Q—Kt4 ch	K—B3
32	Q—B4 ch	K—Kt2
33	Q—Kt5 ch	K—B2
34	Q—B5 ch	K—Kt2
35	R—Q7 ch	R × R
36	Q × R ch	K—R3
37	R—K1	

Having sufficiently harried the black King, White at last has time, on the board and on the clock, to make a *quiet*, but all the more deadly, move.

37	......	R—KKt1
38	Q—Q2 ch	

A decisive diagonal check.

38	......	K—Kt3
39	R—K6 ch	K—B2
40	Q—Q7 ch	Resigns

23. ANTI-MERAN GAMBIT

72

DENKER   **BOTVINNIK**
(Radio Match, U.S.A. *v.* U.S.S.R., 1945)

The following game has given a new lease of life to the Queen's Gambit Declined *by probing the secret resources still to be found in that opening.*

1 P—Q4	P—Q4
2 P—QB4	P—K3
3 Kt—QB3	P—QB3
4 Kt—B3	Kt—B3
5 B—Kt5	

White sharpens the contest, instead of remaining within the confines of the *Semi-Slav*.

5 ......   P×P
Black goes one better and disdains the paths of the *Orthodox Defence*, 5 .... B—K2; 6 P—K3, QKt—Q2; etc. (the normal development); or 5 .... QKt—Q2; 6 P—K3, Q—R4; etc. (*Cambridge Springs Defence*).

6 P—K4
An acute struggle begins between centre and wings.
An interesting diversion occurred in the last game of the match, Bronstein–Botvinnik, *Moscow*, 1951: 6 P—QR4, B—Kt5 (better than either 6 .... P—KR3; or 6 .... QKt—Q2); 7 P—K4, etc.

6 ......   P—Kt4
7 P—K5
Lifeless would be now 7 P—QR4, because of 7 .... B—Kt5; 8 P—K5, P—KR3; 9 B—Q2, B×Kt; 10 B×B, Kt—K5; followed by .... Q—Q4.

7 ......   P—KR3
8 B—R4
Here 8 B—Q2, Kt—Q4; 9 Kt—K4, would be indecisive, as Black remains with an extra pawn and adequate means of defence.
Neither is 8 B×Kt, tempting (Geller–Foltys, *Szczawno Zdroj*, 1950), as, after 8 .... P×B; 9 P—QR4, B—Kt5; 10 KP×P, Q×BP; 11 Kt—K5, P—B4; Black obtains the initiative.

8 ......   P—Kt4
9 Kt×KKtP

Here again giving up a pawn by 9 B—Kt3, produces only a doubtful initiative.

9 ......   P×Kt
10 B×KtP   QKt—Q2
Black can here reinforce his KB3 by 10 .... B—K2.

11 P×Kt
Superficial play. White fails to fathom Black's subtle and carefully prepared plans, which are based on a race for the preponderance on the *long white diagonal*. Thus the capture of the pinned Knight was not as yet a matter of urgency. Best here is Lilienthal's move, 11 P—KKt3.
Premature is 11 Q—B3, because of 11 .... B—QKt2; 12 B—K2, Q—B2; 13 P×Kt, Castles; with promising chances for Black.

11 ......   B—QKt2
12 B—K2   Q—Kt3
Black concentrates his forces for a counter-attack and ignores the KBP, which sooner or later must fall.

13 Castles
Only White continues to make stereotyped moves. The following interlude could have strengthened his chances: 13 P—QR4, P—Kt5; 14 P—R5, Q—R3 (if 14 .... Q—B2; 15 P—R6); 15 Kt—K4, Castles; 16 Q—B2, P—B4; 17 B×P, Q—B3; 18 B—Q3, and there still is a strenuous contest for the initiative, while the white King can select the safest retreat.
Better than castling at once is 13 B—B3.

13 ......   Castles
14 P—QR4
But now, and for purely tactical reasons, this lateral action has lost its effectiveness.

14 ......   P—Kt5
15 Kt—K4
Wrong would be 15 P—R5, Q—B2; with a mating threat.

15 ......   P—B4
Having effected this important thrust with a gain of time, Black now definitely has the upper hand.

16 Q—Kt1   Q—B2

17 Kt—Kt3   P×P
18 B×P
White's "moral success" in having opened the QB file, with threats to the black King, will be brought to nought by White's powerful action in the centre.

18 ......   Q—B3
19 P—B3   P—Q6
The flood gates open and events now move rapidly.
First of all, White must provide against 20 .... Q—B4 ch; followed by .... Q×QB.

20 Q—B1
Or 20 B—K3, B—B4; 21 B×B, Q×B ch; 22 K—R1, Kt—K4; without restraining the momentum of Black's attack. If 20 B×QP, B—B4 ch; 21 K—R1, R×P ch; 22 K×R, R—R1 ch; 23 B—R7, Kt—B1; 24 Kt—K4, Kt×B, 25 K—Kt3, R—Kt1; 26 K—Kt4, Q—Q4; and wins.

20 ......   B—B4 ch
21 K—R1
If 21 B—K3, P—Q7 (too precipitate would be 21.... Kt—K4; 22 B×P ch, followed by 23 Q×B); 22 Q×P, Kt—K4.

21 ......   Q—Q3
22 Q—B4

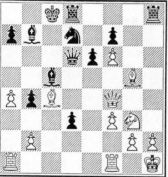

22 ......   R×P ch
A volcanic reply.

23 K×R   R—R1 ch
24 Q—R4
Not 24 B—R6, Q×Q; nor 24 Kt—R5, R×Kt ch; 25 K—Kt3, R×B ch.

24 ......   R×Q ch
25 B×R   Q—B5
    Resigns

If 26 K—R3, Q×KB.
On account of its importance for the theory of the openings as well as owing to the dynamism of Black's attack, this game is one of the most remarkable of the last decade.

73

RAGOSIN   BÖÖK
(Helsinki, 1946)

The frontal assault, which White brings to a successful conclusion in the following game, is most impressive.

1 P—Q4   P—Q4
2 P—QB4   P—K3
3 Kt—QB3   P—QB3
4 Kt—B3   Kt—B3
5 B—Kt5
This line might be called "amphibious" in that White, according to Black's reply, can lead into an orthodox *Queen's Gambit Declined* with the strategy of the pin, or adopt the more incisive lines of the deferred *Queen's Gambit.*
The text-move implies the sacrifice of a pawn and at the same time seeks to avoid the *Meran Variation,*

5 ......   P×P
6 P—K4   P—Kt4
The Achilles heel in Black's formation is his QB3.

7 P—K5   P—KR3
8 B—R4
Unpromising is 8 P×Kt, P×B; 9 P×P, B×P; etc.

8 ......   P—Kt4
9 P×Kt
The whole of this variation is sometimes called the *Soviet Defence.* Another aspect of this defence is 9 Kt×KKtP.

9 ......   P×B
10 Kt—K5
With the threat 11 Kt×KBP, K×Kt; 12 Q—R5 ch, K×P; 13 Q×P(R4) ch, winning the Queen.

10 ......   Q×BP
Parrying the threat indicated above.

11 B—K2
An instructive turn. White threatens eventually to play B—R5, but it is clear that his main object is to occupy the long white

diagonal. It has therefore been proposed to play here 11 P—KKt3.

| 11 ...... | Kt—Q2 |

In order to eliminate the unpleasant Knight, Black gives up a pawn. For if 11 .... B—Q3; White carries out his subsidiary threat, 12 Kt × KtP, P × Kt; 13 B—B3, etc.

Against 11 .... B—Kt5; an ingenious continuation was adopted in a game, Pomar–Tramoyeres, *Spanish Championship, San Sebastian*, 1951: 12 P—R4, B—Kt2; 13 B—B3, Q—K2; 14 Castles, B × Kt; 15 P × B, Castles (15 .... Q—B2; 16 B—R5, R—B1; 17 Q—Kt4, Q—Q3; 18 KR—K1, etc.); 16 R—K1, P—R3; 17 P × P, BP × P; 18 B × B, Q × B; 19 Q—R5, Q—K2; 20 Kt—Kt4, P—B4; 21 Kt × P ch, K—R1 (21 .... K—Kt2; 22 Kt × P ch); 22 Kt—B7 db ch, K—Kt2; 23 Kt—Kt5, R—R1; 24 Kt × P ch, Black resigns.

12 Kt × P(B6)	B—QKt2
13 B—B3	P—R3
14 Castles	

If 14 Q—K2, R—B1.

| 14 ...... | R—KKt1 |

Black should have realised that, for the time being, the struggle centres on his QB3, where he has lost the first bout, but where he could redress the balance by 14 .... R—B1; 15 Kt—K5, B × B; 16 Kt × B, B—Kt2; 17 P—R4, P—Kt5; with, however, an uncertain issue.

Doubtful is 14 .... B—Kt2; 15 P—R4.

15 Kt—Q5

A sudden break-through in the centre. The capture of the Knight is compulsory, as mate is threatened by 16 Kt—B7.

| 15 ...... | P × Kt |
| 16 R—K1 ch | Kt—K4 |

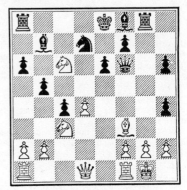

Position after 14 .... R—KKt1

| 17 R × Kt ch | K—Q2 |

In search of a sanctuary.

18 Kt—R5

Avoiding one more stumbling block: if 18 R × P ch, K—B2.

18	R—Kt1
19 Kt × B	R × Kt
20 B × P	R—QKt3
21 Q—B2	B—Q3

If 21 .... R—Kt4; 22 Q—K4, B—Q3; 23 P—B4, and the white forces overrun the position.

22 R—B5	Q × P
23 R × P ch	K—B1
24 Q—B5 ch	

An important preliminary check.

| 24 ...... | K—Kt1 |
| 25 Q—R7 | Resigns |

Black has no defence against the double threat 26 Q × R ch, and 26 R—Kt7 ch.

A clear-cut contest.

24. QUEEN'S PAWN GAME

74

ELISKASES   ROSSETTO
(Mar del Plata, 1950)

The apparent ease with which White wins the following game conceals profound manœuvres, characteristic of Eliskases' style.
At the same time Black commits an error of judgment in indulging in bizarre evolutions such as Kt—KR3—B4; against the particularly sane and logical Colle System, with its famous triangle: pawns at QB3, Q4 and K3.

1	Kt—KB3	P—Q4
2	P—Q4	P—QB3

More usual is 2 .... Kt—KB3; which leaves his opponent in uncertainty whether Black is going to use his QB4 passively, as in the text, or enterprisingly by .... P—QB4.

3	P—K3	P—KKt3

After his preceding move, one would expect Black to play 3 .... B—B4; or even 3 .... B—Kt5.

4	B—Q3	B—Kt2
5	QKt—Q2	Kt—KR3
6	P—B3	Castles
7	Castles	

The first phase of the contest, including castling, is completed. The position can be summed up as follows: White's moves so far are, with some slight transpositions, typical of the *Colle Attack.* White's basic idea is to develop in safety on interior lines, preparing to open up the game by P—K4, followed by a King's side attack.

The standard moves for the defence are: .... P—K3; followed by .... B—Q3. A recognised alternative is also .... P—KKt3; with .... B—Kt2. The ultimate object for Black also is to play .... P—K4. But in this game this pawn remains at K2 until it is captured there on the nineteenth move!

7	......	Kt—Q2
8	P—K4	P×P
9	Kt×P	Kt—KB4
10	B—KB4	Kt—B3

Better is either 10 .... R—K1; or 10 .... Kt—Kt3.

11 Kt×Kt ch

White decides on exchanges, which leave him in control of the centre, a positional advantage which he exploits with consummate skill.

11	......	B×Kt
12	Q—Q2	Q—Kt3
13	KR—K1	P—B4

Now, this is weak, as White can ignore the advance.

14	B×Kt	B×B
15	B—K5	KR—Q1

After 15 .... B×B; 16 R×B, White's various threats become overpowering.
Relatively best is 15 .... K—Kt2; to prevent the irruption of White's Queen.

16 Q—R6

Threatening 17 Kt—Kt5, and Black cannot play 17 .... B×Kt; because of 18 Q—Kt7 mate.

16	......	B×B
17	R×B	P×P

Starting a counter-action, which will require skilful play on the part of White before it is mastered.

18 Kt—Kt5   Q—KB3

A sop to Cerberus, but White insists on more.

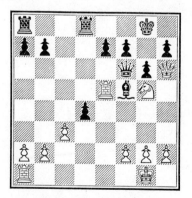

19 R×P

Leaving Black helpless. He cannot take the Rook because of mate in two.

19 ......   Q—Kt2

No better is 19 .... R—Q2; 20 QR—K1.

20 Q—R4

Wisely White refrains from immediate gain, e.g. 20 Q×Q ch, K×Q; 21 R×P ch, K—Kt1; 22 R×KtP, P—Q6; with chances for Black.

20 ......   P×P

21 R×BP   P×P

Or 21 .... Q×R; 22 Kt×Q, P×P; 23 Kt—R6 ch, and wins.

22 R×Q ch   K×R

23 R—K1

The refutation of the clever counter-action which started with Black's seventeenth move. White threatens, after 23 .... P—Kt8(Q); 24 Q×P ch, K—B3; 25 Q—K7 mate.

23 ......   R—Q2

If 23 .... P—KR3; 24 R—K7 ch, with a forced mate. And if 23 .... R—K1; 24 Q—Q4 ch, K—Kt1; 25 Q—B4 ch, K—Kt2; 26 Q—B3 ch (a fine progressive manœuvre), 26 .... K—Kt1; 27 Q—Kt3 ch, K—R1; 28 Q×P ch, and White, having finally liquidated the dangerous pawn, wins easily.

24 Q—QKt4

White shows both energy and circumspection.

24 ......   R—K1

With the optimistic idea: 25 R×R, P—Kt8(Q) ch; 26 Q×Q, B×Q; and White's terrible grip would disappear like a bad dream.

25 Q×P ch   K—R3

26 Kt—B7 ch   Resigns

Because of 26 .... K—R4; 27 P—Kt4 ch, followed by 28 R×R.

A strategic victory.

25. DUTCH DEFENCE

75

BRONSTEIN   BOTVINNIK
(Moscow, 1951)

The principal feature of the memorable match for the Championship of the World between Bronstein and Botvinnik, is that the adversaries were for ever seeking new situations, untried schemes, stresses of battle hitherto unknown.

It is a new kind of strategy that they were trying to create, or at least to design.

1 P—Q4	P—K3
2 P—QB4	P—KB4
3 P—KKt3	

This early *fianchetto* has become popular. Both Alekhine and Botvinnik have adopted it on frequent occasions.

White is left with the option of developing the KKt at K2 or KR3, without interrupting the long white diagonal, or at KB3, according to circumstances.

3	Kt—KB3
4 B—Kt2	B—K2
5 Kt—QB3	Castles
6 P—K3	

A significant moment. This restrained system was introduced by Botvinnik himself in the course of this match.

The usual tendency is to move this pawn to K4 in one move (in order to open the K file) or, if this cannot be done, not to move it at all (so as not to weaken KB3).

6	P—Q4

He decides on the rigid formation of the *Stonewall*, while in their first game, in which the challenger had black, he played the more flexible 6 .... P—Q3 (in a game, Grob–Flohr, *Rosas*, 1935, the continuation was 7 Kt—B3, Q—K1; 8 Q—K2, etc.); 7 KKt—K2, P—B3; 8 Castles, P—K4; 9 P—Q5, Q—K1; 10 P—K4, Q—R4; 11 P×KBP, B×P; and Black has the greater initiative.

7 KKt—K2	P—B3
8 P—Kt3	Kt—K5

Premature.

9 Castles	Kt—Q2
10 B—Kt2	

White's Bishops are favourably placed, and when, as must be expected, the centre is dissolved, one or the other of the Bishops will have an important bearing on the course of the game.

10	QKt—B3
11 Q—Q3	

If 11 P—B3, then not mechanically 11 .... Kt×Kt; 12 Kt×Kt, when White can comfortably effect the thematic thrust P—K4, but rather 11 .... Kt—Kt4; 12 P—KR4, Kt—B2; and Black obtains counter-play in the centre. That is why Bronstein prefers himself to concentrate his energy in the centre.

11	P—KKt4

Botvinnik falls back upon *active defence* throughout the contest. Attack at all hazards has been the watchword of both players, an admirable feature. There were a few draws, but, needless to say, not a few catastrophes.

12 P×P	KP×P
13 P—B3	

This is where Black's 8 .... Kt—K5; is shown to have been premature. If now 13 .... Kt—Q3; 14 B—QR3, and after some exchanges a break-through by P—K4, is threatened.

13	Kt×Kt
14 B×Kt	P—Kt5

The object of this move is to divert White's KBP from supporting the advance P—K4. It is, however, not without its drawbacks. The less aggressive 14 .... B—Q2; would at least allow this Bishop to become effective via K1 and Kt3. As it is, it will remain a "bad Bishop" to the end.

15 P×P	Kt×P
16 B—R3	Kt—R3

A painful, but compulsory retreat. If here 16 .... B—K3; 17 Kt—B4, Q—Q2; 18 B×Kt, P×B; 19 P—K4, P×P; 20 Q×P, B—Q4 (20 .... B—B2; 21 Q—K5, Q—Q3; 22 Q—KB5) 21 Kt×B, P×Kt; 22 Q—K5, Q—Q3; 23 Q—R5, and the weaknesses in Black's camp bring retribution.

17 Kt—B4	B—Q3
18 P—QKt4	

Black's initiative on the K side is cut short, and White transfers the centre of gravity of the contest to the other side.

A characteristic feature of Bronstein's play is his ability to change the scene of action, a procedure which requires exact timing. Here it will be seen that he builds up an overwhelming position on the Q side, only to switch back suddenly to the other wing for decisive action. Nimzowitsch's "alternation" on the grand scale.

18	P—R3
19 P—R4	Q—K2
20 QR—Kt1	P—Kt4

There is now no justification for aggression on this wing. Again the defensive 20 ....B—Q2; is preferable. If then White persists in his Q side advance, Black would obtain more play than in the actual game after 21 P—Kt5, RP×P; 22 P×P, KR—K1; 23 B—Q2, R—R6.

Another method, which allows P—Kt5, but provides compensation on other sectors, is 20 .... Kt—B2; 21 P—Kt5, RP×P; 22 P×P, Kt—Kt4; 23 B—KKt2, Kt—K5; making a stand in the centre.

21 B—KKt2	Kt—Kt5
22 B—Q2	Kt—B3
23 R—Kt2	B—Q2
24 R—R1	Kt—K5

Black has effected both stratagems indicated in the preceding note, but, unfortunately for him, he spoiled this by his compromising twentieth move.

| 25 B—K1 | KR—K1 |
| 26 Q—Kt3 | |

The threats become concrete, e.g.: 27 P×P, RP×P; 28 R×R, R×R; 29 Kt×P, P×Kt; 30 Q×P ch, followed by Q×R.

| 26 ...... | K—R1 |
| 27 R(Kt2)—R2 | Q—B1 |

White threatens to win a pawn by 28 P×P, etc.

| 28 Kt—Q3 | QR—Kt1 |

This decision to abandon the QR file brings about a catastrophe. It could be avoided by 28 .... KR—Kt1. However, in that case White replies 29 Kt—K5, B×Kt; 30 P×B, B—K3; 31 R—QB2, skilfully transferring his objective to QB6.

29 P×P	RP×P
30 R—R7	R—K2
31 Kt—K5	B—K1

If 31 .... B×Kt; 32 P×B, B—K3; 33 P—Kt4, P×P; 34 B—R4, Black is in difficulties, for after 34 .... R×R; 35 R×R, White has serious threats in 36 B×Kt, followed by B—B6 ch.

| 32 P—Kt4 | |

Magically, Bronstein changes front and resumes operations on the K side.

32	P×P
33 B×Kt	P×B
34 B—R4	

A new combatant, dormant hitherto, appears on the battlefield with decisive consequences.

| 34 ...... | R×Kt |

Practically forced. If 34 .... R(K2)—QKt2; 35 Q—K6, B×Kt; 36 Q×B ch, K—Kt1; 37 R×R, R×R; 38 R—R8, etc. Also bad is 34 .... R—KKt2; 35 Q—K6. If 34 .... R—KKt2; 35 R×R, Q—R3; 36 Kt—B7 ch, B×Kt; 37 Q×B, R—KB1; 38 B—B6 ch, Q×B; 39 Q×P mate.

| 35 P×R | B×KP |
| 36 R—KB1 | Q—Kt1 |

Evidently useless is 36 .... B×P ch; 37 K—Kt2.

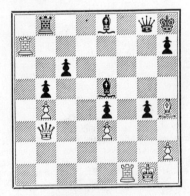

| 37 B—Kt3 | |

A delightful turn. If 37 .... Q×Q; 38 R—B8 ch, Q—Kt1; 39 B×B mate, or 37 .... B×B; 38 Q—B3 ch.

| 37 ...... | B—Kt2 |
| 38 Q×Q ch | Resigns |

White comes out a piece and the double exchange ahead.

The most beautiful game of the match.

26. STAUNTON GAMBIT

76

BARDA   ROSSOLIMO

(Hastings, 1949-50)

The following game is an example of that oft-recurring curiosity: one player deluding himself that he is dictating the course of events, while in reality events are driving him on the downward path.

1 P—Q4	P—KB4
2 P—K4	P × P
3 Kt—QB3	

An interesting line is 3 P—KB3, and if 3 .... P—Q4; 4 P—QB4, etc.

3	Kt—KB3
4 B—KKt5	Kt—B3

A subtle defence. Against 4 .... P—B3; omniscient theory recommends 5 P—B3, while against 4 .... P—KKt3; White's best is an outflanking movement by 5 P—KR4.

Weak is 4 .... P—K3; as played in a short game, Hayden-H. Brown, *London Championship*, 1947: 4 .... P—K3; 5 B × Kt (much better than 5 Kt × P, when Black is relieved of his principal difficulties after 5 .... B—K2), 5 .... Q × B; 6 Kt × P, Q—Q1; 7 Kt—KB3, P—Q3; 8 B—Q3, Kt—Q2; 9 KKt—Kt5, Q—K2; 10 Q—R5ch, P—Kt3; 11 Kt × P ch (very smart, and the beginning of the end), 11 .... P × Kt; 12 B × P ch, P × B; 13 Q × P ch, K—Q1; 14 Kt × P ch, Q × Kt ch; 15 Q × Q, R—R2; 16 Castles QR, R—Kt2; 17 P—KKt3, Black resigns as he is four pawns down in a bad position.

5 P—B3
Although this move is likely to be played sooner or later, it is better to delay it at this point, e.g. 5 P—Q5, Kt—K4; 6 Q—Q4, Kt—B2; 7 B × Kt, KP × B; 8 Kt × P, etc. The text-move allows Black a breathing-space, which enables him to impart an original twist in the opening phase.

5	P—K4

This is the move which, thus early, gives Black the initiative.

6 P—Q5
If 6 Kt × P, B—K2

6	Kt—Q5

7 P × P	B—K2

The threat is 8 .... Kt × QP.

8 B—QB4	P—Q3

Now 8 .... Kt × QP; is doubtful because, after 9 Kt × Kt, B × B; 10 Kt—KB3, Black cannot castle and the white Bishop on the white diagonal would be well worth a pawn.

9 KKt—K2	Kt—Kt5
10 Kt × Kt	

A tricky position. If instead, 10 B × B, Q × B; 11 Kt × Kt, Kt—K6; 12 B—Kt5 ch, K—Q1; 13 Q—Q2, P × Kt; 14 Kt—Q1 (not 14 Q × P, Kt × BP ch), 14 .... Q × P; White clearly has a lost game.

10	B × B
11 B—Kt5 ch	

Tempting, but deceptive. Black has too many threats of his own. White should play 11 Kt—B5.

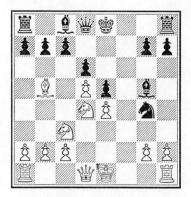

11	P—B3

Sans peur et sans reproche. Evidently not 11 .... B—Q2; 12 Kt—K6, nor, at once, 11 .... K—K2; 12 Kt—K6, B × Kt; 13 P × B, Kt—B3; 14 Kt—Q5 ch, K × P; 15 Castles, etc., with a dynamic advantage for White.

12 Kt × P
The usual procedure in such cases, 12 P × P, threatening 13 P × P dis ch, or 13 P—B7 dis ch, fails here because Black

can play 12 .... Castles; with an over-whelming attack.

In this position which contains dangers for both sides, the question as to who shall be the first to castle is of paramount importance.

12	P × Kt
13 B × P ch	K—K2
14 Castles	

If 14 B × R, Q—Kt3; with too many threats.

| 14 ...... | R—QKt1 |

Here 14 .... Q—Kt3 ch; at once, would not be effective, e.g. 15 K—R1, Kt—B7 ch; 16 R × Kt, Q × R; 17 B × R, and White has more than equality, or 15 .... R—QKt1;

16 Q—B3, and the rôle of the attacker passes to White.

| 15 Q—K2 | Q—Kt3 ch |
| 16 K—R1 | Q—K6 |

The rest is easy to understand. Black strives to retain his extra piece without allowing his position to deteriorate.

17 R—B3	Q × Q
18 Kt × Q	R × P
19 QR—KB1	Kt—B3
20 R—QR3	P—QR3
21 Kt—Kt3	B—Q7
22 P—B3	B—K6
23 Kt—B5 ch	B × Kt
24 P × B	KR—QKt1
Resigns	

27. BENONI COUNTER-GAMBIT

77

FOLTYS   GEREBEN
(Budapest, 1948)

*Psychologically, the choice of an appro-
priate opening is of the utmost importance
for a player's success in a tournament. In
the following murderous encounter, Black is
unfortunate in his choice of a risky defence
against an opponent known and feared for the
precision of his play.*

| 1 P—Q4 | P—QB4 |
| 2 P—Q5 | |

White accepts the challenge. He could
play 2 P—K3 (*Queen's Pawn Game*), or
2 P—K4 (*Sicilian Defence*).

2 ......   P—K4
An unexplored idea is 2 .... P—B4.

| 3 P—K4 | P—Q3 |
| 4 B—Q3 | |

Against 4 Kt—QB3, Black can play
4 .... P—B4.

| 4 ...... | Kt—K2 |
| 5 Kt—K2 | P—B4 |

This attempt to impose his will is to recoil
like a boomerang. More positional is
5 .... Kt—Kt3; followed by .... B—K2;
and .... Castles.

6 P—KB4
Thus early the contest takes a breathless
turn.

6	BP×P
7 B×P	Kt—Q2
8 Castles	Kt—KB3
9 QKt—B3	

Application of the simple principle:
development of the pieces without any loss
in time or space.

| 9 ...... | B—Kt5 |
| 10 P—KR3 | B—R4 |

Futile would be the gain of a pawn by
10 .... Kt×B; 11 Kt×Kt, B×Kt;
12 Q×B, Kt×P; on account of 13 P×P,
followed by 14 Q—R5 ch.

11 K—R2
Coolly White maintains the tension in the
centre. The exchange 11 P×P, P×P; would

be premature and lighten his opponent's
task. If 11 Q—Q3, Q—Kt3; with counter-
threats.

| 11 ...... | B—Kt3 |
| 12 Kt—Kt3 | Q—Kt3 |

Black does not give up his aspirations
to attack. More prudent is 12 .... Q—Q2.

13 P×P
At the right moment White espies an
opportunity for tactical disturbances in
the centre, before Black places his King in
comparative security by castling.

| 13 ...... | P×P |
| 14 P—Q6 | Kt(K2)—Kt1 |

The only move, e.g. 14 .... Kt—B1;
15 R×Kt, P×R; 16 P—Q7 ch, or 14 ....
Kt—B3; 15 R×Kt, P×R; 16 Kt—Q5, or
14 .... Castles; 15 P×Kt, R×Q;
16 P×B(Q) ch, R×Q; 17 R×R, all to
White's advantage.

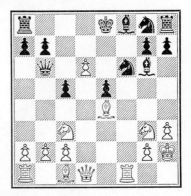

15 P—Q7 ch
This pawn's progress has been impressive.
Black is compelled to accept the sacrifice,
for 15 .... K—Q1; stands condemned after
16 B—Kt5, B—K2; 17 Q—B3, and Black is
threatened from all sides.

| 15 ...... | Kt×P |
| 16 Kt—Q5 | Q—Q3 |

If 16 .... Q—Q1; 17 B×B ch, P×B;
18 Q—Kt4.

17 B×B ch   P×B

18 Kt—K4   Q—QB3
19 B—Kt5
The key to the combination initiated with White's thirteenth move. The black King remains pinned and desolate in the centre.

19 ......   Kt—R3
If 19 .... Kt—K2; 20 P—B4, and Black is still unable to castle. And if 19 .... P—B5 (to prevent White from fortifying his centre with 20 P—B4); there follows 20 Q—B3, with the terrible threat, 21 Q—B7 mate (e.g. 20 .... Q×Kt; 21 Kt—Q6 ch, mating or winning the Queen).

20 P—B4   Kt—Kt3
Or 20 .... Kt—B2; 21 Q—Kt4 (threat

22 Q—K6 ch, Q×Q; 23 Kt—B7 mate), 21 .... Kt×B; 22 Q×Kt, and Black cannot reply 22 .... R—R4; because of 23 Kt—B7 ch, Q×Kt; 24 Q×KtP ch, followed by Q×R.

21 Q—B3   Kt×P
No better is 21 .... Kt×Kt; 22 P×Kt, Q—Q2; 23 B×Kt, etc.

22 B×Kt   Castles
With much trouble Black has succeeded in castling, and he hopes to recover his piece, as two hostile pieces are attacked.

23 B×P   Resigns
(23 .... B×B; 24 Kt—K7 ch, or 23 .... R—Kt1; 24 B×B, etc.)

28. PROTO-INDIAN DEFENCE

78

TESCHNER — TARTAKOWER
(Southsea, 1951)

A novelty? Frequently modern masters create something new by reverting to an ancient line of play and by adding to it some novel points of their own.

1 P—Q4   P—Q3
The oldest form of *Indian Defence*, which allows White to build up a centre, with the intention of attacking it forthwith. There are some fine points in this defence which do not occur in the more usual types of *Indian Defences*. It may be added that 1 .... P—Q3; has a universal character, as it is adapted for play against both P—K4 and P—Q4.

2 P—K4
The most natural continuation. Against 2 P—QB4, Black replies without fear 2 .... P—K4.

2 ......   Kt—KB3
3 Kt—QB3   P—KKt3
A minor success. Black now has a *King's Indian Defence*, while White lacks the useful co-operation of a pawn at QB4.

4 P—B4
Also a kind of central phalanx. A quiet development is 4 Kt—B3, B—Kt2; 5 B—K2, etc. More enterprising is the course of the prototype, Schallopp–Paulsen, *Nuremberg*, 1883: 5 P—KR3, QKt—Q2; 6 P—K5, Kt—KKt1; 7 B—KB4, etc.
A modern system named after its protagonist, Pirc, goes on, after 5 B—K2, with 5 .... Castles; 6 Castles, QKt—Q2; 7 B—KKt5, P—B4; 8 P—Q5 (or as in a game, Kostic–Pirc, *Ljubljana*, 1950: 8 P—K5, BP×P; 9 P×Kt, P×P; 10 Q×P, P×B; 11 Q×QP, P—Kt5; 12 Kt—Q4, B—K4; 13 Q—Q5, Q—Kt4; 14 QR—Q1, Kt—B3, and Black has the initiative), 8 .... P—KR3; 9 B—KB4, Q—Kt3; 10 Q—B1, K—R2; etc., with equal chances.
A plan, as simple as it is vigorous, is proposed by the Parisian master, Thiellemont: 4 B—Kt5, B—Kt2; 5 P—K5, and if 5 .... P×P; 6 P×P, Q×Q ch; 7 R×Q,

Black is suddenly faced with awkward problems.

4 ......   B—Kt2
5 Kt—B3   Castles
6 B—K2
Instead of this unpretentious development, 6 B—Q3, deserves consideration.

6 ......   P—B4
Taking advantage of a tactical opportunity to challenge the centre.

7 P×P
A psychological error. White expects only the peaceful issue: 7 .... P×P; 8 Q×Q, R×Q; with equality. But Black has more ambitious plans.
Against 7 P—Q5, Black would play 7 .... P—K3; 8 P×P, B×P; or 7 .... P—QR3; 8 P—QR4, Q—B2; etc.

7 ......   Q—R4
With the threat 8 .... Kt×P; and it is now seen that, in view of this turn, 6 B—Q3, would have been more useful than 6 B—K2.

8 Kt—Q2
After 8 Castles, Q×P ch; 9 K—R1, Kt—Kt5; 10 Q—K1, B×Kt; 11 Q×B, Q×Q; 12 P×Q, Kt—QB3; Black's advantage is taking shape.

8 ......   Q×BP
And now Black has recovered his pawn without White being able to castle and without exchanging Queens.

9 Kt—Kt3   Q—Kt3
10 B—B3   Kt—B3
11 Kt—Q5
If 11 Q—K2, in order to drive away the black Queen from the critical diagonal by B—K3, Black still has the last word after 11 .... P—K4; 12 B—K3, Kt—Q5; etc.

11 ......   Kt×Kt
12 P×Kt   Kt—Q5
13 Kt×Kt   B×Kt
14 P—B3   B—B7 ch
15 K—B1   P—QR4
The key-stone of Black's conception.
If, instead, 15 .... P—KR4 (to prevent 16 P—KKt4); there follows 16 Q—K2,

B—R5 (not 16 .... B—QB4; 17 P—QKt4, winning the Bishop); 17 B—K3, and White, having regained control of the disputed diagonal, has palpably the better game.

16 Q—K2	B—QB4
17 P—KKt4	B—Q2
18 K—Kt2	

White has achieved artificial castling, but Black has preserved his command of the black diagonal.

18	P—K3
19 P × P	P × P
20 P—KR4	

White also strives to open a line of attack.

| 20 ...... | QR—K1 |
| 21 P—Kt5 | |

Not yet 21 P—R5, P—Kt4.

| 21 ...... | P—K4 |
| 22 P—R5 | KP × P |

Black fires the first shot.

| 23 B—Q5 ch | K—Kt2 |

More astute than 23 .... K—R1; because now 24 P—R6 ch, K—R1; would make the black King's retreat the more secure.

| 24 Q—B3 | R—B4 |

A bold Rook, which threatens on one side the Bishop at Q4, on the other the KKtP, while maintaining its vertical pressure. Still more precise, however, is to delegate this threefold function to both Rooks with 24 .... R—K4.

| 25 B × BP | |

The turning point in the game. White still hopes to "fish in troubled waters." If, for instance, 25 .... R × KB; 26 P—R6 ch, K—R1; 27 B—K5 ch, K—Kt1 (capturing the Bishop leads to a mate in two); 28 Q × R ch, B—K3; 29 Q—Q2, P × B; 30 KR—K1, White, in spite of Black's superiority in material, still has some resources.

| 25 ...... | Q × P ch (see diag.) |

A move which required exact calculation. Much less decisive is the gain of the Queen

for two Rooks by 25 .... R—K6; 26 B × R, R × Q; 27 B × B, Q × B; 28 B × R, Q × P ch; 29 K—B2, and White can still put up a fight.

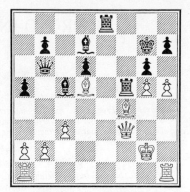

Position after 25 B × BP

26 K—Kt3	Q—B7 ch
27 Q × Q	B × Q ch
28 K × B	

Sad, but unavoidable. If 28 K—B3, B—K6.

28	R × B ch
29 K—Kt3	R—B4
30 P × P	R × P ch

The King-hunt begins.

| 31 K—B2 | R—B1 ch |

The Rooks will win a clear piece.

| 32 K—K3 | |

Not 32 B—B7, P × P; nor 32 B—B3, B—Kt5; 33 R × P ch, K × P; etc.

| 32 ...... | R—K4 ch |
| 33 B—K4 | |

If 33 K—Q4, R—B5 ch; 34 K—Q3, B—B4 ch (not, at once, 34 .... R × B ch; 35 K—K3, and White recovers his piece); 35 K—Q2, R × B ch; 36 K—K3, R—K5 ch; and wins.

33	B—B4
34 R × P ch	K × P
35 R—R4	R(B1)—K1
36 R—Kt4 ch	K—B2
Resigns	

INDIAN DEFENCES

29. OLD INDIAN DEFENCE

79

GOLOMBEK   WAHLTUCH
(National Club Championship,
London, 1950)

The following instructive contest demonstrates how cautiously Black must proceed if he is not to fall a victim to modern, or to be more precise, ultra-modern methods.

1 P—Q4	Kt—KB3
2 P—QB4	P—Q3

A defence frequently adopted by Tchigorin, whose idea was to open up Black's game by .... P—K4; at the earliest opportunity.

3 P—KKt3
A move practically unknown in Tchigorin's time and well suited to Golombek's mainly positional style of play.

3	QKt—Q2

More counter-play is provided by 3 .... P—B3; 4 B—Kt2, B—B4; 5 Kt—QB3, P—K4; 6 P—K4, B—Kt5; 7 KKt—K2, P×P; 8 Q×P, QKt—Q2; with a satisfactory development. Incidentally, it is possible, without disadvantage, to lead into the *King's Indian Defence* with 3 .... P—KKt3.

4 B—Kt2	P—K4
5 Kt—KB3	

White already is in a position to pay little attention to Black's plans and to complete his development at leisure, in the knowledge that Black can at best maintain but not improve his position. Of course 5 .... P—K5; loses a pawn after 6 Kt—Kt5.

5	B—K2

The adherents of the *Tchigorin System* (instead of 5 .... P—KKt3; and .... B—Kt2) are few but faithful. A different plan, with an inversion of moves, was followed in a game, Euwe–Réti, *Mährisch-Ostrau*, 1923: 5 .... P—B3; 6 Kt—B3, P×P; 7 Kt×P, Kt—Kt3; 8 Q—Q3, P—Q4.

6 Kt—B3	P—B3

This, with the next move, completes the Tchigorin scheme.

7 Castles	Q—B2
8 P—K4	

An interesting point here: while White has so far made self-evident moves, Black has gone on playing the routine moves of the *Tchigorin System* until the moves ran out.

8	P—QR4

An interesting continuation is 8 .... Kt—B1; 9 P—KR3, B—Q2; 10 B—K3, P—KR3; 11 R—B1, etc. But there is no call for experiments. Simplest is 8 .... Castles; followed by .... R—K1; and an ultimate re-grouping by .... B or Kt—B1.

9 P—Kt3	P×P
10 Kt×P	Kt—B4

An advanced post of the kind which does not last.

11 P—KR3
Stopping the black QB's only useful outlet.

11	P—R3

This and the next move are what might be called *coups d'embarras*. They show that Black follows no set plan. This will result in his having to castle on the Q side, in direct line of an attack supported by the Bishop on the long white diagonal.

12 B—K3	P—KKt3
13 Q—Q2	B—Q2
14 QR—Q1	Castles QR

Can it be that he hopes that White may take the KRP, after which Black, with an open KR file, would get a chance of exerting his well-known ingenuity and attacking powers. But Golombek is too experienced a player and carries on quietly with his own schemes.

15 P—R3	Kt—K3
16 P—B4	P—R4
17 P—QKt4	Kt—K1

If 17 .... P×P; 18 P×P, and the open QR file is at White's mercy.

18 Kt—Kt3	B—B3
19 Kt×P	P—B4

The threat was 20 Kt—R4, but the text-move lets in the Knight elsewhere in equally

decisive fashion. The lesser evil is therefore 19 .... B × Kt; 20 Q × B, R—Kt1.

20 Kt—Q5   Q—Kt1
21 Kt × B   Kt × Kt (see diag.)
Black now expects 22 Q × P, Q × Q;
23 R × Q, which is dismal enough, but White
finds an even more damaging, and at the
same time, elegant continuation.

22 P—K5   Resigns
He cannot play 22 .... P × KP; because
of 23 B × P ch, K—B2; 24 Q—Q6 mate. If
22 .... Kt—K1; 23 B × P ch, K—B2;
24 P × P ch, K—Kt3; 25 P × P ch, Kt × P
(25 .... K—R2; 26 P—B6 dis ch);
26 B × Kt ch, K × B; and now White has the
choice of four mates!

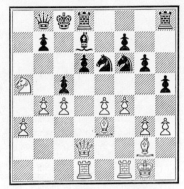

Position after 21 .... Kt × Kt

30. KING'S INDIAN DEFENCE

80

KOTOV   GELLER
(U.S.S.R. Championship, 1949)

The following game is striking, not only on account of its tactical beauty, but ,also because of its important theoretical value.

1 P—Q4	Kt—KB3
2 P—QB4	P—KKt3
3 Kt—QB3	

Nowadays, 3 P—KKt3, avoiding the *Grünfeld Defence*, has become popular.

| 3 ...... | B—Kt2 |

Here Black can still play 3 .... P—Q4; but not without risk.

4 P—KKt3	Castles
5 B—Kt2	P—Q3
6 Kt—B3	QKt—Q2
7 Castles	P—K4
8 P—K4	

The *normal position* of the *King's Indian Defence.*

| 8 ...... | P×P |

Extensive analysis has shown that the waiting moves, 8 .... R—K1; and 8 .... P—B3; have their disadvantages.

| 9 Kt×P | Kt—B4 |
| 10 P—B3 | |

A difficult decision. 10 R—K1, leaves the KBP vulnerable, but the text-move weakens the black diagonal on which stands the King.

White can, however, play 10 P—KR3, keeping the KBP free for some future attack.

| 10 ...... | KKt—Q2 |

Manœuvring on interior lines. In a game, Kottnauer–Geller, *Szczawno Zdroj*, 1950, which reached this position by an inversion of moves, Black went on here 10 .... P—B3; 11 B—K3, P—QR4; 12 Q—Q2, P—R5; and also succeeded in gaining the upper hand.

It may be added that in this type of position it is usual to play .... P—QR4; at once, but here Black does not fear 11 P—QKt4, as his Knight has a good square at K3.

| 11 B—K3 | P—QB3 |

A move characteristic of the *Boleslavsky System*, thanks to which the black Queen gains in mobility, while the weakness at Black's Q3 is difficult to attack.

| 12 Q—Q2 | P—QR4 |
| 13 QR—Q1 | Kt—K4 |

Typical of Geller's enterprising style. More solid, however, is 13 .... Kt—Kt3; 14 P—Kt3, Q—K2.

| 14 P—Kt3 | P—R5 |
| 15 Kt(Q4)—K2 | |

Inviting Black's QKt to relinquish its observation post, after which White could capture the QRP with impunity.

More "concentric" is 15 P—B4.

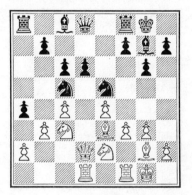

| 15 ...... | P×P |

A remarkably deep conception. Black loses a piece, but remains with passed pawns which paralyse White's game.

| 16 B×Kt | Kt×P |
| 17 Q—B1 | P×P |

Here 17 .... P—Kt7; is insufficient. After 18 Q—B2, P×B; 19 R×Q, R×R; 20 R—Q1, B—K3; 21 P—B4, Black has no means of increasing the pressure.

18 K	Q—R4
19 Q×	B—K3
20 Q—B1	P×B
21 Kt(R2)—B3	P—QKt4
22 Kt—Kt1	

Excessive optimism. Preferable here is
22 P—B4, e.g. 22 .... B—Kt6; 23 R—Q6,
P—Kt5; 24 P—K5, giving back the piece
for a gain in space.

22	P—Kt5
23 Kt—B4	B—Kt6
24 R—Q6	

Wiser is 24 Kt—Q2, B×R; 25 R×B.

| 24 ...... | P—B5 |
| 25 R×BP | P—B6 |

The moving forest!

26 Kt—Q5

Played apparently on the assumption that
Black could not risk the exchange of pieces
and capture of the pawn at his Q4, because
of White's Bishop raking the long diagonal.

26	B×Kt
27 P×B	Q×P
28 P—B4	Q—Q5 ch
29 K—R1	R—R7

Foreshadowing the climax of Black's
strategy, a sudden swoop on the opposite
wing. The immediate threat is 30 ....
R×B; 31 K×R, Q—K5 ch.

| 30 B—B3 | R—QKt7 |
| 31 P—B5 | B—K4 |

To prevent the Bishop from being shut
in by 32 P—B6.

| 32 Q—K1 | R—Q1 |
| 33 B—K4 | K—Kt2 |

Astutely tempting White to give check,
after which the black King obtains a more
secure retreat.

34 P—B6 ch	K—Kt1
35 R—R6	P—R4
36 R—R5	P—R5

Starting on the last lap. Of course, if
37 P×P, R×P mate.

37 B×P

A desperate bid for salvation.

37 ...... R×P ch

Thus each player has prepared a disagree-
able surprise for his opponent.

38 K×R	B×P ch
39 Q×B	P×Q ch
40 K—R3	P×B
Resigns	

White is lost.
A grand fight, covering the whole board.

81

DR. STREHLE   GYGLI
(Swiss Championship, 1946)

*Here again the players castle on opposite
sides, and here again, the result is a ferocious
fight. But the large-scale strategy is enriched
by some additional finesses.*

| 1 P—Q4 | Kt—KB3 |
| 2 P—QB4 | |

Against 2 Kt—KB3, the *King's Indian
Defence* is less insistent, as White can
then quite well play 3 Kt—B3, P—Q4;
4 B—B4, B—Kt2; 5 P—K3, Castles;
6 P—KR3, with the better chances.

2	P—KKt3
3 Kt—QB3	B—Kt2
4 P—K4	P—Q3
5 B—K2	

A *finesse* in the opening. After the normal 5 Kt—B3, Black can safely castle,
whereas now; 5 .... Castles; leaves Black
open to an immediate K side attack.

5 ...... Castles

More cautious is 5 .... QKt—Q2;
6 Kt—B3, P—K4; 7 Castles, and now only
7 .... Castles. White then has the choice
between the rather lifeless 8 P×P, P×P;
9 Q—B2, P—B3; with a level game, or the
more static 8 P—Q5, P—QR4; 9 Q—B2,
Kt—B4; etc., or, finally, the acrobatic
8 R—K1, R—K1; 9 B—B1, P—B3 (Boleslavsky's speciality); 10 P—QKt3, etc., with
a contest rich in strategic ideas.

6 P—KR4

With this move the battle is engaged on
the terrain chosen by White.

6	P—KR4
7 Kt—R3	P—B3
8 Kt—Kt5	B—Q2

Directed, in conjunction with .... Q—B1;
against White's P—KKt4. Black's first
care in this defence should be to enforce
.... P—K4; and .... QKt—Q2; now
impossible, should be played early.

9 P—B3 P—K4

Of course, now 10 P—KKt4, would not be
prevented by 9 .... Q—B1; and 8 ....
B—Q2; is clearly shown to have been a misconception.

| 10 B—K3 | P—Kt3 |
| 11 Q—Q2 | P—R4 |

Preparing an attack in case White should
castle on the Queen's side. But White is not to
be deterred: his own attack is more advanced.

12 Castles QR   Q—B2

Black clearly banks on the chances of his attack.

13 P—KKt4	P—Kt4
14 P × RP	Kt × RP
15 QR—Kt1	P—Kt5
16 Kt—Q1	P × P

Black has no good move, but 16 .... B—K1; to get the QKt into play, is the lesser evil. The text-move leads to the exchange of Black's KB, leaving the King with still fewer defenders.

17 B × P	B × B
18 Q × B	Kt—B5
19 Q—K3	P—Q4 (see diag.)
20 P—R5	

Very fine play.

| 20 ...... | P × KP |

Not 20 .... Kt × P; 21 R × Kt, etc.

21 R—R4

Forcing the exchange of yet another black defender.

| 21 ...... | Kt × B ch |
| 22 Q × Kt | Q—K4 |

Black makes the best of a bad position.

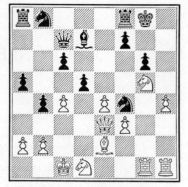

Position after 19 .... P—Q4

23 P—B4	Q—B3
24 QR—R1	B—B4
25 P × P	B × P
26 Q—R2	Q—Q5

Hoping against hope for 27 .... Q × BP ch; 28 K—Kt1, P—K6 dis ch; etc.

| 27 R—R8 ch | K—Kt2 |
| 28 Kt—K6 ch | Resigns |

A beautiful finishing touch. After 28 .... P × Kt; there follows 29 Q—R6 ch, K—B3; 30 Q × R ch, with a forced mate.

31. GRÜNFELD DEFENCE

82

BRONSTEIN   BOLESLAVSKY
(First Match Game, Moscow, 1950)

Another of Bronstein's games which must be counted as a classic in chess literature. Energy and imagination prevail, but in addition the game is of great theoretical value for this particular variation. Bronstein, as White, manages to infuse new life into a line of play long thought to be inadequate.

1 P—Q4	Kt—KB3
2 P—QB4	P—KKt3
3 Kt—QB3	P—Q4
4 P×P	

Reverting to an old continuation, which had fallen into disrepute as it corresponds with Black's desire for an immediate settlement in the centre.

4	Kt×P
5 P—K4	

A positional continuation is 5 P—KKt3.

5	Kt×Kt

He prefers not to lose time by a withdrawal of the Knight.

6 P×Kt	P—QB4

So far we have the original Grünfeld plan, which is based on the idea that Black's pawn majority on the Q side, together with White's difficulty in taking advantage of his strong centre, should give Black the better chances.

7 B—QB4

This early *sortie* of the Bishop allows a more flexible development of the KKt than 7 Kt—B3.

7	B—Kt2
8 Kt—K2	P×P

A more expectative continuation, played in the second game of the Botvinnik–Bronstein *match*, is 8 .... Castles; 9 Castles, Kt—Q2; 10 B—KKt5, P—KR3; 11 B—K3, Q—B2; 12 R—B1, P—R3; 13 Q—Q2 (thanks to his tenth move, B—KKt5, White has gained an important *tempo* for his attack), 13 .... K—R2; 14 B—Q3, P—QKt4; 15 Kt—B4, with a fine initiative for White.

9 P×P	Kt—B3

An interesting idea here is 9 .... Q—R4 ch; 10 B—Q2, Q—R4.

10 B—K3	Castles
11 Castles	B—Kt5

An ingenious manœuvre. If at once 11 .... Kt—R4; 12 B—Q3, B—K3 (a good alternative is 12 .... P—Kt3; 13 R—B1, P—K4); 13 P—Q5, B×R; 14 Q×B, P—B3; 15 B—KR6, R—K1; 16 Kt—B4, B—Q2; 17 P—K5, with a very strong attack for the exchange. The great theorist Znosko-Borovsky prefers 11 .... P—Kt3; 12 R—B1, B—Kt2.

12 P—B3	Kt—R4
13 B—Q3	

A picturesque situation. Unsubstantial is 13 B×P ch, R×B; 14 P×B, R×R ch; 15 Q×R, Q—Q2; 16 P—KR3, Kt—B5; and Black's initiative is ample compensation for the lost pawn.

13	B—K3
14 P—Q5	

This sacrifice of the exchange is in the spirit of this variation. Useless is 14 Q—R4, P—QR3; 15 Q—Kt4, P—QKt4; 16 KR—Q1, R—Kt1.

14	B×R
15 Q×B	P—B3

Otherwise there follows 16 B—KR6, and White recovers the exchange.

16 B—KR6	Q—Kt3 ch (see diag.)

He hopes, not only to maintain his advantage in material, but also to gain space. Preferable is 16 .... R—K1.

17 K—R1

An interesting fact: the same players, with some minor transpositions, chose the identical moves in the Candidates' Tournament at *Budapest*, 1950.

Both players appeared to be satisfied with their chances. But here Bronstein has a well-prepared reply, while, in the previous encounter, he played rather anxiously 17 Kt—Q4, and only drew after 17 .... B—Q2; 18 R—Kt1, Q—B4; 19 R—QB1, Q—Kt3; 20 B×R, R×B; etc.

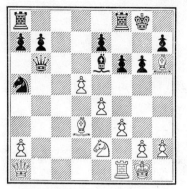

Position after 16 .... Q—Kt3 ch

17 ......   KR—Q1
This appears to refute White's designs, but had Boleslavsky foreseen his future difficulties he would willy-nilly have given back the exchange by 17 .... B—Q2.

18 R—Kt1   Q—B4
If 18 .... Q—B2; 19 B—KB4, and if 18 .... Q—Q3; 19 Q—B3.

19 B—Q2
A dynamic retreat. 19 R—Kt5, leads to nothing after 19 .... Q—R6.

19 ......   P—Kt3
If 19 .... P—QR3; 20 B—Kt4, Q—B2; 21 R—QB1, Q—Kt3; 22 B×KP, and Black's game collapses.

20 B—Kt4   Q—B2
21 R—QB1   Q—Kt2
If 21 .... Q—Q2; 22 Kt—Q4, B—B2; 23 B—Kt5, leaving Black no peace.

22 Q—Kt1
Threatening two black pieces at the same time.

22 ......   QR—Kt1
A good example of the psychology of the attack! The defender becomes worried and is more often than not in time trouble, when even a grandmaster is likely to overlook simple things. The only way to save the piece is 22 .... B—B1; but after 23 B×Kt, P×B; 24 Q×Q, B×Q; 25 R—B7, etc. White still has a great positional advantage and many threats.

23 P×B
The rest is a slow death for Black.

23 ......   Kt—B3

24 B—B3   Kt—K4
25 B—Kt5   R(Q1)—QB1
26 B×Kt   R×R ch
27 Q×R   P×B
28 B—Q7   Q—R3
29 Kt—Kt3   Q×P
30 P—R4   R—KB1
31 Q—Kt5   R—B3
32 Q×R   Resigns

A Queen's sacrifice, even when fairly obvious, always rejoices the heart of the chess-lover.

83

FINE   NAJDORF
(Match, New York, 1949)

To know how to adorn a purely positional treatment with tactical finesse (see White's moves 21 and 28 in the following game) is the attribute of the great player.

1 P—Q4   Kt—KB3
2 P—QB4   P—KKt3
3 Kt—QB3   P—Q4
4 B—B4
A continuation which is more ambitious than its innocent appearance leads one to suppose. Its strategic meaning has been elucidated in a game Tartakower–Frydman, *Lodz*, 1935.

4 ......   B—Kt2
5 P—K3   Castles
6 Q—Kt3
White can win a pawn by 6 P×P, Kt×P; 7 Kt×Kt, Q×Kt; 8 B×P, but then most players would prefer Black's game with its superior development, which is well worth a pawn. This is shown in a game Swihart–Hall, *correspondence, U.S.A.*, 1950: 8 .... Kt—B3; 9 Kt—B3, B—B4; 10 P—QR3, QR—B1; 11 B—Kt3, B—B7; 12 Q—Q2, Kt—R4; 13 P—K4, Q×P ch; 14 Q—K3, Kt—Kt6; 15 R—R2, Q×Q ch; 16 P×Q, B—Kt8; White resigns: he loses the Rook. An amusing finish.

6 ......   P—B3
7 Kt—B3   P—Kt3
A surprising move for a player of Najdorf's temperament. By allowing White to exchange pawns, he virtually surrenders an open QB file and condemns his own Queen's Bishop to comparative inactivity. He should himself exchange pawns. After 7 .... P×P; 8 B×P, QKt—Q2; 9 Castles KR, Kt—Kt3; 10 B—K2, B—K3; Black has a satisfactory game.

8 R—B1	B—Kt2
9 P×P	P×P
10 B—K2	Kt—B3
11 Castles	R—B1
12 P—KR3	P—KR3
13 Q—R4	P—R3

The Q side is evidently Black's weak point.

14 Kt—K5	Kt×Kt
15 B×Kt	Kt—Q2
16 B×B	

On positional grounds this move is open to question. White's QB was much more effective than Black's KB. Moreover, White's efforts are clearly centred on the Q side, and, as the exchange in the text solves all K side problems, Black can now concentrate on redressing the balance on the Q side. One would have expected 16 B—Kt3, contributing to the pressure on the Q side.

16	K×B
17 R—B2	P—K3
18 Q—Kt4	Kt—Kt1
19 KR—B1	Kt—B3
20 Q—R3	Q—K2

Black has managed to get a satisfactory position, but he now shows a pacifism which will bring its own retribution. By playing 20 .... P—QKt4; 21 Kt—Kt1, Q—R4; he could have established a lasting equality.

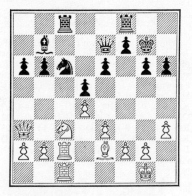

21 Kt—R4
An excellent move! If now 21 .... P—QKt4; 22 Q×Q, Kt×Q; 23 Kt—B5, Black has no adequate reply. If 21 .... Q—Q1; 22 B×P, wins.

21	Q×Q
22 P×Q	P—QKt4
23 Kt—Kt6	

Now better than 23 Kt—B5, Kt—R4; 24 Kt×B, R×R; 25 R×R, Kt×Kt; 26 R—B7, R—QKt1; and Black can hold out.

| 23 ...... | R—B2 |
| 24 P—QR4 | P×P |

He cannot play 24 .... P—Kt5; 25 B×P, B×B; 26 R×Kt.

25 Kt×RP
His threat is 26 Kt—B5, winning the RP.

25 ......   KR—B1
In order to prevent 26 Kt—B5. If, for instance, 25 .... R—QR1; 26 Kt—B5, Kt—Q1; 27 Kt×P ch, Kt×Kt; 28 R×R, Kt×R; 29 R×Kt, White wins a valuable pawn.

| 26 Kt—Kt6 | R—QKt1 |
| 27 P—QR4 | |

Undue precipitancy here would have untoward consequences, e.g. 27 B×P, B×B; 28 R×Kt, R×R; 29 R×R, B—Kt4; 30 R—Q6, K—B1; 31 Kt—Q7 ch, B×Kt; 32 R×B, R—Kt8 ch; 33 K—R2, R—Kt7; and Black has established equality. After the text-move, however, the threat B×P, is real and unanswerable.

| 27 ...... | R—Q1 |
| 28 B×P | |

Q.E.D.! The fight for Black's QRP during the last five moves has been dramatic.

28	B×B
29 R×Kt	R×R
30 R×R	R—QKt1
31 P—R5	R—Kt2

This will cost a second pawn, but at least the Rook will get into play.

32 Kt×P	R—Kt8 ch
33 K—R2	B—Q6
34 R—Kt6	R—R8

Not 34 .... P×Kt; 35 R×R, B×R; 36 P—R6, and the pawn queens!

35 Kt—Kt4	B—B5
36 P—R6	P—B4
37 R—B6	B—Kt6
38 R—B7 ch	K—B3
39 P—R7	P—Kt4

Black puts up a desperate defence, which, however, is of no avail against his opponent's consummate technical skill.

40 Kt—B6   Resigns
Because of the threat, 41 Kt—K5, P—Kt5; 42 P—R4, with an unavoidable mate by R—B7.

84

G. KRAMER — NAJDORF
(New York, 1948–9)

There are some players whose vivid temperaments appear to infuse their forces with dynamic life. This is illustrated in the following beautiful game, in which Najdorf's pawns and Knights execute lightning manœuvres.

1 P—Q4	Kt—KB3
2 P—QB4	P—KKt3
3 Kt—QB3	P—Q4
4 Q—Kt3	

The *Amsterdam Attack* which was tried out in the Euwe–Alekhine *match*, 1935. The move is intended to prevent the consolidation of Black's centre, but it was found that the better and more rational course is first 4 Kt—B3, B—Kt2; and only then 5 Q—Kt3.

4	P×P

Against the passive 4 .... P—B3; White can continue his co-ordinated development with 5 Kt—B3, or 5 B—B4, or even the quiet 5 P—K3. Too peaceful is the exchange, 5 P×P.

5 Q×BP	B—Kt2

Full of pitfalls is the continuation .... B—K3; as in Sokor–Volck, *Leningrad*, about 1938: 6 Q—Kt5 ch (risky. Preferable is 6 Q—Q3, followed by P—K4), 6 .... Kt—B3; 7 Kt—B3, Kt—Q4; 8 Q×P (the Queen cannot afford to capture the QKtP in this variation. Best is 8 P—K4, Kt—Kt5; 9 Q—R4, B—Q2; 10 Q—Q1), 8 ... Kt(Q4)—Kt5 (Black already threatens to win the Queen by 9 .... R—QKt1; to say nothing of the exchange by 9 .... Kt—B7 ch); 9 B—B4, B—R3; 10 B×P, Kt×QP; 11 B×Q, Kt(Q5)—B7 ch; 12 K—Q1, R×B ch; 13 Kt—Q5, B×Kt; 14 Q—B7, B×Kt dis ch; 15 Q×R ch, K×Q; 16 KP×B, K—B2; White resigns. He loses the Rook, for if 17 QR—Kt1, R—Q1 ch; 18 K—K2, R—Q7 mate. Black's play is a dazzling exhibition of combinative skill.

6 Kt—B3	Castles

Black is well-advised to complete his development unperturbed rather than to attack the Queen, which seems to offer a tempting target.

7 P—K4	

The further course of the game presents a striking example of modern methods.

White has a splendid centre, but the modernist looks upon such a centre as an appropriate target, and once it is disrupted the disrupter obtains much scope for attacking play. This style, however, demands the utmost accuracy.

7	Kt—R3

The first "modern" move, developing the Knight on the ill-famed R file. The object, however, is to attack the centre with 8 .... P—B4; which White cannot safely prevent, e.g. 8 P—QKt4, B—K3; 9 P—Q5, Kt×KP; 10 Q×KKt, B×Kt ch, etc., or 10 Kt×Kt, B×P; followed by .... B×R. Against Smyslov's move, 7 .... B—Kt5; the following can be recommended: 8 B—K3, KKt—Q2; 9 Kt—KKt5. The most solid continuation for Black is 7 .... P—B3; 8 Q—Kt3, P—QKt4; 9 B—K2, Q—R4; etc. In a game, Kmoch–Prins, *Amsterdam*, 1940, 7 .... P—Kt3; was played with a tragi-comic ending as follows: 8 P—K5, B—K3; 9 P×Kt, B×Q; 10 P×B, K×P; 11 B×B, Kt—B3; 12 B—K3, Kt—Kt5; 13 Castles KR, Kt—B7; 14 QR—Q1, Kt×B; 15 P×Kt, P—QB4; 16 Kt—KKt5, P—K3; 17 R×Pch; Black resigns.

8 B—K2	

If 8 B—K3, or Q—R4, Black plays 8 .... P—B4.

8	P—B4
9 Castles	P×P
10 R—Q1	

An artificial plan which gives Black the opportunity for a brilliant reply. Best is 10 Kt×P. Against 10 .... Kt×P; White has the counter-surprise, 11 Kt—B6.

10	P—K4

Thanks to this deflecting manœuvre Black is able to maintain his advanced pawn.

11 Kt×KP	Kt—Q2

Another stratagem full of subtlety.

12 Kt×Kt	B×Kt

By clever manœuvring, Black has established his passed pawn and White is definitely on the defensive.

13 Kt—Q5	R—B1
14 Q—Kt3	Kt—B4

Note how smoothly Black has brought all his forces into play.

15 Q—QR3	R—K1
16 P—B3	P—B4
17 Q×P	P×P

18 P×P	Kt×P
19 B—B3	B—QB3
20 Kt—Kt4	

White no doubt thinks that he has surmounted his difficulties and his position can
easily be re-established by Kt×B. Black's
apparent threat to win the Queen is inoperative, e.g. 20 .... R—R1; 21 Kt×B, Q—B2;
22 Kt—K7 ch, Q×Kt; 23 Q—Kt6. But
Black had the following combination in
mind long before the present position
arose.

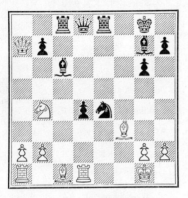

20	Kt—B7

Superlative play, as will be seen from the
following variations:

21 K×Kt, Q—R5 ch; 22 K—B1,
B—Kt4 ch; followed by 23 .... R—K8 ch.

If 21 K×Kt, Q—R5 ch; 22 P—Kt3,
Q×RP ch; 23 K—B1, B×B; 24 R—Q2,
R—K8 ch; 25 K×R, Q—Kt8 mate. There
are other variations, all of them equally
forcible.

21 Kt×B	Kt×R

With the threat of mate at K8.

22 B—Q2	P×Kt
23 R×Kt	P—Q6
24 Q—R6	Q—Q5 ch
25 K—R1	Q×P

The combinative play is not yet over.
If now 26 Q×QP, QR—Q1; 27 Q—B4 ch,
K—R1; 28 Q—B4, R×B; 29 Q×R, Q×Q;
30 R×Q, R—K8 mate. Of course, Black,
with the exchange and two passed pawns,
has an easy win. The rest needs no
comment.

26 Q—B4 ch	K—R1
27 P—KR3	P—B4
28 P—QR4	Q—Q5
29 Q×Q	B×Q
30 B—KKt4	R—B2

31 B—QR5	R—B2
32 B—Kt6	R—B7
33 P—R5	P—Q7
34 K—R2	R—K8
35 K—Kt3	R×R
Resigns	

(If 36 B×R, R—B8.)
A remarkable game.

Pseudo-Grünfeld

85

FAIRHURST   RHODES
(Felixstowe, 1949)

*It is difficult to be brief when describing
Mr. Fairhurst's style. Is it the constant
search for new situations, for unknown
schemes and tensions as yet untested? Is it
his creative spirit which has enabled him to
enrich the theory of the openings by fertile
and energetic ideas (e.g. his highly individual-
istic treatment of the defence against the
Colle System)? In one word, is it his
constructiveness? Were Mr. Fairhurst not
an engineer already, he should become one.*

1 P—Q4	Kt—KB3
2 P—QB4	P—KKt3
3 P—KKt3	

The panacea of modernist chess.

3	B—Kt2

If Black intends to play .... P—Q4; as in
the *Grünfeld Defence* proper (3 Kt—QB3,
P—Q4); he can equally play it at this stage.
He can also prepare it by 3 .... P—B3;
4 B—Kt2, P—Q4.

4 B—Kt2	P—Q4

This *Pseudo-Grünfeld*, after White has
developed his KB in *fianchetto*, looks risky,
but is nevertheless gaining adherents.

5 P×P	Kt×P
6 Kt—KB3	

Better than at once 6 P—K4, for after the
text-move Black may in the meantime
commit himself to some less favourable
course, as indeed happens in this game.

6	Castles
7 Castles	P—QB4

The Southport expert also is fond of
experiments and disregards the solid 7 ....
P—QB3. An alternative is 7 .... Kt—Kt3.

8 P—K4	Kt—Kt3

The retreat, 8 .... Kt—KB3; would
expose him to an immediate attack:

9 P—K5, Kt—Q4; 10 Q—K2, Kt—QB3;
11 P×P, and White has a dominating
position.

9 P—Q5
Instead of the text-move, White can
safely play 9 P×P, Q×Q; 10 R×Q, but the
complications conjured up by the text-move
suit his style.

9 ......   P—K3
10 B—Kt5
A fine provocative manœuvre, thanks to
which White succeeds in mobilising his
forces, as it were, under fire.

10 ......   P—B3
11 B—K3   Kt—R3
If, instead, 11 .... P×P; there follows
12 B×P, P×P; 13 B×R, Q×Q; 14 R×Q,
K×B; 15 Kt—Q4, with advantage to White.

12 Kt—B3   P×P
Or 12 .... Kt—B5; 13 B—B1, P—K4;
14 Kt—QKt5, B—Q2; 15 P—QR4, Q—Kt3;
16 P—Kt3, Kt—R4; 17 R—K1, and White
has the better game.

13 P×P   R—K1
14 Kt—Q2
A masterly move which provokes a
further weakening of Black's position by
.... P—B4. Now Black's game collapses
in an astonishingly short space of time.

14 ......   P—B4
15 Q—Kt3   K—R1
16 KR—Q1   B—Q2
17 P—QR4
White multiplies his threats: hereafter the
white pieces fall into place as smoothly as
the pieces of a jigsaw puzzle nearing completion.

17 ......   Q—Kt1
He cannot allow the white Queen to
capture the QKtP. The alternative, 17 ....
Q—B1; loses the Knight after 18 P—R5.

18 P—R5   Kt—B1

Within immediate reach of comparative
safety by 19 .... Kt—Q3!

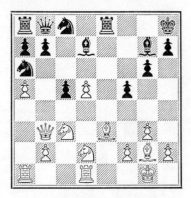

19 Kt—B4
The right move at the right time—that
is the secret of success. On a full board,
Black is now practically in *Zugzwang*.

19 ......   P—QKt4
In view of the threat 20 B—B4, Black
makes a desperate effort to free his game.

20 P×P e.p.   P×P
21 B—B4   Q—R2
22 Kt—Kt5   Q—Kt2
If 22 .... B×Kt; 23 Q×B, R—Q1;
24 P—Q6, and Black has no defence.

23 P—Q6   R—K5
An *"appeasement" sacrifice.* If 23 ....
B—QB3; 24 P—Q7.

24 B×R   P×B
25 Kt—K5
Threatening 26 Kt—B7 ch, and mate in
two. Of course, 25 .... KB×Kt; leads to
mate on the move.

25 ......   P—R3
26 Q—B7   Resigns
A masterpiece both in the preparation for
the attack and in its flawless and powerful
execution.

32. QUEEN'S INDIAN DEFENCE

86

EUWE　　　　　　**KERES**

(Rotterdam, 1940)

No one who studies the following game will accuse us of fulsomeness if we render homage to the extreme elegance with which mind triumphs over matter.

1 P—Q4	Kt—KB3
2 P—QB4	P—K3
3 Kt—KB3	P—QKt3
4 P—KKt3	

The modern continuation.

| 4 ...... | B—Kt2 |
| 5 B—Kt2 | B—K2 |

The simplest; Black preserves his forces for the defence. 5 .... B—Kt5 ch; does nothing towards freeing his game; while, after the more imaginative 5 .... P—B4; White exercises a lasting pressure after 6 P—Q5, P×P; 7 Kt—R4, etc.

| 6 Castles | Castles |
| 7 Kt—B3 | Kt—K5 |

Sämisch's manœuvre, which prevents White's intended occupation of the centre, say after 7 .... P—Q3; by 8 Q—B2, followed by P—K4.

8 Q—B2

A sound, but too simplifying continuation is 8 Kt×Kt, B×Kt; 9 Kt—K1, B×B; 10 Kt×B, etc.

| 8 ...... | Kt×Kt |
| 9 Q×Kt | |

More imaginative, but also more binding is 9 P×Kt.

| 9 ...... | P—Q3 |
| 10 Q—B2 | P—KB4 |

Tactically, he has to avoid the well-known trap, 11 Kt—Kt5, etc., while strategically he must prevent White's expansion by P—K4.

| 11 Kt—K1 | Q—B1 |

A battle of *imponderabilia*, in which accurate timing to a fraction is essential. If 11 .... B×B; 12 Kt×B, Q—B1; 13 Kt—B4, some difficulties would ensue for Black.

12 P—K4

The turning point. The drawbacks of the move are not easy to foresee. Steadier is the completion of his development by 12 P—Kt3, followed by B—Kt2, and QR—Q1.

| 12 ...... | Kt—Q2 |
| 13 P—Q5 | |

White refrains from exchanging 13 P×P, P×P; as he hopes to exploit Black's weakness at K6.

| 13 ...... | BP×P |
| 14 Q×P | |

If 14 B×P, Kt—B3.

| 14 ...... | Kt—B4 |
| 15 Q—K2 | B—KB3 |

Parrying the threat, 16 P—QKt4.

| 16 B—R3 | R—K1 |
| 17 B—K3 | |

If 17 P—QKt4, not 17 .... B×R; 18 P×Kt, etc., but 17 .... P×P. Now the threat 18 B×Kt, seems to crown White's honest endeavours.

| 17 ...... | Q—Q1 |
| 18 B×Kt | |

Dr. Euwe, the great logician, does not believe in miracles and expects only the normal reply 18 .... QP×B; when 19 B×P ch, K—R1; 20 Kt—Q3, etc., secures for him a comfortable advantage.

| 18 ...... | P×B |

Abruptly reversing the rôles. If now 19 B—K3, P—Q5; 20 B—Kt2, B×B; 21 Kt×B, P×B; 22 Kt×P, B—Q5; 23 Q—Q2, B×Kt; 24 P×B, it is White and not Black who carries the burden of a weak KP.

| 19 B—K6 ch | K—R1 |
| 20 R—Q1 | |

White must give back the piece, for if 20 B—QR3, Q—K2.

| 20 ...... | QP×B |
| 21 Kt—Kt2 | |

Or 21 P×P, QB×P; 22 R×B, Q—K2; etc., and again Black has things his own way.

| 21 ...... | P—Q5 |
| 22 P—B4 | |

A necessary reinforcement in view of the threat 22 .... B—B1. White thus hopes to maintain his advanced post at K6 as a compensation for his lost pawn, e.g. 22 .... Q—Q3; 23 P—B5, Q—B3; 24 P—KR4, QR—Q1; 25 R—Q3, etc.

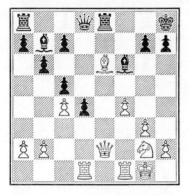

22	P—Q6

The black forces spring into action.

23 R×P	Q×R

Few players, anywhere or at any time, would have even thought of a conception such as this.

24 Q×Q	B—Q5 ch

An important intermediary check.

25 R—B2
After 25 K—R1, R×B; 26 P—KR4, QR—K1; etc., White is just one move too late to avoid ultimate loss.

25	R×B
26 K—B1	QR—K1
27 P—B5	

Attempted salvation. If 27 R—Q2, B—K5; 28 Q—R3, B—B4; with .... B—R6; in view.

27	R—K4
28 P—B6	P×P
29 R—Q2	

Clearly not 29 R×P, B×Kt ch; 30 K×B, R—K7 ch.

29	B—B1

A decisive regrouping. Threat: 30 .... B—R6; followed by .... R—K8 mate.

30 Kt—B4	R—K6
31 Q—Kt1	R—B6 ch
32 K—Kt2	R×Kt

A superb conception. Thanks to the mobility of his Rooks, Keres is able to assert the superiority of his Bishops over the hostile Queen.

33 P×R	R—Kt1 ch
34 K—B3	B—Kt5 ch
Resigns	

For after 35 K—K4, R—K1 ch; 36 K—Q3, B—B4 mate, or 36 K—Q5, B—B6 ch; followed by mate. A game of great artistry.

87

HOROWITZ   DENKER
(U.S.A. Championship, 1947)

The unwavering manner in which White gradually gains space, to wind up in fortissimo *style, deserves all praise.*

1 P—Q4	Kt—KB3
2 P—QB4	

After 2 Kt—KB3, an immediate *fianchetto* by 2 .... P—QKt3; can well be played, while, after the text-move, 2 .... P—QKt3; ("*Wild West*" *Indian*) would be rash because of 3 Kt—QB3, B—Kt2; 4 P—Q5.

2	P—K3
3 Kt—KB3	P—QKt3
4 P—KKt3	

The duel between the two opposed Bishops is engaged. Unreasonable, and causing the loss of precious time, is 4 P—QR3, to prevent a possible check. This is illustrated in a curious little game, Nürnberg—Dr. Rödl, *Riedenburg*, 1947: 4 P—QR3, B—Kt2; 5 Kt—B3, Kt—K5; 6 Q—B2, Kt×Kt; 7 Q×Kt, B—K2; 8 B—B4, B—KB3; 9 Q—Q2, P—Q3; 10 P—K3, Kt—Q2; 11 B—K2 (White appears to have made eleven perfectly natural moves and yet he is already lost), 11 .... P—KKt4; White resigns, for after 12 B—Kt3, P—Kt5; 13 Kt—Kt1, B×KtP; his game is ruined. The finish is unexpected, amusing and—not unmerited.

4	B—Kt2
5 B—Kt2	B—Kt5 ch

With a view to simplification.

6 QKt—Q2
More scientific is 6 B—Q2, B×B ch; 7 Q×B, followed by Kt—B3, and White has a sound position and a hold on the centre.

6	Kt—K5

A pointless sally in view of Black's lack of development. It will result only in the exchange of his developed pieces, with improved chances for White. 6 .... Castles; soon followed by .... P—Q4; is the correct continuation.

7 Castles	Kt×Kt
8 B×Kt	B×B
9 Q×B	Castles
10 Q—B2	

Bringing about a variation of the famous *Monticelli trap*, e.g. 10 .... P—Q3 (or even 10 .... P—KR3); 11 Kt—Kt5, Q×Kt; 12 B×B, winning the exchange.

10	Kt—B3
11 QR—Q1	P—Q3

Now 11 .... P—Q4; is no longer adequate, because, after 12 P×P, P×P; 13 R—B1, White controls the QB file and Black's QBP is backward.

12 P—Q5	P×P

Black is compelled to exchange, because after 12 .... Kt—Kt1; 13 P×P, P×P; 14 Kt—Kt5, White wins. We see here an opening trap worth remembering in this type of position.

13 P×P	Kt—Kt5
14 Q—B4	P—QR4
15 P—QR3	Kt—R3

If 15 .... B—R3; 16 Q—Kt3, B×P; 17 P×Kt, winning two pieces for Rook and pawn.

16 P—QKt4	Q—Q2
17 R—Q4	

A strong move which centralises the Rook and provides against .... Q—R5.

17	KR—K1
18 P—K3	P×P
19 P×P	P—QKt4
20 Q—Q3	B—B1

Black has no satisfactory reply. He cannot eliminate his backward pawn by 20 .... P—QB4; on account of 21 P×P e.p., Q×P; 22 R×P.

21 R—B1	R—Kt1
22 R—KB4	Q—Q1
23 P—R4	P—R3
24 Q—B3	B—Q2
25 R—R1	Q—B1
26 K—R2	R—Kt3
27 Kt—Q4	Kt—Kt1
28 R—QB1	Q—R3

A last fling. If 29 Q×P, R—QB1; and White loses the Queen.

29 P—Kt4	B—B1

If 29 .... R—QB1; the deflection of all the black forces becomes still more marked.

30 Q×P	R—Kt2
31 Q—B3	Kt—Q2

Making as quickly as possible for the K side, but it momentarily encumbers his second rank.

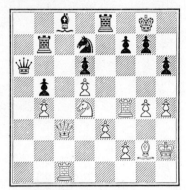

32 Q×B	

Brilliant and decisive.

32	R×Q
33 R×R ch	Kt—B1

If 33 .... K—R2; 34 B—K4 ch, P—B4 (34 .... P—Kt3; 35 R×P mate); 35 R×P, etc.

34 Kt—K6	

A beautiful point, supplementing the preceding sacrifice.

34	P—Kt3
35 R×Kt ch	K—R2
36 R(B4)×P ch	R×R
37 R×R ch	K—R1
38 B—K4	Q—R8
39 B×P	Resigns

An excellent win by Horowitz.

88

	O'KELLY
PIRC	DE GALWAY

(Amsterdam, 1950)

Some victories can be described as overpoweringly aggressive, others methodical, others again as combinative. The following fine game is remarkable in that it does not belong to any one of these types, but combines all their characteristics.

1 Kt—KB3	Kt—KB3
2 P—Q4	P—QKt3

In this sequence of moves, a very good continuation, in which Black seeks to secure the early control of his K4. 2 .... P—K3; is in the nature of a waiting move; reserving a choice of continuations, e.g. 3 P—B4, P—QKt3 (*Queen's Indian*); or 3 P—B4, P—Q4 (*Queen's Gambit Declined*).

3 P—K3

With this move White begins to develop his game on the lines of the *Colle System.* When openings get intermingled in this manner it is easy for one side or the other to go wrong.

3 ......   B—Kt2
4 B—Q3

As the *Colle System* is based on the ultimate advance, P—K4, which square Black endeavours to control in the *Queen's Indian,* this clash of systems is particularly interesting.

4 ......   P—B4
5 Castles   P—K3
6 QKt—Q2   Kt—B3
7 P—B3

And here is the famous *Colle Triangle.* Other attempts have had little success, e.g. 7 P—QR3, or 7 P—B4, or 7 P—QKt3, followed by B—Kt2, or at once 7 P×P, P×P; etc.

7 ......   Q—B2

Black is experimenting, but goes astray. If he wishes to remain within the *Indian* complex, he can continue with 7 .... R—B1; or without any finessing 7 .... B—K2. The simplest is 7 .... P—Q4; whereby he obtains the normal formation against the *Colle System.*

8 P—QR3

Premature would be the thematic advance, 8 P—K4, P×P; 9 P×P, Kt—QKt5.

8 ......   P×P

Here again he could and should play 8 .... P—Q4. The move chosen by Black prevents White's P—K4, but, on the other hand, he opens the white Queen's Bishop's diagonal.

9 KP×P   B—K2
10 R—K1   Kt—Q4

The Knight is making for KB5, but this attempt to force an attack at all costs is clearly unpositional.

11 Kt—B4   Kt—B5

The last move in a plan which never looked right. It is true that 11 .... Castles QR; 12 QKt—K5, Kt×Kt; 13 Kt×Kt, QR—B1; 14 P—B4, etc., would be rash. On the other hand, 11 .... Castles KR; would be tantamount to entering the lion's den.

The most rational therefore is 11 .... P—Q3; but it would be an admission that Black's strategy (7 .... Q—B2), and especially the preceding move (10 .... Kt—Q4), followed the wrong course.

12 B×Kt   Q×B

The exchange B×Kt, has probably taken Black by surprise, as White thereby is deprived of the advantage of the "two Bishops."

The black Queen's vulnerable position offers ample compensation.

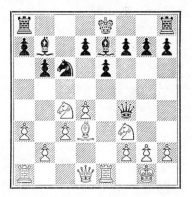

13 P—Q5

A powerful move. After 13 .... P×P; 14 QKt—K5, White commands the open file and Black is exposed to similar dangers as in the game.

13 ......   Kt—Q1
14 Kt(B4)—K5   P—QR3

He must prevent 15 B—Kt5, which would be decisive, e.g. if 14 .... B×QP; 15 B—Kt5, Castles; 16 Kt×QP, R—K1; 17 Kt×P, wins the exchange.

15 P—KKt3   Q—R3

If 15 .... Q—B3; 16 Kt—Kt4, and the Queen has no move.

16 Kt—Kt4   Q—R4
17 Kt(B3)—K5

The interplay of the Knights is pretty. He now threatens 18 Kt—B6 ch, winning the Queen.

17 ......   P—Kt3
18 B—K2

Restoring the threat.

18 ......   Q—B4
19 P—Q6   Resigns

The main threat is 19 .... B—KB1; 20 B—Q3, Q—Kt4; 21 P—KB4, and Black has the choice of Charybdis or Scylla, losing the Queen or being mated (21 .... Q—R4; 22 Kt—B6 mate). On the other hand, if 19 .... B—KB3; 20 B—Q3, is equally forcible.

33. NIMZO-INDIAN DEFENCE

89

CAPABLANCA   **MIKENAS**
(Buenos Aires, 1939)

The 1939 Olympiad was Capablanca's noble swan-song, for he had the best result on Board I, ahead of his perennial rival, Alekhine. In the following game we find the same lucid, energetic and elegant style which distinguished the play of his halcyon days.

1 P—Q4	Kt—KB3
2 P—QB4	P—K3
3 Kt—QB3	B—Kt5
4 Q—B2	

It is not surprising that, of a number of possible lines of play, Capablanca should choose the Capablanca continuation.

4	Kt—B3

The *Milner-Barry Variation* (akin to the *Zürich Variation* 4 Q—Kt3, Kt—B3), a constructive line of play, which tries to establish a bridge-head in the middle of the board after .... P—Q3; .... Q—K2; eventually .... R—K1; and finally .... P—K4.

5 Kt—B3	P—Q4

A scheme elaborated by masters of the U.S.S.R. and which is claimed to be as viable as the usual 5 .... P—Q3.

6 P—QR3
Capablanca upholds his principle, whether with White or with Black, not to allow the pinning Bishop to remain unchallenged for any length of time. Playable also is, first 6 P—K3, Castles; and then only 7 P—QR3.

6	B × Kt ch
7 Q × B	P—QR4

Against a noncommittal move, such as 7 .... Castles; White could already secure an additional trump by 8 P—QKt4, with possible action on the Q side.

8 P—QKt3
A necessary measure to prevent the blockade of his own Q side by 8 .... P—R5.

8	Castles
9 B—Kt5	P—R3
10 B × Kt	

Again "real Capablanca." He has no fear of simplifications, provided they enable him to gain time.

10	Q × B
11 P—K3	B—Q2
12 B—Q3	

To all appearance the contest is following a peaceable course.

12	KR—B1

There is here an indication of a possible counter-offensive on the Q side. Perhaps Black hopes to provoke 13 P—B5, which would put an end to the tension in the centre. This would allow Black to re-transfer the centre of gravity to his K4 after 13 .... R—K1; threatening 14 .... P—K4.

13 Castles KR
With an almost Olympic serenity, Capablanca allows his fretful adversary to go his own way. The psychological advantage of the great Cuban's waiting policy frequently consisted in the fact that his opponents, left without the guidance of direct threats, lost their way in the labyrinth of numerous possibilities.

13	P—R5

If Black remains passive, White, who has completed his mobilisation, will go over to the attack in the centre by P—K4.

14 P—QKt4	P × P
15 B × P	Kt—R2

More natural would seem 15 .... Kt—K2; but then 16 Kt—K5, B—K1; 17 P—Kt5, would seriously impede Black's plans.

16 Kt—K5	B—K1
17 P—B4	P—QKt3
18 Q—Q3	

An unostentatious but all the more effective manœuvre. It seems, in the first place, to be directed against Black's Kt—Kt4—Q3. It can also help a re-grouping by Q—K4 and B—Q3. And yet, the real threat is quite different.

18	R—Q1

Black has lost his bearings, but still hopes to carry out his illusory intention, ... P—QB4. However, 18 .... P—Kt3; would seriously weaken his King's field.

Best is 18 .... Kt—B3; trying to clear up the position and, in any event, bringing back a useful piece into the zone of battle.

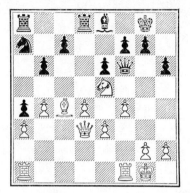

19 P—B5
The ice-breaker. White's object is to eliminate the obstacle of Black's KP, while bringing the KB file to life.

19 ......   P—QKt4
A desperate counter-measure, played perhaps in the hope of 20 B—R2, Q × Kt; and Black wins.

20 P × P
An elegant turn.

20 ......   P × B
21 R × Q   P × Q
22 P × P ch   B × P
Black must give back the piece and remains with a pawn minority.

23 R × B   Kt—Kt4
24 R—B2   R—Q4
Or 24 .... R—K1; 25 R—Q2, etc.

25 Kt × P
This gain of a second pawn, foreseen on White's twentieth move, settles the issue.

25 ......   R—K1
A last hope: 26 R—K2, R × QP.

26 R—B3   Resigns

90
KERES   BOTVINNIK
(Leningrad, 1941)

Frequently the circumstances surrounding a game of chess are quite as interesting as the game itself.

In the following contest, Keres selected on his eighth move a novelty (Castles QR) with which his opponent, Botvinnik, had been taken by surprise the previous year. It was an unfortunate choice, for Botvinnik played a far more energetic continuation and won handsomely.

And the moral of this tale: you cannot catch a great player twice with the same artifice.

Botvinnik, as did his predecessor, Alekhine, constantly tries to improve his game. Capablanca, however, preferred to rely on his intuition, while Lasker thought that his rationalism rendered him immune from the surprises of chess theory.

1 P—Q4   Kt—KB3
2 P—QB4   P—K3
3 Kt—QB3   B—Kt5
4 Q—B2   P—Q4
Peremptorily preventing the advance P—K4, but the text-move leaves him no elasticity in the centre.

5 P × P   P × P
6 B—Kt5
The game now has the characteristics of the orthodox *Queen's Gambit Declined, Exchange Variation*. A quiet line is 6 P—K3, Castles; 7 B—Q3, P—QKt3; 8 Kt—K2, etc. A well-founded positional continuation is 6 P—QR3, B × Kt ch; 7 P × B, etc.

6 ......   P—KR3
Forcing White to an immediate decision.

7 B—R4
More cautious is 7 B × Kt, Q × B; 8 P—QR3, B × Kt ch; 9 Q × B, and the contest levels off.

7 ......   P—B4
Keeping an eye on the K side, he becomes active on the Q side. But he must not show too much zeal with 7 .... P—KKt4; 8 B—Kt3, Kt—K5; 9 P—B3, Kt × B; 10 P × Kt, when White's game gains in scope on the K side.

8 Castles
Original but risky.

8 ......   B × Kt
An important exchange! Having been taken by surprise in his game against Mikenas in the preceding U.S.S.R. Championship in 1940, by White castling on the Q side, when he replied with less precision 8 .... Castles; Botvinnik on this occasion elaborates a more efficacious counter-action.

9 Q × B   P—KKt4
10 B—Kt3   P × P

He has no hesitation in opening the sluice-gates.

11	Q×P	Kt—B3
12	Q—QR4	B—B4
13	P—K3	R—QB1

He refrains from looking after his own King (13 .... Castles) but rushes matters on the Q side.

14 B—Q3   Q—Q2

Already decisive, as the QB file springs to life.

15	K—Kt1	B×B ch
16	R×B	Q—B4
17	P—K4	

It is clear that neither 17 K—B2, Castles; 18 K—Q2, Kt—K5 ch; 19 K—K2, Kt—B4; etc., nor 17 Q—R3, Kt—QKt5; can save White.

17 ......   Kt×P
18 K—R1   Castles

Making a graceful exit.

19 R—Q1

White appears to have consolidated his position, since his King has escaped persecution and his back rank is again guarded.

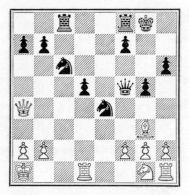

19 ......   P—Kt4

A *deflecting sacrifice.*

20 Q×KtP

Against 20 Q—R3, Black still plays 20 .... Kt—Q5.

20 ......   Kt—Q5
21 Q—Q3   Kt—B7 ch
22 K—Kt1

If now 22 .... Kt×B; 23 RP×Kt,

White is saved. But Black has a withering reply at his disposal.

22 ......   Kt—Kt5
Resigns

91

B. H. WOOD   P. DEVOS
(Soest-Baarn, 1948)

In the following game, the British Master falls a victim to a "theoretical variation"—in other words, a variant derived from previous analysis.

This in no way detracts from the merit of his opponent, who, in this contest, displays as much imagination as analytical power. On the whole, a game which is a credit to both players.

1	P—Q4	Kt—KB3
2	P—QB4	P—K3
3	Kt—QB3	B—Kt5
4	Q—B2	P—Q4
5	P—QR3	

This dogmatic continuation leads to more incisive play than 5 P×P.

5	......	B×Kt ch
6	Q×B	Kt—K5
7	Q—B2	P—QB4

Black must hasten to disturb the centre, for, if quietly, 7 .... Castles; 8 P—K3, followed by 9 B—Q3, White's chances are already improving.

Another attempt which caused much analytical ink to flow is here 7 .... Kt—QB3; followed by 8 .... P—K4. This is the *San Remo Variation,* which is full of the unexpected.

8 QP×P   Kt—QB3

This pawn sacrifice helps to accelerate Black's mobilisation. If, however, 8 .... Kt×QBP; 9 P—QKt4, Kt—K5; 10 B—Kt2, P—QKt3; 11 P—Kt3, P—B4; 12 B—Kt2, etc.

9 P×P

Not 9 P—QKt4, because of 9 .... Q—B3. More peaceful continuations are 9 P—K3, Q—R4 ch; 10 B—Q2, Kt×B; 11 Q×Kt, or 9 Kt—B3, Q—R4 ch; 10 B—Q2, Kt×B; 11 Q×Kt, etc.

9 ......   P×P
10 Kt—B3

The threat to maintain his "plus" on the Q side by 11 P—QKt4, has now become real.

10 ......   B—B4

The Bishop, set free by his opponent's ninth move, appears on the battlefield and Black threatens 11 .... Kt—Kt6. Less ambitious is 10 .... Q—R4 ch; 11 B—Q2, Q×BP; and, although Black has recovered his pawn, the end-game would be in White's favour after 12 Q×Q, Kt×Q; 13 P—K3, Kt—Kt6; 14 R—Q1, Kt×B; 15 R×Kt, etc.

11 P—QKt4

Sans peur, but perhaps not *sans reproche*.

11 ......   Castles

Black proves equal to the situation. Of little value would be 11 .... Kt—Kt6; because of 12 Q—Kt2, Kt×R; 13 Q×P, e.g. 13 .... KR—B1; 14 B—R6, Q—K2; 15 Q×R ch, Q×Q; 16 B×Q, K×B; 17 P—Kt3, followed by B—Kt2, winning the Knight, or 13 .... K—Q2; 14 Q×P ch, Kt—K2; 15 B—Kt5, with a winning attack.

Interesting also is 11 .... P—Q5 (threat in earnest: 12 .... Kt—Kt6); 12 Q—Kt2, Q—B3; 13 P—K3, Castles QR; with equal chances.

12 B—Kt2

He continues his development with a pistol pointed at his head.

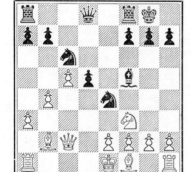

12 ......   P—Q5

A serious emergency.

A memorable game, Euwe–Najdorf, *Mar del Plata*, 1947, went 12 .... Kt—Kt6; 13 Q—B3, P—Q5; 14 Kt×P, Kt×Kt; 15 BP×Kt, Kt—B7 ch.

13 Q—B4

The optimism of Mr. Wood—who has, by his eleventh move braved so many dangers—is a happy trait in his temperament, but at times leads to disaster.

13 ......   R—K1
14 Kt×P

Better is, in any case, 14 B×P. Taking the innocent pawn is too precipitate, and more cautious is 14 R—Q1, although even then Black has dangerous threats as long as the white King remains exposed in the centre.

14 ......   Q—B3

Without a moment's delay the black forces overrun the terrain and multiply their threats. First and foremost is the threat 15 .... Kt×KBP.

15 R—R2

Perhaps the least evil. If, e.g., 15 P—B3, Q—R5 ch; 16 P—Kt3, Kt×KKtP; 17 P×Kt, Q×P ch; 18 K—Q2, QR—Q1; and wins. And if 15 Kt×B, Q×B; 16 R—Q1, Kt—B6; 17 Kt—K3, R×Kt; 18 P×R, Kt×R; 19 K×Kt, Q—Kt8 ch; 20 K—Q2, R—Q1 ch; 21 K—B3, R—Q8; 22 Q—Kt4, R—B8 ch; 23 K—Q2, Q—B7 mate.

15 ......   B—K3

Wrong now would be 15 .... Kt×KBP; because of 16 Kt×Kt.

16 Kt×B	Q×P ch
17 K—Q1	R×Kt
18 B—B3	

He tries to guard his three sickly squares QB2, K1 and Q4. After 18 B—B1, which guards two squares only, there follows—if nothing worse—18 .... R—Q1 ch; 19 K—B2, R—Q5; 20 Q—Kt5 (or 20 Q—Kt3, R×P; etc.), 20 .... R—Q7 ch; followed by .... Kt—Q5 ch; and .... Kt×Q.

| 18 ...... | R—Q1 ch |
| 19 K—B2 | Q—K6 |

The Belgian Master conducts the attack with deadly precision, preventing, above all, the emancipation of the white pieces.

20 P—KR4

A desperate attempt to bring his KR into the fray via R3.

20	R—Q7 ch
21 B×R	Q×B ch
22 K—Kt3	Kt—Q5 ch
23 K—R4	Q—Q8 ch
24 K—R5	R—R3 ch
25 Q×R	Q—R5 ch

A magnificent conception, in which Black gives up the whole of his artillery.

26 K×Q	Kt—B6 ch
27 K—R5	Kt—Kt6 mate

A pure mate is the climax of the combination.

92

BOTVINNIK   CAPABLANCA
(Avro, 1938)

In the following magnificent game, Botvinnik plays steadfastly for a win.

1 P—Q4	Kt—KB3
2 P—QB4	P—K3
3 Kt—QB3	B—Kt5
4 P—K3	

The *Rubinstein Variation*, which has become *la grande mode* since it has been linked with the *Sämisch Variation* (4 P—QR3), of which the object is to enforce P—K4.

4 ......   P—Q4

An unrestrained line of play is: 4 .... Castles; 5 Kt—K2, R—K1; 6 P—QR3, B—B1; keeping his KB for the defence of his interior lines.

Another continuation is 4 .... P—B4; 5 P—QR3, B×Kt ch; 6 P×B, etc., reverting to the *Sämisch Variation*. An original attempt by Black to avoid these dangers is seen in a game, Geller–Golombek, *Budapest*, 1952: 4 .... P—B4; 5 P—QR3, P×P; 6 P×B, P×Kt; 7 Kt—B3, P×P; 8 B×P, P—Q4; 9 P—B5, P—QKt3; 10 B—Kt5 ch, B—Q2; 11 B×B ch, KKt×B; 12 Q—B2, Kt—QB3; 13 B×P, Kt×KtP; 14 Q—Kt1, R—KKt1; 15 P—B6, Kt×P; 16 Q×RP, Kt—B3 (a miraculous salvation!); 17 B×Kt, Q×B; 18 Q×P ch, K—Q2; 19 Kt—K5 ch, Kt×Kt; 20 Q×R, Kt—B6 ch; 21 P×Kt, Q×R ch; 22 K—K2, Q—R7 ch; drawn by perpetual check.

5 P—QR3	B×Kt ch
6 P×B	P—B4
7 BP×P	KP×P
8 B—Q3	Castles
9 Kt—K2	

More flexible than 9 Kt—B3.

9 ......   P—QKt3

10 Castles

A reasoned continuation at this point is Mme. Chaudé's idea, 10 P—QR4.

10 ......   B—R3

Capablanca, the simplifier.

11 B×B	Kt×B
12 B—Kt2	

Botvinnik is a severe critic of his own play. He was the first to find fault with the lack of precision shown by the text-move. According to him, he should at once play 12 Q—Q3, inducing 12 .... Q—B1; with a more modest role for the black Queen than in the game.

12 ......   Q—Q2

The Cuban at once seizes the opportunity of giving his game greater elasticity.

13 P—QR4

Of course, now, if 13 Q—Q3, Q—R5.

13 ......   KR—K1

But here 13 .... P×P; 14 BP×P, KR—B1; is more effective.

14 Q—Q3   P—B5

He pays too much attention to the Q side and too little to the repercussions which are bound to occur in the centre.

15 Q—B2   Kt—Kt1

Starting on a long but promising journey.

16 QR—K1	Kt—B3
17 Kt—Kt3	Kt—QR4
18 P—B3	Kt—Kt6
19 P—K4	Q×P

Each player has achieved his object: Black has his pawn; White will have his attack.

20 P—K5	Kt—Q2
21 Q—B2	P—Kt3
22 P—B4	P—B4

Trying to stop the onset of White's KBP.

23 P×P e.p.	Kt×BP
24 P—B5	R×R
25 R×R	R—K1
26 R—K6	R×R
27 P×R	K—Kt2
28 Q—B4	

The crisis draws near. White's Queen has secured two important files in the absence of the opposing Queen. The white QRP was the bait which drew the enemy forces away.

28 ......   Q—K1

A return ticket.

29 Q—K5   Q—K2

The Queen is back again—a short-lived satisfaction.

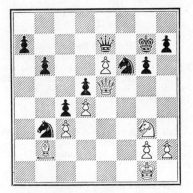

30 B—R3

A sacrificial combination of unusual beauty. It has a multiple function. Not only will the black Queen again be cut off from the critical zone, but the passed pawn will become mobile.

30 ......   Q×B

Compulsory, for if 30 .... Q—K1; 31 Q—B7 ch, K—Kt1; 32 B—K7, Kt—Kt5; 33 Q—Q7, etc., or 30 .... Q—Q1; 31 B—Q6, etc. Black accepts the sacrifice the more willingly, as he himself has a serious threat after, say, 31 P—K7, by 31 .... Q—B8 ch; 32 Kt—B1, Kt—Q7.

31 Kt—R5 ch

The point of the point. The first sacrifice was made in order to make this complementary sacrifice possible.

31 ......   P×Kt

If 31 .... K—R3; 32 Kt×Kt, Q—B8 ch; 33 K—B2, Q—Q7 ch; 34 K—Kt3, Q×BP ch; 35 K—R4, Q×P ch; 36 Kt—Kt4, with a counter-check.

32 Q—Kt5 ch   K—B1
33 Q×Kt ch

Luckily with check, so that Black obtains no breathing space.

33 ......   K—Kt1

Or 33 .... K—K1; 34 Q—B7 ch, and mate to follow.

34 P—K7

With a concurrent threat of mate. Now begins a long series of counter-checks by Black. That in the end these would become exhausted needed exact calculation on the part of White.

34 ......   Q—B8 ch

35 K—B2   Q—B7 ch
36 K—Kt3   Q—Q6 ch
37 K—R4   Q—K5 ch
38 K×P

A necessary pause, to put a stop to the perpetual check. If 38 K—Kt5, Q—K6 ch.

38 ......   Q—K7 ch

There is no salvation: 38 .... Q—Kt3 ch; 39 Q×Q ch, P×Q ch; 40 K×P, and the white pawn queens.

39 K—R4   Q—K5 ch
40 P—Kt4   Q—K8 ch
41 K—R5   Resigns

A memorable game.

93

LILIENTHAL   NAJDORF

(Saltsjöbaden, 1948)

The following most artistic game has also a considerable theoretical value. It constitutes an impressive link in the turbulent life, the greatness and decadence, of a curious variation.

1 P—Q4   Kt—KB3
2 P—QB4   P—K3
3 Kt—QB3   B—Kt5
4 P—QR3

In spite of its anti-positional appearance, the *Sämisch Variation* has many adherents among contemporary masters.

4 ......   B×Kt ch
5 P×B   P—B4

This reply in the *Sicilian* manner leads to lively exchanges. A fairly resistant structure results from 5 .... Castles: with the possible continuation: 6 P—B3, Kt—R4; 7 Kt—R3, P—KB4; 8 P—K4, P×P; 9 B—Kt5, Q—K1; 10 P×P, P—K4; with chances for both sides.

6 P—K3

This position can also occur in the *Rubinstein Variation*. Less consistent is the "Sämisch plan" proper: 6 P—B3, because of 6 .... P—Q4; 7 P—K3, Castles; 8 BP×P, Kt×P; 9 B—Q2, Kt—QB3; and Black secures the initiative.

6 ......   Kt—B3

He has in view an early action on the Q side, comprising the moves .... P—QKt3; .... B—R3; .... Kt—QR4; the object being to exploit the weakness of White's pawns on the QB file. Good also is 6 .... Castles; 7 B—Q3, Kt—B3; etc. The more

incisive 6 .... P—Q4; is doubtful on
account of 7 BP×P, KP×P; 8 B—Q3,
Castles; 9 Kt—K2, etc. The most circum-
spect is, at once, 6 .... P—QKt3; 7 B—Q3,
B—Kt2; 8 P—B3, Kt—B3; etc.

7 B—Q3   P—QKt3

It is clear that the moves .... Castles,
.... P—Q3; .... P—QKt3; are part of this
defensive system, but it is important to play
them in the correct order. 7 .... Castles;
fulfils more closely the requirements of the
situation.

Another interesting plan was tried in a
game Szabó–Keres, *Budapest*, 1950: 7 ....
P—K4; 8 Kt—K2, P—Q3; 9 Castles
(9 P—K4, Kt—KR4), 9 .... Q—K2
(9 .... Castles; 10 P—K4, Kt—KR4;
11 B—K3, P—QKt3; 12 P—B4, with a
dynamic advantage to White); 10 P—K4,
Kt—Q2; 11 P—B4, P—QKt3; 12 Kt—Kt3,
P—Kt3; etc.

8 Kt—K2   Castles
9 P—K4

White quite rightly hastens to make this
thematic advance, which threatens, not only
10 P—K5, but also 10 B—Kt5. Note also
that White has succeeded in carrying out his
primary plan without having recourse to
the supporting P—B3. Good, but dilatory,
is 9 Castles. Too slow is 9 Kt—Kt3,
B—R3; 10 B—Kt2, R—B1; for then Black's
action on the Q side anticipates White's
attack in the centre.

9 ......   Kt—K1

An important decision. By this manœuvre, retrograde, preventive and elastic,
Black evades both the threats mentioned
above, and now has the possibility to play
.... P—B4; in reply to P—B4, digging
himself in on the K side, after which he can
concentrate his efforts on the weak points in
White's Queen's wing. This beautiful idea
is due to the great Capablanca, who applied
it in a similar position against P. Johner,
Carlsbad, 1929.

10 Castles   P—Q3

As long as this move is not yet necessary,
a more assertive line of play is 10 ....
B—R3.

11 P—K5

Intrepid play! Very good too is 11 P—B4,
P—B4 (not 11 .... B—R3; 12 P—B5);
12 P—Q5, Kt—R4; 13 QP×P, B×P;
14 P×P, B—B2; etc.

11 ......   QP×P

More resistent is 11 .... B—Kt2

12 P×KP   B—Kt2

A terrible blunder would be 12 ....
Kt×P; 13 B×P ch, followed by 14 Q×Q.
But a defensive position could be built up
by 12 .... B—R3; 13 B—B4, Kt—R4;
14 Q—B2, P—Kt3.

13 B—B4   P—B4

This restless counter-measure is based on
tactical considerations, but will fail against
tactical surprises. More cautious is 13 ....
P—Kt3.

14 P×P e.p.   P—K4

Too dogmatic. He should make the best
of 14 .... Kt×P; although, other things
being equal, the weakness of Black's KP would
then give White some definite advantage.

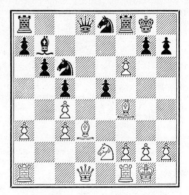

15 P×P

A combination of which the manifold
features will become apparent later.

15 ......   R×B
16 Kt×R   P×Kt
17 B×P ch

This additional sacrifice illustrates clearly
the danger of depriving the King of his
natural defenders.

17 ......   K×B

If 17 .... K×P; 18 Q—R5, Q—B3;
19 QR—Q1, B—B1; 20 Q×Kt, K×B;
21 R—Q5, etc.

18 Q—R5 ch   K×P
19 QR—Q1   Q—B3

If 19 .... Q—B2; 20 Q—Kt4 ch, followed by R—Q7, and if 19 .... Q—B1;
20 KR—K1, Kt—B3; 21 Q—Kt5 ch,
K—B2; 22 R—Q6. It is seen that Black is

unable to prevent the triumphal irruption of the hostile Rooks.

20	R—Q7 ch	K—B1
21	R×B	Kt—Q1
22	R—Q7	Kt—KB2
23	Q—Q5	R—Kt1

Although the material is more or less equal, Black must succumb because his forces lack co-ordination. He cannot play 23 .... R—Q1; 24 R×Kt ch, followed by Q×R.

| 24 | R—K1 | P—B6 |

A last attempt in view of the threat, 25 R—K6, Q—Kt2 (25 .... Q×P; 26 QR×Kt ch, K×R; 27 R—K3 dis ch); 26 KR—K7, etc. If 24 .... Kt—Kt2; 25 R×Kt ch, Q×R; 26 Q—Q6 ch, followed by Q×R ch. Again, if 24 .... Kt—Kt4; 25 R—K5.

| 25 | R—K3 | Resigns |

For if 25 .... Q—Kt3; 26 QR×Kt ch, Q×R; 27 R×P, Kt—B3; 28 Q—Q6 ch, followed by Q×R. And if 25 .... Kt(K1)—Q3; 26 R×BP, Q—Kt3; 27 R×Kt, etc.

Thus we have seen, in this game, the *history of an idea* (9 .... Kt—K1) with its ups and downs in turn for one or other of the players.

34. CATALAN SYSTEM

94

ALEKHINE   BOGOLJUBOW
(Exhibition Game, Warsaw, 1943)

The following is one of the many incomparable games which Alekhine has bequeathed to the world.

1 P—Q4	P—Q4
2 P—QB4	P—K3
3 Kt—KB3	Kt—KB3
4 P—KKt3	

The *Catalan Gambit*, which, properly speaking, is the *Grünfeld Defence* with a move in hand.

4 ......   P×P

Bringing about the schema of the *Queen's Gambit*. Against the rather slow *Catalan System*, the text-move is quite satisfactory for Black, provided that he can solve the problem of the development of his QB. The drawback to an early .... P×P; in the *Queen's Gambit*—namely, that White can retake with the KB, gaining time and following up with a strong advance in the centre—does not apply here. On the other hand Black is exposed to danger on the long white diagonal, and, with correct play, advantage and drawback should cancel each other out.

5 Q—R4 ch

It is clear that White must not play with fire and delay the recovery of his pawn. Against 5 B—Kt2, P—QR3; can be recommended.

In a game Veitch–J. Penrose, *Buxton*, 1950, White played 5 QKt—Q2, which led to the following harrowing finish: 5 .... P—B4; 6 P×P (he has nothing better than 6 Q—R4 ch, recovering his pawn), 6 .... B×P; 7 B—Kt2 (this plausible move, strangely enough, spells instant downfall), 7 .... B×P ch; 8 K×B, Kt—Kt5 ch; 9 K—K1 (9 K—Kt1, Q—Kt3 ch; leads to mate), 9 .... Kt—K6; White resigns. After 10 Q—R4 ch, B—Q2; the Queen has no move!

5 ......   Q—Q2

Although Black will force the exchange of Queens by this manœuvre, he remains with the problem of the development of his QB

unsolved, and this ultimately will cost him the game.

Too passive is 5 .... P—B3. 5 .... B—Q2; was played in a game, Lundin–Benkö, *Bad Gastein*, 1948: 6 Q×BP, B—B3; 7 B—Kt2, QKt—Q2; 8 Castles, B—Q4; 9 Q—Q3, B—K5; 10 Q—K3, P—B4; 11 Kt—B3, B—B3; 12 R—Q1, Q—Kt3; 13 P—Q5, B—Kt4; 14 P×P, P×P; 15 Kt×B, Q×Kt; 16 Q×P ch, B—K2; 17 Kt—Kt5, Black resigns (17 .... R—KB1; 18 B—B4, etc.).

The most active continuation is 5 .... QKt—Q2.

6 Q×BP	Q—B3
7 QKt—Q2	Q×Q
8 Kt×Q	B—Kt5 ch
9 B—Q2	B×B ch
10 QKt×B	

If 10 KKt×B, Kt—B3; 11 Kt—B3, Kt—QKt5; and Black has good counterchances. After the text-move, White has three advantages: (*1*) The open Q file; (*2*) the diagonal KR1—QR8, and (*3*) the weakness of the opposing Bishop. Bogoljubow attempts too venturesome a solution: it will be seen with what result.

10	Kt—B3
11 B—Kt2	B—Q2
12 Castles KR	Castles QR

This is the overbold attempt. The correct method is 12 .... Castles KR; followed by .... KR—Q1; .... QR—B1; and .... B—K1; after which Black's position, although difficult, should be tenable.

13 QR—B1	KR—K1
14 Kt—B4	

Preventing .... P—K4; and threatening 15 Kt(B3)—K5, R—B1; 16 Kt×Kt, B×Kt; 17 B×B, P×B; 18 P—K3, followed by Kt—K5, or Kt—R5, winning the pawn on Black's QB3.

14	R—K2
15 P—QR3	

The beginning of the decisive Q side advance.

15	B—K1
16 KR—Q1	Kt—Q4
17 P—QKt4	Kt—Kt3

Better is 17 .... P—QR3; but it leaves

a bad weakness at Black's QB4, on which square White can later establish a Knight.

18 P—Kt5   Kt—Kt1

If 18 .... Kt×Kt; 19 P×Kt, Kt×P; 20 P×P ch, K×P; 21 Kt—K5 dis ch, K—B1; 22 Kt—B6, B×Kt; 23 B×B, R—Q3; 24 R—B3, followed by R—R1, winning the Knight.

19 Kt×Kt ch   RP×Kt
20 P—QR4   P—KB3
21 B—R3   B—Q2

Now at last it looks as if Black will be able to free himself by .... P—K4; but "when one sups with the Devil, one needs a long spoon."

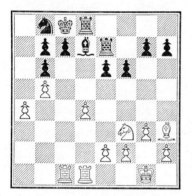

22 Kt—Q2

A devastating surprise, threatening Kt—B4, followed by Kt—Q6, or Kt×P mate—and if 22 .... P—K4; 23 Kt—B4, B×B; then 24 Kt×P is still mate.

22 ......   R—B1
23 B—Kt2

Preventing Black from escaping by .... K—Q1; and threatening to win the QKtP by Kt—B4.

23 ......   P—B3
24 Kt—B4   K—B2
25 P—K4   P×P

This loses quickly, but Black is defenceless against the threat of 26 P—Q5, KP×P; 27 KP×P, P×QP (otherwise 28 P—Q6 ch); 28 B×P, followed by Kt—R5 dis ch, and Kt×P ch.

26 P×P   B×P

Hoping, after 27 Kt—R3 dis ch, B—B3; 28 P—Q5, R—Q2; to have some slight chance with the two passed Q side pawns. But White plays so as to force the exchange of pawns in the centre first, which allows his Bishop to take part in the attack with decisive effect.

27 P—Q5   P×P
28 Kt—R3 dis ch   B—B3
29 P×P   R—Q2
30 Kt—Kt5 ch   K—Q1
31 P×B   P×P
32 Kt—Q4   Resigns

Black loses the QBP, since he must guard against Kt—K6 ch, and his game is therefore past hope.

Strategically and tactically a masterly game.

The notes to the above game are largely those by C. H. O'D Alexander in his excellent book, *Alekhine's Best Games, 1938–45.*

35. BUDAPEST DEFENCE

95
GOLOMBEK — BISGUIER
(Southsea, 1950)

Black, in the following game, handicaps himself by adopting a variation of doubtful value, a handicap which even his great talent does not enable him to overcome against a player known for his skill in demolishing "variations."

It is said that an ounce of common sense can outweigh a ton of "variations."

1 P—Q4	Kt—KB3
2 P—QB4	P—K4
3 P × P	Kt—K5

The *Fajarowicz Variation*, which contains subtle threats, but is hardly as sound as the usual 3 .... Kt—Kt5. Let us illustrate the normal line of play by two miniature games. Donovan–Bisguier, *Detroit*, 1950: 3 .... Kt—Kt5; 4 Kt—KB3, Kt—QB3; 5 P—QR3, P—Q3; 6 P—K3, B—B4; 7 P × P, B × P; 8 B—K2, Q—B3; 9 Kt—Q4, Kt × BP; 10 K × Kt, B—B7 dis ch; 11 Kt—B3, B × Q; 12 R × B, Kt—K4; 13 Kt—Q2, Kt—Kt5 ch; 14 K—Kt1, B × P ch; White resigns.

Whyte–M. Davis, *Hastings*, 1951-2: 3 .... Kt—Kt5; 4 P—K4, P—Q3 (in gambit style. If 4 .... Kt × KP; 5 P—B4 is playable, or as recommended by Fine, 5 B—K2, followed by Kt—KB3); 5 P × P, B × P; 6 B—K2, P—KB4; 7 B × Kt (much better is 7 P × P, as played by Capablanca *v.* Tartakower, *Bad Kissingen*, 1928), 7 .... P × B; 8 Q—Q5, Kt—B3; 9 P—QR3, Kt—Q5 (a remarkable move. If 10 Q × Kt, B—Kt5 ch; wins the Queen. The real threat is 10 .... B—K3; 11 Q—R5 ch, P—Kt3; 12 Q—R6, Kt—B7 ch; 13 K—B1 or 13 K—K2, B—B5; 14 B × B, B × P mate, or 13 .... B—B5; 14 B × B, Q—Q8 mate); 10 P—B5, B—K2; 11 K—B1, B—K3; 12 Q × Q ch, R × Q; 13 Kt—QB3, B—B5 ch, White resigns. If 14 K—K1, Kt—B7 mate, and if 14 KKt—K2, Kt × Kt; 15 Kt × Kt, R—Q8 mate. A memorable little game.

4 Kt—KB3	Kt—QB3
5 QKt—Q2	Kt—B4
6 P—KKt3	P—Q3
7 P × P	Q × P

Clearly with the intention to castle on the Queen's side, the wisdom of which is questionable, when White is developing his KB at Kt2. Preferable is 7 .... B × P.

8 B—Kt2	B—B4
9 P—QR3	P—QR4
10 Castles	Castles

He burns his bridges. Less ambitious, but safer, is 10 .... R—Q1.

11 P—QKt4

With fine positional judgment White gives up a pawn with the sole purpose of obtaining control of the open QR file—in connection with the long white diagonal, an important asset.

11	P × P
12 P × P	Kt × P
13 R—R8 ch	K—Q2
14 R × R ch	K × R
15 B—Kt2	P—KB3
16 Kt—Q4	B—Q2
17 Kt—K4	

Although, normally, the defender benefits by exchanges, the maxim does not hold good when the attacker can thereby lessen the number of his opponent's developed pieces.

17	Kt × Kt
18 B × Kt	B—R6
19 R—K1	P—QB4

White threatened 20 Q—Kt3, followed by 21 R—Q1, or, alternatively, 21 P—B5.

20 Kt—B5	Q × Q
21 R × Q ch	K—B2
22 B—B1	Kt—B3
23 B—B4 ch	Kt—K4
24 R—Kt1	B × Kt

He cannot play 24 .... P—QKt3; because, after 25 R—R1, his position is wide open.

25 B × B	B—Q3

He could obtain Bishops of opposite colours, but it would not help. According to Mr. Golombek's own analysis, after 25 .... P—KKt4; 26 B × Kt ch, P × B; 27 B—K4, P—Kt3; 28 R—R1, B—Q3; 29 R—R7 ch, K—B1; 30 B × P, White has a simple win.

26 B—K4	P—QKt3
27 B—Q5	P—KKt4
28 B—Q2	Kt—B3
29 R—R1	B—K4
30 R—R2	

Restricting the black Bishop's mobility.

30 ......   R—QKt1

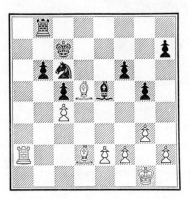

31 P—B4

A new actor enters the scene.

31	P × P
32 P × P	B—Q3
33 P—K3	P—Kt4
34 R—R6	R—Kt3

Better is 34 .... Kt—Kt5; when, again as demonstrated by Mr. Golombek himself, the win would take longer after 35 R—R7 ch,

K—Kt3; 36 R—Q7, B—B2; 37 B—K6, and White has penetrated into Black's position.

The rest is an object lesson in the handling of the "two Bishops" in an ending.

35 P × P	R × R
36 P × R	K—Kt3
37 K—B2	Kt—Kt5
38 B—B4	Kt × P
39 K—B3	Kt—B2
40 K—K4	B—K2
41 K—B5	K—B3
42 P—K4	Kt—Kt4
43 K—K6	B—Q1
44 B—Q5 ch	K—Kt3
45 K—Q7	B—B2
46 K—K7	Kt—Q5
47 K × P	Kt—B6
48 B—B1	Kt × P
49 P—K5	Kt—Kt5 ch
50 K—B5	P—R4
51 B—B3	Kt—B7
52 B × P	Kt—Q6
53 B—K3	K—B3
54 K—K4	P—B5
55 B—K8 ch	K—Kt2
56 B—Kt5	Resigns

The best game in the tournament which fully deserves the frequently misused adjectives: strictly logical, and positionally sound and powerful.

36. ENGLISH OPENING

96

TARTAKOWER   LOTHAR SCHMID
(Southsea, 1950)

The most instructive feature in the following bitter contest is the manner in which preparations are made "behind the front."

1 P—QB4	P—K4

An active reply.

2 Kt—QB3	Kt—KB3
3 Kt—B3	Kt—B3
4 P—K4	

Nimzowitsch's move in the *English Four Knights'*. The incisive continuation, 4 P—Q4, is met by 4 .... P×P; 5 Kt×P, B—Kt5; etc., but 4 P—K3, is better than its reputation.

4	B—Kt5

Better than 4 .... P—Q3; which should not be played early, unless White himself refrains from advancing the QP to Q4.

5 P—Q3	P—Q3
6 B—K2	

Nimzowitsch tried also 6 P—KKt3, followed by B—Kt2.

6	P—KR3

Is this precaution really necessary? In a game Fine–Dake, *Mexico City*, 1935: 6 .... Castles; 7 Castles, B×Kt; 8 P×B, Q—K2; 9 Kt—K1, Kt—K1; 10 Kt—B2, P—B4; led to equality.

7 P—KR3	Q—K2
8 Castles	Castles
9 B—K3	

There is nothing to be gained by 9 Kt—Q5, Kt×Kt; 10 BP×Kt, Kt—Q1; which locks up the centre, while leaving Black sufficient freedom of action.

9	B×Kt
10 P×B	Kt—Q2
11 P—Kt4	

Directed against the threatened .... P—B4.

11	Kt—B4
12 Q—Q2	P—KKt4

In preparation for .... Kt—K3.

13 K—Kt2	P—B3
14 R—R1	K—Kt2

A well-conceived manœuvre, anticipating White's onslaught on the KR file.

15 R—R2	B—Q2
16 QR—R1	R—R1
17 Kt—K1	

It is a case of strengthening the KP by P—B3 in order to enforce the central P—Q4.

17	Kt—K3
18 P—KR4	QR—KKt1

Black's defence is very skilful.

19 P×P	RP×P
20 P—B3	Q—Q1

He vacates his K2 for the benefit of his QKt, and provides additional support for his KR1.

21 P—Q4	

A thematic advance.

21	Kt—K2
22 R×R	

Slightly premature. After so much preparatory manœuvring "behind the front," White should have continued with 22 Kt—Q3.

22	R×R
23 R×R	K×R

Not, of course, 23 .... Q×R; when Black loses his QB or his KKtP after 24 P×P.

24 P—B5	P×QP
25 P(B3)×P	P—Q4

Ingenious. If now 26 P×P, Kt×P(Q4); 27 Kt—B2, Kt(K3)—B5 ch; Black would exchange both the white Bishops and would at least draw. Weak, however, would be 25 .... P×P; because of 26 P—Q5.

26 Kt—Q3	B—B3

An active defence.

27 P—K5	Kt—Kt3
28 P×P	Q×P
29 K—B2	

So far, Black has refused to be intimidated, and has succeeded in counteracting all White's attempts at a break-through.

This is why White has here recourse to an astute waiting move, improving his King's position in view of coming events.

29 ......   Kt(K3)—B5

The desire to mask the weakness of his KKtP is understandable. A painful blunder would be 29 .... Kt×QP; 30 Q—B3 (or Q—Kt2), and Black loses the Knight. If 29 .... K—Kt2; to guard the Queen, White gains space by 30 Kt—Kt4. If 29 .... B—Kt4; White has a small positional advantage, as in the game, after 30 Kt—K5, B×B; 31 Kt×Kt ch, Q×Kt; 32 K×B, etc.

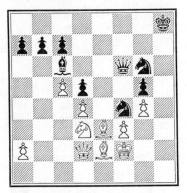

30 Kt—K5

A fight for squares. Of course 30 Kt×Kt, would lose a Bishop, and 30 B×Kt, P×B; would win for Black. The text-move is a fine counter which turns the tables.

30 ......   Kt×Kt

Plausible but fatal. Weak too would be 30 .... Kt×B; 31 B×P. The best defence is 30 .... B—K1; when 31 B—B1, would maintain the tension.

31 P×Kt   Q—R3

Clearly not 31 .... Q×P; 32 B—Q4, and wins.

32 B×Kt   P×B
33 Q—Q4

Centralisation *in excelsis.*

33 ......   K—Kt1

If 33 .... Q—R5 ch; 34 K—Kt2, Q—Kt6 ch; 35 K—B1, and the white King escapes.

34 K—Kt2

Decisive, Black's pieces are tied to the defence of his weak pawns, White has command of the terrain.

34	K—B2
35 B—Q3	K—K2
36 B—B5	B—K1
37 P—K6	

Rash would be 37 Q×QP, because of 37 .... Q—R3.

| 37 ...... | B—Kt3 |
| 38 Q×QP | Resigns |

97

| DENKER | RABAR |
| (*U.S.A.*) | (*Jugoslavia*) |

(Radio Match, 1950)

In the following game we see a quadruple fianchetto, but the course of events is neither monotonous nor symmetrical. Black early on loses control of his Q4, which leads to further difficulties.

| 1 P—QB4 | Kt—KB3 |
| 2 Kt—KB3 | P—B4 |

There are openings, such as the *Four Knights'*, where Black can safely imitate White's first moves, but the *English Opening* is not one of them. Better is 2 .... P—KKt3; leading into some variation of the *King's Indian Defence.*

3 P—Q4

Opening a central file and assuming control of his Q4.

| 3 ...... | P×P |
| 4 Kt×P | P—KKt3 |

Better here, or even on the next move, is .... P—Q4.

| 5 Kt—QB3 | B—Kt2 |
| 6 P—KKt3 | |

A surprising move, he could increase his hold on the centre by 6 P—K4.

6 ......   Castles

He misses his last chance of having a say in the centre by 6 .... P—Q4.

| 7 B—Kt2 | Kt—B3 |
| 8 Castles | |

Another good continuation, which avoids exchanges is 8 Kt—B3.

8	Kt×Kt
9 Q×Kt	P—Q3
10 Q—Q2	

Although the black Knight has no useful discovery, White shows rare judgment in retiring the Queen to the unlikely square Q2. The point is that the white QB will

be more effective at Kt2 than on its present
diagonal, and after P—Kt3, the Knight will
require protection.

10	......	Q—B2
11	P—Kt3	B—Q2
12	B—Kt2	B—B3
13	P—K4	

After all, he can play P—K4, with great
effect. Black's only counter-chance, which
he misses, is a diversion on the Q side by
13 .... P—QR4. He leaves this until the
twenty-fifth move, when it is no longer
effective.

13	......	P—Kt3
14	P—B4	QR—Q1

Black already lacks space for manœuvring,
which is why it is difficult to suggest anything better. If 14 .... P—K3; 15 Kt—Kt5,
and wins after 15 .... B×Kt; 16 P—K5.

15	QR—K1	Kt—Q2
16	R—B2	

A discreet preparation for the doubling of
Rooks.

16	......	Kt—B4
17	Kt—Q5	

The sword of Damocles falls.

17	......	B×Kt

Now he has no option, for after 17 ....
Q—Kt2; there follows 18 P—QKt4, Kt—K3;
19 P—KB5, Kt—B2; 20 Kt×P ch, K—R1;
21 Q—R6, B×B; 22 P×P, P×P;
23 R×R ch, etc.

18	B×B	

The black King loses his most effective
defender.

18	......	K×B
19	KP×B	QR—K1
20	KR—K2	

It is clear that White's complete mastery
of the K file constitutes a winning advantage,
the only remaining interest being the skilful
way in which White deals with the situation.

20	......	P—B3

Out of the frying-pan into the fire. Now
Black's weakened K3 becomes the target of
White's machinations.

21	P—KR4	Q—Q2

Preventing 22 B—R3.

22	P—QKt4	Kt—Kt2
23	K—R2	

Securing KR3 for the Bishop, and now
the black Queen must give way.

23	......	Q—B2
24	Q—Q4	R—B2
25	B—R3	P—QR4

Long overdue.

26	P—R3	P×P
27	P×P	R—QR1

Paralysed in the centre, Black tries to make
up leeway on the Q side.

28	B—K6	R(B2)—B1
29	P—Kt4	K—R1
30	P—KKt5	R—R5
31	P×P	P×P

Recapturing with the Rook is equally
bad. After 32 B—R3, the K file is wide
open, as it is after the text-move.

32	B—R3	Q—Kt2
33	R—K7	R—R7 ch
34	K—Kt1	Q—R3

If 34 .... R—B2; 35 R—K8 ch, R—B1;
36 R(K1)—K7, Q—Kt1; 37 B—K6, R×R;
38 Q×P ch, etc.

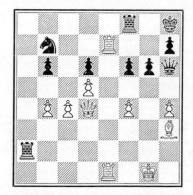

35 R—K8

The final assault. If 35 R×Kt, Q×RP;
36 Q—K3, R—R6; etc. Black can still put
up a defence.

35	......	Q×RP
36	R×R ch	K—Kt2
37	Q—K3	R—R6

A last trap: if 38 Q×R, Q×R ch; but—
White announces mate in four.
(38 Q—K7 ch, K—R3; 39 Q×P ch,
K×Q; 40 R—K7 ch, K—R3; 41 R—R8
mate.) A fine performance.

37. RÉTI-ZUKERTORT

98

HEBERGER   KUNERTH
(Weilheim, 1949)

The following game shows that the initiative is by no means the first player's exclusive and absolute prerogative.

1	Kt—KB3	Kt—KB3
2	P—KKt3	P—Q4
3	P—B4	P—B3
4	P—Kt3	P—KKt3
5	B—QKt2	B—Kt2
6	B—Kt2	Castles
7	Castles	P × P
8	P × P	B—K3
9	Q—B2	

So far, White has followed the *Réti System*, according to which he refrains from occupying the centre, but keeps it under observation and distant control by pieces. The ultimate object, however, is to occupy the centre at a time when it will be more effective than at the beginning. Here White misses the right moment, and when he does occupy the centre, it is as a defensive measure, which is fatal.

9	......	Q—B1
10	Kt—Kt5	

This is where White should have played 10 P—Q4, followed by QKt—Q2.

10	......	B—Q2
11	R—K1	P—KR3
12	Kt—KB3	B—R6
13	B—R1	

A well-known stratagem, which avoids the exchange of a valuable Bishop. But in this particular case it is not worth the time wasted. Now or never is the moment to develop the QKt.

13	......	QKt—Q2
14	P—Q3	

Even now 14 P—Q4, would give White a fair game.

14	......	R—K1
15	Kt—K5	Kt × Kt
16	B × Kt	Q—B4

Black takes over!

17	P—B4	Kt—Kt5
18	P—K4	

He occupies the centre several moves late; by his unruly seventeenth move (P—B4,

instead of the retreat, B—QB3), White has changed the positional character of the struggle.

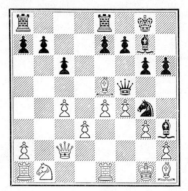

18	......	B × B

A brilliant offer of the Queen. If 19 P × Q, Black mates in three.

19	P × B	Q × P(K4)
20	Q—B3	QR—Q1
21	R—Q1	

If White exchanges Queens, he loses a second pawn in a hopeless position.

21	......	Q—B4 ch
22	P—Q4	P—K4

Very fine play, offering the Queen a second time. If 23 P × Q, Black mates in two.

23	Q—R3	R × P

Offering the Queen a third time. If 24 Q × Q, Black mates on the move. If 24 R—Q3, Black offers the Queen a fourth and final time with 24 .... R × R dis ch; White resigns.

The repeated offer of the Queen is very attractive and most unusual.

99

TARTAKOWER   A. R. B. THOMAS
(Southsea, 1951)

The following game is a magnificent illustration of the theme: "How to take advantage of your opponent's mistakes."

1 Kt—KB3   P—Q4
2 P—KKt3

This is often named the *Barcza Opening*. It is in reality an inversion of the *King's Indian Defence*. When, as in this game, White follows up with P—Q4, it could well be called the *Réti-Catalan*.

2 ......   Kt—KB3

An enterprising continuation, 2 .... B—B4; was successfully tried in a game, Dr. David–Dr. Balogh, *Budapest*, 1948: 2 .... B—B4; 3 B—Kt2, Kt—Q2; 4 P—B4, P—QB3; 5 P×P, P×P; 6 Q—Kt3 (plausible, but premature), 6 .... Kt—B4; 7 Q—Kt5 ch, B—Q2; 8 Q×Kt (essential is 8 Q—Kt4, P—K4; 9 Q—B3), 8 .... R—B1; White resigns.

3 B—Kt2   P—K3
4 Castles   P—B4

A bold use of the QBP. If 4 .... P—B3; 5 P—Q4, B—K2; 6 P—B4, Castles; 7 Kt—B3, White has some advantage in space.

5 P—Q4

The right moment for White to establish his rights in the centre.

5 ......   Kt—B3

The natural development. More artificial is 5 .... QKt—Q2; more vague, 5 .... P×P; 6 Kt×P, P—K4; while 5 .... B—K2; would lose time.

6 P—B4

Notwithstanding its risky appearance, this move is now necessary to disturb the centre and, if possible, to extend the range of the KB.

6 ......   QP×P

He disdains the defensive by 6 .... B—K2; and takes up the challenge.

7 Q—R4

Another sound plan is 7 Kt—K5 (Keres–Klein, *Anglo-Soviet Radio Match*, 1946).

7 ......   B—Q2
8 P×P

In order to gain an important *tempo*. Inoffensive would be, at once, 8 Q×BP, P×P; 9 Kt×P, R—B1; 10 Kt—QB3, Kt×Kt; 11 Q×Kt, B—B4; 12 Q—Q1, B—B3; with equality.

8 ......   B×P

Another idea is 8 .... Kt—QR4; 9 Q—B2, B×P; 10 Kt—K5, P—KR3; etc.

9 Q×BP   B—K2

A reasoned retreat. Neither 9 .... Q—Kt3; 10 Kt—B3, Kt—K2; 11 Kt—K5, nor 9 .... Q—K2; 10 B—Kt5, etc., is satisfactory.

10 Kt—B3   R—QB1

Or 10 .... Castles; 11 R—Q1, Q—R4; and Black evades the hostile pressure.

11 Q—KR4

Risky and not yet necessary. Better is 11 Q—Q3, or 11 P—K4, widening his command of space.

11 ......   Castles

Black is quite unconcerned and first completes his development.

12 P—K4

White underestimates the danger to his Queen, which, after this move and Black's reply, is cut off from the centre and the Q side. Playable, rather, is 12 R—Q1.

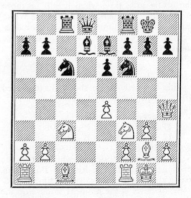

12 ......   P—K4

Bravo! At a stroke White's position has become tragic.

13 B—R3

This loses ingloriously. He should in any event try 13 R—Q1, or 13 B—Kt5, P—KR3; 14 B×Kt, B×B; 15 Q—R5.

13 ......   Kt—Q5

Excellent judgment. White expected 13 .... Kt—KKt5; at this point, when the Queen escapes after 14 Kt—KKt5, P—KR3; 15 B×Kt, P×Kt; 16 Q—R3.

14 Kt×P

If 14 Kt×Kt, Black wins an important pawn after 14 .... P×Kt; 15 Kt—K2, B×B; 16 Q×B, Kt×P.

14 ......   Kt—Kt5

The death sentence for the white Queen.

15	B×Kt	B×Q
16	Kt×B	P—B4
17	Kt×R	P×B
18	B—K3	

If 18 P×B, Q×P; 19 B—B4, R×QKt; 20 B—Kt3, R×B ch; 21 BP×R, Kt—K7 ch; 22 K—B2, Q×RP ch; etc.

18	......	Kt—B6 ch
19	K—R1	Q×Kt
20	P×B	Q—Q3
	Resigns	

Black has taken advantage of his opportunity in a masterly manner.

38. BIRD'S OPENING

100

GROB   Mme. CHAUDÉ
           DE SILANS

(Match, Zürich, 1951)

*Once again Mme. Chaudé de Silans shows
that she can provide worthy opposition for any
master.*

1 P—KB4   P—Q4

Allowing White to play the *Dutch Defence*
with a move in hand. Schlechter's plan is
considered more resistant: 1 .... Kt—KB3;
2 Kt—KB3, P—KKt3; followed by ....
B—Kt2. This, however, came to grief in a
game, H. Brown–Dr. Friedman, *London*,
1949, 3 P—K3, B—Kt2; 4 P—Q4, Castles;
5 QKt—Q2, P—Q4; 6 B—Q3, P—B4;
7 P—B3, Q—B2 (here Black should play
7 .... P—Kt3; and after .... B—Kt2; and
.... QKt—Q2; his position is entirely
satisfactory); 8 Castles, P×P; 9 KP×P,
Q×KBP (intending to return with her booty
to QB2); 10 Kt—Kt5, Q—K6 ch; 11 K—R1,
B—Kt5; 12 Kt(Q2)—B3, Black resigns. If
12 .... B×Kt; 13 R×B, the Queen is caught
in hostile territory. An intriguing little piece.

An important side line is the *From
Gambit*: 1 .... P—K4; 2 P×P, P—Q3;
3 P×P, B×P. Of this there is a forcible
example in a game, Krasner–Antonoff,
Paris, 1949: 2 P×P (or 2 P—K4, the *King's
Gambit*), 2 .... P—Q3; 3 P×P, B×P;
4 Kt—KB3, P—KKt4; 5 P—Q4, P—Kt5;
6 Kt—Kt5, P—KB4 (an abortive attempt to
capture the KKt in broad daylight);
7 P—K4, B—K2; 8 Kt—KR3, P×Kt;
9 Q—R5 ch, K—B1; 10 B—QB4, B—Kt5 ch,
11 P—B3, Q—K2; 12 Castles, P—Kt4;
13 B×Kt, K×B; 14 R—B3, Q×P;
15 R—Kt3 ch, K—B1; 16 B—R6 ch,
K—K2; 17 R—K3, Black resigns.

2 Kt—KB3   Kt—KB3
3 P—K3   P—K3
4 P—QKt3   P—B4
5 B—Kt2   Kt—B3
6 B—Kt5   B—Q2

Black has allowed her opponent to carry
out an *encircling strategy*, but refuses to allow
her pawns to be weakened (6 .... P—QR3;
7 B×Kt ch, P×B; 8 Kt—K5, etc.).

7 Castles   B—K2
8 P—Q3

This prevents .... Kt—K5; and prepares
for his own QKt—Q2, and an advance in the
centre.

8 ......   Castles
9 QKt—Q2   P—QR3
10 B×QKt   B×B
11 Q—K2

He spends too much time on preparations.
The move in keeping with the general situation is 11 Kt—K5.

11 ......   P—QKt4

Now Black not only preserves her QB,
but provides for it a promising field of
activity on the long diagonal.

12 K—R1   R—B1
13 P—KKt4

An ingenious pawn sacrifice. If now
13 .... Kt×P; 14 Kt—Kt5, B×Kt;
15 Q×Kt, White has a powerful attack.
Black, however, finds a strong counter,
which delays the capture.

13 ......   P—Q5

Strong play. If 14 P×P, P×P; Black's
pawn is safe, as the KKt is pinned. Black
then threatens 15 .... Kt×P; followed by
.... Kt—K6.

14 P—K4   Kt×KtP

Well-timed. Black must have seen
through the complications of the next
moves.

15 Kt × P	P × Kt
16 Q × Kt	P—B4

The key-move.

17 Q—K2	B—Kt5
18 QR—K1	B—Kt2

A threat to White's QBP.

19 Q—Q1	P × P
20 P × P	P—K4

The death-blow.

21 P—B5	Q—Kt4
22 R—B2	KR × P

23 R—Kt2	Q—R3
24 P × R	B × Kt

White has succeeded in warding off the first assault but now succumbs to the second.

25 R × P

A bad move in a lost position, but there is no saving clause. If 25 R—K2, B—K6; followed by .... R—B1.

25	B—B5
Resigns	

Mme. Chaudé de Silans played this game in exemplary fashion.

INDEX OF PLAYERS

Page numbers in italics refer to players of additional games quoted for reference

A CATALOGUE OF SELECTED DOVER BOOKS
IN ALL FIELDS OF INTEREST

A CATALOGUE OF SELECTED DOVER BOOKS
IN ALL FIELDS OF INTEREST

LEATHER TOOLING AND CARVING, Chris H. Groneman. One of few books concentrating on tooling and carving, with complete instructions and grid designs for 39 projects ranging from bookmarks to bags. 148 illustrations. 111pp. 7⅞ x 10.
23061-9 Pa. $2.50

THE CODEX NUTTALL, A PICTURE MANUSCRIPT FROM ANCIENT MEXICO, as first edited by Zelia Nuttall. Only inexpensive edition, in full color, of a pre-Columbian Mexican (Mixtec) book. 88 color plates show kings, gods, heroes, temples, sacrifices. New explanatory, historical introduction by Arthur G. Miller. 96pp. 11⅜ x 8½.
23168-2 Pa. $7.50

AMERICAN PRIMITIVE PAINTING, Jean Lipman. Classic collection of an enduring American tradition. 109 plates, 8 in full color—portraits, landscapes, Biblical and historical scenes, etc., showing family groups, farm life, and so on. 80pp. of lucid text. 8⅜ x 11¼.
22815-0 Pa. $5.00

WILL BRADLEY: HIS GRAPHIC ART, edited by Clarence P. Hornung. Striking collection of work by foremost practitioner of Art Nouveau in America: posters, cover designs, sample pages, advertisements, other illustrations. 97 plates, including 8 in full color and 19 in two colors. 97pp. 9⅜ x 12¼.
20701-3 Pa. $4.00
22120-2 Clothbd. $10.00

AN ATLAS OF ANATOMY FOR ARTISTS, Fritz Schider. Finest text, working book. Full text, plus anatomical illustrations; plates by great artists showing anatomy. 593 illustrations. 192pp. 7⅞ x 10¾.
20241-0 Clothbd. $6.95

THE GIBSON GIRL AND HER AMERICA, Charles Dana Gibson. 155 finest drawings of effervescent world of 1900-1910: the Gibson Girl and her loves, amusements, adventures, Mr. Pipp, etc. Selected by E. Gillon; introduction by Henry Pitz. 144pp. 8¼ x 11⅜.
21986-0 Pa. $3.50

STAINED GLASS CRAFT, J.A.F. Divine, G. Blachford. One of the very few books that tell the beginner exactly what he needs to know: planning cuts, making shapes, avoiding design weaknesses, fitting glass, etc. 93 illustrations. 115pp.
22812-6 Pa. $1.75

CREATIVE LITHOGRAPHY AND HOW TO DO IT, Grant Arnold. Lithography as art form: working directly on stone, transfer of drawings, lithotint, mezzotint, color printing; also metal plates. Detailed, thorough. 27 illustrations. 214pp.
21208-4 Pa. **$3.50**

DESIGN MOTIFS OF ANCIENT MEXICO, Jorge Enciso. Vigorous, powerful ceramic stamp impressions — Maya, Aztec, Toltec, Olmec. Serpents, gods, priests, dancers, etc. 153pp. 6⅛ x 9¼. 20084-1 Pa. **$2.50**

AMERICAN INDIAN DESIGN AND DECORATION, Leroy Appleton. Full text, plus more than 700 precise drawings of Inca, Maya, Aztec, Pueblo, Plains, NW Coast basketry, sculpture, painting, pottery, sand paintings, metal, etc. 4 plates in color. 279pp. 8⅜ x 11¼. 22704-9 Pa.**$5.00**

CHINESE LATTICE DESIGNS, Daniel S. Dye. Incredibly beautiful geometric designs: circles, voluted, simple dissections, etc. Inexhaustible source of ideas, motifs. 1239 illustrations. 469pp. 6⅛ x 9¼. 23096-1 Pa. **$5.00**

JAPANESE DESIGN MOTIFS, Matsuya Co. Mon, or heraldic designs. Over 4000 typical, beautiful designs: birds, animals, flowers, swords, fans, geometric; all beautifully stylized. 213pp. 11⅜ x 8¼. 22874-6 Pa. **$5.00**

PERSPECTIVE, Jan Vredeman de Vries. 73 perspective plates from 1604 edition; buildings, townscapes, stairways, fantastic scenes. Remarkable for beauty, surrealistic atmosphere; real eye-catchers. Introduction by Adolf Placzek. 74pp. 11⅜ x 8¼. 20186-4 Pa. $2.75

EARLY AMERICAN DESIGN MOTIFS. Suzanne E. Chapman. 497 motifs, designs, from painting on wood, ceramics, appliqué, glassware, samplers, metal work, etc. Florals, landscapes, birds and animals, geometrics, letters, etc. Inexhaustible. Enlarged edition. 138pp. 8⅜ x 11¼. 22985-8 Pa. $3.50
23084-8 Clothbd. $7.95

VICTORIAN STENCILS FOR DESIGN AND DECORATION, edited by E.V. Gillon, Jr. 113 wonderful ornate Victorian pieces from German sources; florals, geometrics; borders, corner pieces; bird motifs, etc. 64pp. 9⅜ x 12¼. 21995-X Pa. **$3.00**

ART NOUVEAU: AN ANTHOLOGY OF DESIGN AND ILLUSTRATION FROM THE STUDIO, edited by E.V. Gillon, Jr. Graphic arts: book jackets, posters, engravings, illustrations, decorations; Crane, Beardsley, Bradley and many others. Inexhaustible. 92pp. 8⅛ x 11. 22388-4 Pa. $2.50

ORIGINAL ART DECO DESIGNS, William Rowe. First-rate, highly imaginative modern Art Deco frames, borders, compositions, alphabets, florals, insectals, Wurlitzer-types, etc. Much finest modern Art Deco. 80 plates, 8 in color. 8⅜ x 11¼. 22567-4 Pa. $3.50

HANDBOOK OF DESIGNS AND DEVICES, Clarence P. Hornung. Over 1800 basic geometric designs based on circle, triangle, square, scroll, cross, etc. Largest such collection in existence. 261pp. 20125-2 Pa. $2.75

150 MASTERPIECES OF DRAWING, edited by Anthony Toney. 150 plates, early 15th century to end of 18th century; Rembrandt, Michelangelo, Dürer, Fragonard, Watteau, Wouwerman, many others. 150pp. 8⅜ x 11¼.   21032-4 Pa. **$4.00**

THE GOLDEN AGE OF THE POSTER, Hayward and Blanche Cirker. 70 extraordinary posters in full colors, from Maîtres de l'Affiche, Mucha, Lautrec, Bradley, Cheret, Beardsley, many others. 9⅜ x 12¼.   22753-7 Pa. **$5.95**
21718-3 Clothbd. **$7.95**

SIMPLICISSIMUS, selection, translations and text by Stanley Appelbaum. 180 satirical drawings, 16 in full color, from the famous German weekly magazine in the years 1896 to 1926. 24 artists included: Grosz, Kley, Pascin, Kubin, Kollwitz, plus Heine, Thöny, Bruno Paul, others. 172pp. 8½ x 12¼.   23098-8 Pa. **$5.00**
23099-6 Clothbd. **$10.00**

THE EARLY WORK OF AUBREY BEARDSLEY, Aubrey Beardsley. 157 plates, 2 in color: Manon Lescaut, Madame Bovary, Morte d'Arthur, Salome, other. Introduction by H. Marillier. 175pp. 8½ x 11.   21816-3 Pa. **$4.00**

THE LATER WORK OF AUBREY BEARDSLEY, Aubrey Beardsley. Exotic masterpieces of full maturity: Venus and Tannhäuser, Lysistrata, Rape of the Lock, Volpone, Savoy material, etc. 174 plates, 2 in color. 176pp. 8½ x 11.   21817-1 Pa. **$4.00**

DRAWINGS OF WILLIAM BLAKE, William Blake. 92 plates from Book of Job, Divine Comedy, Paradise Lost, visionary heads, mythological figures, Laocoön, etc. Selection, introduction, commentary by Sir Geoffrey Keynes. 178pp. 8½ x 11.
22303-5 Pa. **$4.00**

LONDON: A PILGRIMAGE, Gustave Doré, Blanchard Jerrold. Squalor, riches, misery, beauty of mid-Victorian metropolis; 55 wonderful plates, 125 other illustrations, full social, cultural text by Jerrold. 191pp. of text. 8⅛ x 11.
22306-X Pa. **$6.00**

THE COMPLETE WOODCUTS OF ALBRECHT DÜRER, edited by Dr. W. Kurth. 346 in all: Old Testament, St. Jerome, Passion, Life of Virgin, Apocalypse, many others. Introduction by Campbell Dodgson. 285pp. 8½ x 12¼.   21097-9 Pa. **$6.00**

THE DISASTERS OF WAR, Francisco Goya. 83 etchings record horrors of Napoleonic wars in Spain and war in general. Reprint of 1st edition, plus 3 additional plates. Introduction by Philip Hofer. 97pp. 9⅜ x 8¼.   21872-4 Pa. **$3.50**

ENGRAVINGS OF HOGARTH, William Hogarth. 101 of Hogarth's greatest works: Rake's Progress, Harlot's Progress, Illustrations for Hudibras, Midnight Modern Conversation, Before and After, Beer Street and Gin Lane, many more. Full commentary. 256pp. 11 x 14.   22479-1 Pa. **$7.95,**

PRIMITIVE ART, Franz Boas. Great anthropologist on ceramics, textiles, wood, stone, metal, etc.; patterns, technology, symbols, styles. All areas, but fullest on Northwest Coast Indians. 350 illustrations. 378pp.   20025-6 Pa. **$3.75**

MOTHER GOOSE'S MELODIES. Facsimile of fabulously rare Munroe and Francis "copyright 1833" Boston edition. Familiar and unusual rhymes, wonderful old woodcut illustrations. Edited by E.F. Bleiler. 128pp. 4½ x 6⅜. 22577-1 Pa. $1.50

MOTHER GOOSE IN HIEROGLYPHICS. Favorite nursery rhymes presented in rebus form for children. Fascinating 1849 edition reproduced in toto, with key. Introduction by E.F. Bleiler. About 400 woodcuts. 64pp. 6⅞ x 5¼. 20745-5 Pa. $1.50

PETER PIPER'S PRACTICAL PRINCIPLES OF PLAIN & PERFECT PRONUNCIATION. Alliterative jingles and tongue-twisters. Reproduction in full of 1830 first American edition. 25 spirited woodcuts. 32pp. 4½ x 6⅜. 22560-7 Pa. $1.25

THE NIGHT BEFORE CHRISTMAS, Clement Moore. Full text, and woodcuts from original 1848 book. Also critical, historical material. 19 illustrations. 40pp. 4⅝ x 6. 22797-9 Pa. $1.35

THE KING OF THE GOLDEN RIVER, John Ruskin. Victorian children's classic of three brothers, their attempts to reach the Golden River, what becomes of them. Facsimile of original 1889 edition. 22 illustrations. 56pp. 4⅝ x 6⅜. 20066-3 Pa. $1.50

DREAMS OF THE RAREBIT FIEND, Winsor McCay. Pioneer cartoon strip, unexcelled for beauty, imagination, in 60 full sequences. Incredible technical virtuosity, wonderful visual wit. Historical introduction. 62pp. 8⅜ x 11¼. 21347-1 Pa. $2.50

THE KATZENJAMMER KIDS, Rudolf Dirks. In full color, 14 strips from 1906-7; full of imagination, characteristic humor. Classic of great historical importance. Introduction by August Derleth. 32pp. 9¼ x 12¼. 23005-8 Pa. $2.00

LITTLE ORPHAN ANNIE AND LITTLE ORPHAN ANNIE IN COSMIC CITY, Harold Gray. Two great sequences from the early strips: our curly-haired heroine defends the Warbucks' financial empire and, then, takes on meanie Phineas P. Pinchpenny. Leapin' lizards! 178pp. 6⅛ x 8⅜. 23107-0 Pa. $2.00

WHEN A FELLER NEEDS A FRIEND, Clare Briggs. 122 cartoons by one of the greatest newspaper cartoonists of the early 20th century — about growing up, making a living, family life, daily frustrations and occasional triumphs. 121pp. 8½ x 9½. 23148-8 Pa. $2.50

ABSOLUTELY MAD INVENTIONS, A.E. Brown, H.A. Jeffcott. Hilarious, useless, or merely absurd inventions all granted patents by the U.S. Patent Office. Edible tie pin, mechanical hat tipper, etc. 57 illustrations. 125pp. 22596-8 Pa. $1.50

THE DEVIL'S DICTIONARY, Ambrose Bierce. Barbed, bitter, brilliant witticisms in the form of a dictionary. Best, most ferocious satire America has produced. 145pp. 20487-1 Pa. $1.75

THE BEST DR. THORNDYKE DETECTIVE STORIES, R. Austin Freeman. The Case of Oscar Brodski, The Moabite Cipher, and 5 other favorites featuring the great scientific detective, plus his long-believed-lost first adventure — 31 New Inn — reprinted here for the first time. Edited by E.F. Bleiler. USO 20388-3 Pa. $3.00

BEST "THINKING MACHINE" DETECTIVE STORIES, Jacques Futrelle. The Problem of Cell 13 and 11 other stories about Prof. Augustus S.F.X. Van Dusen, including two "lost" stories. First reprinting of several. Edited by E.F. Bleiler. 241pp.
20537-1 Pa. $3.00

UNCLE SILAS, J. Sheridan LeFanu. Victorian Gothic mystery novel, considered by many best of period, even better than Collins or Dickens. Wonderful psychological terror. Introduction by Frederick Shroyer. 436pp. 21715-9 Pa. $4.00

BEST DR. POGGIOLI DETECTIVE STORIES, T.S. Stribling. 15 best stories from EQMM and The Saint offer new adventures in Mexico, Florida, Tennessee hills as Poggioli unravels mysteries and combats Count Jalacki. 217pp. 23227-1 Pa. $3.00

EIGHT DIME NOVELS, selected with an introduction by E.F. Bleiler. Adventures of Old King Brady, Frank James, Nick Carter, Deadwood Dick, Buffalo Bill, The Steam Man, Frank Merriwell, and Horatio Alger — 1877 to 1905. Important, entertaining popular literature in facsimile reprint, with original covers. 190pp. 9 x 12. 22975-0 Pa. $3.50

ALICE'S ADVENTURES UNDER GROUND, Lewis Carroll. Facsimile of ms. Carroll gave Alice Liddell in 1864. Different in many ways from final Alice. Handlettered, illustrated by Carroll. Introduction by Martin Gardner. 128pp. 21482-6 Pa. $2.00

ALICE IN WONDERLAND COLORING BOOK, Lewis Carroll. Pictures by John Tenniel. Large-size versions of the famous illustrations of Alice, Cheshire Cat, Mad Hatter and all the others, waiting for your crayons. Abridged text. 36 illustrations. 64pp. 8¼ x 11. 22853-3 Pa. $1.50

AVENTURES D'ALICE AU PAYS DES MERVEILLES, Lewis Carroll. Bué's translation of "Alice" into French, supervised by Carroll himself. Novel way to learn language. (No English text.) 42 Tenniel illustrations. 196pp. 22836-3 Pa. $3.00

MYTHS AND FOLK TALES OF IRELAND, Jeremiah Curtin. 11 stories that are Irish versions of European fairy tales and 9 stories from the Fenian cycle — 20 tales of legend and magic that comprise an essential work in the history of folklore. 256pp. 22430-9 Pa. $3.00

EAST O' THE SUN AND WEST O' THE MOON, George W. Dasent. Only full edition of favorite, wonderful Norwegian fairytales — Why the Sea is Salt, Boots and the Troll, etc. — with 77 illustrations by Kittelsen & Werenskiöld. 418pp.
22521-6 Pa. $4.50

PERRAULT'S FAIRY TALES, Charles Perrault and Gustave Doré. Original versions of Cinderella, Sleeping Beauty, Little Red Riding Hood, etc. in best translation, with 34 wonderful illustrations by Gustave Doré. 117pp. 8⅛ x 11. 22311-6 Pa. $2.50

EARLY NEW ENGLAND GRAVESTONE RUBBINGS, Edmund V. Gillon, Jr. 43 photographs, 226 rubbings show heavily symbolic, macabre, sometimes humorous primitive American art. Up to early 19th century. 207pp. 8⅜ x 11¼.
21380-3 Pa. $4.00

L.J.M. DAGUERRE: THE HISTORY OF THE DIORAMA AND THE DAGUERREOTYPE, Helmut and Alison Gernsheim. Definitive account. Early history, life and work of Daguerre; discovery of daguerreotype process; diffusion abroad; other early photography. 124 illustrations. 226pp. 6⅙ x 9¼.
22290-X Pa. $4.00

PHOTOGRAPHY AND THE AMERICAN SCENE, Robert Taft. The basic book on American photography as art, recording form, 1839-1889. Development, influence on society, great photographers, types (portraits, war, frontier, etc.), whatever else needed. Inexhaustible. Illustrated with 322 early photos, daguerreotypes, tintypes, stereo slides, etc. 546pp. 6⅛ x 9¼.
21201-7 Pa. $5.95

PHOTOGRAPHIC SKETCHBOOK OF THE CIVIL WAR, Alexander Gardner. Reproduction of 1866 volume with 100 on-the-field photographs: Manassas, Lincoln on battlefield, slave pens, etc. Introduction by E.F. Bleiler. 224pp. 10¾ x 9.
22731-6 Pa. $6.00

THE MOVIES: A PICTURE QUIZ BOOK, Stanley Appelbaum & Hayward Cirker. Match stars with their movies, name actors and actresses, test your movie skill with 241 stills from 236 great movies, 1902-1959. Indexes of performers and films. 128pp. 8⅜ x 9¼.
20222-4 Pa. $2.50

THE TALKIES, Richard Griffith. Anthology of features, articles from Photoplay, 1928-1940, reproduced complete. Stars, famous movies, technical features, fabulous ads, etc.; Garbo, Chaplin, King Kong, Lubitsch, etc. 4 color plates, scores of illustrations. 327pp. 8⅜ x 11¼.
22762-6 Pa. $6.95

THE MOVIE MUSICAL FROM VITAPHONE TO "42ND STREET," edited by Miles Kreuger. Relive the rise of the movie musical as reported in the pages of Photoplay magazine (1926-1933): every movie review, cast list, ad, and record review; every significant feature article, production still, biography, forecast, and gossip story. Profusely illustrated. 367pp. 8⅜ x 11¼.
23154-2 Pa. $7.95

JOHANN SEBASTIAN BACH, Philipp Spitta. Great classic of biography, musical commentary, with hundreds of pieces analyzed. Also good for Bach's contemporaries. 450 musical examples. Total of 1799pp.
EUK 22278-0, 22279-9 Clothbd., Two vol. set $25.00

BEETHOVEN AND HIS NINE SYMPHONIES, Sir George Grove. Thorough history, analysis, commentary on symphonies and some related pieces. For either beginner or advanced student. 436 musical passages. 407pp.
20334-4 Pa. $4.00

MOZART AND HIS PIANO CONCERTOS, Cuthbert Girdlestone. The only full-length study. Detailed analyses of all 21 concertos, sources; 417 musical examples. 509pp.
21271-8 Pa. $6.00

THE FITZWILLIAM VIRGINAL BOOK, edited by J. Fuller Maitland, W.B. Squire. Famous early 17th century collection of keyboard music, 300 works by Morley, Byrd, Bull, Gibbons, etc. Modern notation. Total of 938pp. 8⅜ x 11.
ECE 21068-5, 21069-3 Pa., Two vol. set $15.00

COMPLETE STRING QUARTETS, Wolfgang A. Mozart. Breitkopf and Härtel edition. All 23 string quartets plus alternate slow movement to K156. Study score. 277pp. 9⅜ x 12¼.
22372-8 Pa. $6.00

COMPLETE SONG CYCLES, Franz Schubert. Complete piano, vocal music of Die Schöne Müllerin, Die Winterreise, Schwanengesang. Also Drinker English singing translations. Breitkopf and Härtel edition. 217pp. 9⅜ x 12¼.
22649-2 Pa. $5.00

THE COMPLETE PRELUDES AND ETUDES FOR PIANOFORTE SOLO, Alexander Scriabin. All the preludes and etudes including many perfectly spun miniatures. Edited by K.N. Igumnov and Y.I. Mil'shteyn. 250pp. 9 x 12.
22919-X Pa. $6.00

TRISTAN UND ISOLDE, Richard Wagner. Full orchestral score with complete instrumentation. Do not confuse with piano reduction. Commentary by Felix Mottl, great Wagnerian conductor and scholar. Study score. 655pp. 8⅛ x 11.
22915-7 Pa. $11.95

FAVORITE SONGS OF THE NINETIES, ed. Robert Fremont. Full reproduction, including covers, of 88 favorites: Ta-Ra-Ra-Boom-De-Aye, The Band Played On, Bird in a Gilded Cage, Under the Bamboo Tree, After the Ball, etc. 401pp. 9 x 12.
EBE 21536-9 Pa. $6.95

SOUSA'S GREAT MARCHES IN PIANO TRANSCRIPTION: ORIGINAL SHEET MUSIC OF 23 WORKS, John Philip Sousa. Selected by Lester S. Levy. Playing edition includes: The Stars and Stripes Forever, The Thunderer, The Gladiator, King Cotton, Washington Post, much more. 24 illustrations. 111pp. 9 x 12.
USO 23132-1 Pa. $3.50

CLASSIC PIANO RAGS, selected with an introduction by Rudi Blesh. Best ragtime music (1897-1922) by Scott Joplin, James Scott, Joseph F. Lamb, Tom Turpin, 9 others. Printed from best original sheet music, plus covers. 364pp. 9 x 12.
EBE 20469-3 Pa. $7.50

ANALYSIS OF CHINESE CHARACTERS, C.D. Wilder, J.H. Ingram. 1000 most important characters analyzed according to primitives, phonetics, historical development. Traditional method offers mnemonic aid to beginner, intermediate student of Chinese, Japanese. 365pp.
23045-7 Pa. $4.00

MODERN CHINESE: A BASIC COURSE, Faculty of Peking University. Self study, classroom course in modern Mandarin. Records contain phonetics, vocabulary, sentences, lessons. 249 page book contains all recorded text, translations, grammar, vocabulary, exercises. Best course on market. 3 12" 33⅓ monaural records, book, album.
98832-5 Set $12.50

MANUAL OF THE TREES OF NORTH AMERICA, Charles S. Sargent. The basic survey of every native tree and tree-like shrub, 717 species in all. Extremely full descriptions, information on habitat, growth, locales, economics, etc. Necessary to every serious tree lover. Over 100 finding keys. 783 illustrations. Total of 986pp.
20277-1, 20278-X Pa., Two vol. set $9.00

BIRDS OF THE NEW YORK AREA, John Bull. Indispensable guide to more than 400 species within a hundred-mile radius of Manhattan. Information on range, status, breeding, migration, distribution trends, etc. Foreword by Roger Tory Peterson. 17 drawings; maps. 540pp.
23222-0 Pa. $6.00

THE SEA-BEACH AT EBB-TIDE, Augusta Foote Arnold. Identify hundreds of marine plants and animals: algae, seaweeds, squids, crabs, corals, etc. Descriptions cover food, life cycle, size, shape, habitat. Over 600 drawings. 490pp.
21949-6 Pa. $5.00

THE MOTH BOOK, William J. Holland. Identify more than 2,000 moths of North America. General information, precise species descriptions. 623 illustrations plus 48 color plates show almost all species, full size. 1968 edition. Still the basic book. Total of 551pp. 6½ x 9¼.
21948-8 Pa. $6.00

HOW INDIANS USE WILD PLANTS FOR FOOD, MEDICINE & CRAFTS, Frances Densmore. Smithsonian, Bureau of American Ethnology report presents wealth of material on nearly 200 plants used by Chippewas of Minnesota and Wisconsin. 33 plates plus 122pp. of text. 6⅛ x 9¼.
23019-8 Pa. $2.50

OLD NEW YORK IN EARLY PHOTOGRAPHS, edited by Mary Black. Your only chance to see New York City as it was 1853-1906, through 196 wonderful photographs from N.Y. Historical Society. Great Blizzard, Lincoln's funeral procession, great buildings. 228pp. 9 x 12.
22907-6 Pa. $6.95

THE AMERICAN REVOLUTION, A PICTURE SOURCEBOOK, John Grafton. Wonderful Bicentennial picture source, with 411 illustrations (contemporary and 19th century) showing battles, personalities, maps, events, flags, posters, soldier's life, ships, etc. all captioned and explained. A wonderful browsing book, supplement to other historical reading. 160pp. 9 x 12.
23226-3 Pa. $4.00

PERSONAL NARRATIVE OF A PILGRIMAGE TO AL-MADINAH AND MECCAH, Richard Burton. Great travel classic by remarkably colorful personality. Burton, disguised as a Moroccan, visited sacred shrines of Islam, narrowly escaping death. Wonderful observations of Islamic life, customs, personalities. 47 illustrations. Total of 959pp.
21217-3, 21218-1 Pa., Two vol. set $10.00

INCIDENTS OF TRAVEL IN CENTRAL AMERICA, CHIAPAS, AND YUCATAN, John L. Stephens. Almost single-handed discovery of Maya culture; exploration of ruined cities, monuments, temples; customs of Indians. 115 drawings. 892pp.
22404-X, 22405-8 Pa., Two vol. set $9.00

CONSTRUCTION OF AMERICAN FURNITURE TREASURES, Lester Margon. 344 detail drawings, complete text on constructing exact reproductions of 38 early American masterpieces: Hepplewhite sideboard, Duncan Phyfe drop-leaf table, mantel clock, gate-leg dining table, Pa. German cupboard, more. 38 plates. 54 photographs. 168pp. 8⅜ x 11¼.   23056-2 Pa. $4.00

JEWELRY MAKING AND DESIGN, Augustus F. Rose, Antonio Cirino. Professional secrets revealed in thorough, practical guide: tools, materials, processes; rings, brooches, chains, cast pieces, enamelling, setting stones, etc. Do not confuse with skimpy introductions: beginner can use, professional can learn from it. Over 200 illustrations. 306pp.   21750-7 Pa. $3.00

METALWORK AND ENAMELLING, Herbert Maryon. Generally conceded best all-around book. Countless trade secrets: materials, tools, soldering, filigree, setting, inlay, niello, repoussé, casting, polishing, etc. For beginner or expert. Author was foremost British expert. 330 illustrations. 335pp.   22702-2 Pa. $4.00

WEAVING WITH FOOT-POWER LOOMS, Edward F. Worst. Setting up a loom, beginning to weave, constructing equipment, using dyes, more, plus over 285 drafts of traditional patterns including Colonial and Swedish weaves. More than 200 other figures. For beginning and advanced. 275pp. 8¾ x 6⅜.   23064-3 Pa. $4.50

WEAVING A NAVAJO BLANKET, Gladys A. Reichard. Foremost anthropologist studied under Navajo women, reveals every step in process from wool, dyeing, spinning, setting up loom, designing, weaving. Much history, symbolism. With this book you could make one yourself. 97 illustrations. 222pp.   22992-0 Pa. $3.00

NATURAL DYES AND HOME DYEING, Rita J. Adrosko. Use natural ingredients: bark, flowers, leaves, lichens, insects etc. Over 135 specific recipes from historical sources for cotton, wool, other fabrics. Genuine premodern handicrafts. 12 illustrations. 160pp.   22688-3 Pa. $2.00

DRIED FLOWERS, Sarah Whitlock and Martha Rankin. Concise, clear, practical guide to dehydration, glycerinizing, pressing plant material, and more. Covers use of silica gel. 12 drawings. Originally titled "New Techniques with Dried Flowers." 32pp.   21802-3 Pa. $1.00

THOMAS NAST: CARTOONS AND ILLUSTRATIONS, with text by Thomas Nast St. Hill. Father of American political cartooning. Cartoons that destroyed Tweed Ring; inflation, free love, church and state; original Republican elephant and Democratic donkey; Santa Claus; more. 117 illustrations. 146pp. 9 x 12.
22983-1 Pa. $4.00
23067-8 Clothbd. $8.50

FREDERIC REMINGTON: 173 DRAWINGS AND ILLUSTRATIONS. Most famous of the Western artists, most responsible for our myths about the American West in its untamed days. Complete reprinting of *Drawings of Frederic Remington* (1897), plus other selections. 4 additional drawings in color on covers. 140pp. 9 x 12.
20714-5 Pa. **$5.00**

HOW TO SOLVE CHESS PROBLEMS, Kenneth S. Howard. Practical suggestions on problem solving for very beginners. 58 two-move problems, 46 3-movers, 8 4-movers for practice, plus hints. 171pp. 20748-X Pa. $3.00

A GUIDE TO FAIRY CHESS, Anthony Dickins. 3-D chess, 4-D chess, chess on a cylindrical board, reflecting pieces that bounce off edges, cooperative chess, retrograde chess, maximummers, much more. Most based on work of great Dawson. Full handbook, 100 problems. 66pp. 7⅞ x 10¾. 22687-5 Pa. $2.00

WIN AT BACKGAMMON, Millard Hopper. Best opening moves, running game, blocking game, back game, tables of odds, etc. Hopper makes the game clear enough for anyone to play, and win. 43 diagrams. 111pp. 22894-0 Pa. $1.50

BIDDING A BRIDGE HAND, Terence Reese. Master player "thinks out loud" the binding of 75 hands that defy point count systems. Organized by bidding problem—no-fit situations, overbidding, underbidding, cueing your defense, etc. 254pp. EBE 22830-4 Pa. $3.00

THE PRECISION BIDDING SYSTEM IN BRIDGE, C.C. Wei, edited by Alan Truscott. Inventor of precision bidding presents average hands and hands from actual play, including games from 1969 Bermuda Bowl where system emerged. 114 exercises. 116pp. 21171-1 Pa. $1.75

LEARN MAGIC, Henry Hay. 20 simple, easy-to-follow lessons on magic for the new magician: illusions, card tricks, silks, sleights of hand, coin manipulations, escapes, and more —all with a minimum amount of equipment. Final chapter explains the great stage illusions. 92 illustrations. 285pp. 21238-6 Pa. $2.95

THE NEW MAGICIAN'S MANUAL, Walter B. Gibson. Step-by-step instructions and clear illustrations guide the novice in mastering 36 tricks; much equipment supplied on 16 pages of cut-out materials. 36 additional tricks. 64 illustrations. 159pp. 6⅝ x 10. 23113-5 Pa. $3.00

PROFESSIONAL MAGIC FOR AMATEURS, Walter B. Gibson. 50 easy, effective tricks used by professionals —cards, string, tumblers, handkerchiefs, mental magic, etc. 63 illustrations. 223pp. 23012-0 Pa. $2.50

CARD MANIPULATIONS, Jean Hugard. Very rich collection of manipulations; has taught thousands of fine magicians tricks that are really workable, eye-catching. Easily followed, serious work. Over 200 illustrations. 163pp. 20539-8 Pa. $2.00

ABBOTT'S ENCYCLOPEDIA OF ROPE TRICKS FOR MAGICIANS, Stewart James. Complete reference book for amateur and professional magicians containing more than 150 tricks involving knots, penetrations, cut and restored rope, etc. 510 illustrations. Reprint of 3rd edition. 400pp. 23206-9 Pa. $3.50

THE SECRETS OF HOUDINI, J.C. Cannell. Classic study of Houdini's incredible magic, exposing closely-kept professional secrets and revealing, in general terms, the whole art of stage magic. 67 illustrations. 279pp. 22913-0 Pa. $3.00

THE MAGIC MOVING PICTURE BOOK, Bliss, Sands & Co. The pictures in this book move! Volcanoes erupt, a house burns, a serpentine dancer wiggles her way through a number. By using a specially ruled acetate screen provided, you can obtain these and 15 other startling effects. Originally "The Motograph Moving Picture Book." 32pp. 8¼ x 11.   23224-7 Pa. $1.75

STRING FIGURES AND HOW TO MAKE THEM, Caroline F. Jayne. Fullest, clearest instructions on string figures from around world: Eskimo, Navajo, Lapp, Europe, more. Cats cradle, moving spear, lightning, stars. Introduction by A.C. Haddon. 950 illustrations. 407pp.   20152-X Pa. $3.50

PAPER FOLDING FOR BEGINNERS, William D. Murray and Francis J. Rigney. Clearest book on market for making origami sail boats, roosters, frogs that move legs, cups, bonbon boxes. 40 projects. More than 275 illustrations. Photographs. 94pp.
20713-7 Pa. $1.25

INDIAN SIGN LANGUAGE, William Tomkins. Over 525 signs developed by Sioux, Blackfoot, Cheyenne, Arapahoe and other tribes. Written instructions and diagrams: how to make words, construct sentences. Also 290 pictographs of Sioux and Ojibway tribes. 111pp. 6⅛ x 9¼.   22029-X Pa. $1.75

BOOMERANGS: HOW TO MAKE AND THROW THEM, Bernard S. Mason. Easy to make and throw, dozens of designs: cross-stick, pinwheel, boomabird, tumblestick, Australian curved stick boomerang. Complete throwing instructions. All safe. 99pp.   23028-7 Pa. $1.75

25 KITES THAT FLY, Leslie Hunt. Full, easy to follow instructions for kites made from inexpensive materials. Many novelties. Reeling, raising, designing your own. 70 illustrations. 110pp.   22550-X Pa. $1.50

TRICKS AND GAMES ON THE POOL TABLE, Fred Herrmann. 79 tricks and games, some solitaires, some for 2 or more players, some competitive; mystifying shots and throws, unusual carom, tricks involving cork, coins, a hat, more. 77 figures. 95pp.   21814-7 Pa. $1.50

WOODCRAFT AND CAMPING, Bernard S. Mason. How to make a quick emergency shelter, select woods that will burn immediately, make do with limited supplies, etc. Also making many things out of wood, rawhide, bark, at camp. Formerly titled Woodcraft. 295 illustrations. 580pp.   21951-8 Pa. $4.00

AN INTRODUCTION TO CHESS MOVES AND TACTICS SIMPLY EXPLAINED, Leonard Barden. Informal intermediate introduction: reasons for moves, tactics, openings, traps, positional play, endgame. Isolates patterns. 102pp. USO 21210-6 Pa. $1.35

LASKER'S MANUAL OF CHESS, Dr. Emanuel Lasker. Great world champion offers very thorough coverage of all aspects of chess. Combinations, position play, openings, endgame, aesthetics of chess, philosophy of struggle, much more. Filled with analyzed games. 390pp.   20640-8 Pa. $4.00

SLEEPING BEAUTY, illustrated by Arthur Rackham. Perhaps the fullest, most delightful version ever, told by C.S. Evans. Rackham's best work. 49 illustrations. 110pp. 7⅞ x 10¾. 22756-1 Pa. $2.00

THE WONDERFUL WIZARD OF OZ, L. Frank Baum. Facsimile in full color of America's finest children's classic. Introduction by Martin Gardner. 143 illustrations by W.W. Denslow. 267pp. 20691-2 Pa. $3.00

GOOPS AND HOW TO BE THEM, Gelett Burgess. Classic tongue-in-cheek masquerading as etiquette book. 87 verses, 170 cartoons as Goops demonstrate virtues of table manners, neatness, courtesy, more. 88pp. 6½ x 9¼. 22233-0 Pa. $2.00

THE BROWNIES, THEIR BOOK, Palmer Cox. Small as mice, cunning as foxes, exuberant, mischievous, Brownies go to zoo, toy shop, seashore, circus, more. 24 verse adventures. 266 illustrations. 144pp. 6⅝ x 9¼. 21265-3 Pa. $2.50

BILLY WHISKERS: THE AUTOBIOGRAPHY OF A GOAT, Frances Trego Montgomery. Escapades of that rambunctious goat. Favorite from turn of the century America. 24 illustrations. 259pp. 22345-0 Pa. $2.75

THE ROCKET BOOK, Peter Newell. Fritz, janitor's kid, sets off rocket in basement of apartment house; an ingenious hole punched through every page traces course of rocket. 22 duotone drawings, verses. 48pp. 6⅞ x 8⅜. 22044-3 Pa. $1.50

CUT AND COLOR PAPER MASKS, Michael Grater. Clowns, animals, funny faces . . . simply color them in, cut them out, and put them together, and you have 9 paper masks to play with and enjoy. Complete instructions. Assembled masks shown in full color on the covers. 32pp. 8¼ x 11. 23171-2 Pa. $1.50

THE TALE OF PETER RABBIT, Beatrix Potter. The inimitable Peter's terrifying adventure in Mr. McGregor's garden, with all 27 wonderful, full-color Potter illustrations. 55pp. 4¼ x 5½. USO 22827-4 Pa. $1.00

THE TALE OF MRS. TIGGY-WINKLE, Beatrix Potter. Your child will love this story about a very special hedgehog and all 27 wonderful, full-color Potter illustrations. 57pp. 4¼ x 5½. USO 20546-0 Pa. $1.00

THE TALE OF BENJAMIN BUNNY, Beatrix Potter. Peter Rabbit's cousin coaxes him back into Mr. McGregor's garden for a whole new set of adventures. A favorite with children. All 27 full-color illustrations. 59pp. 4¼ x 5½. USO 21102-9 Pa. $1.00

THE MERRY ADVENTURES OF ROBIN HOOD, Howard Pyle. Facsimile of original (1883) edition, finest modern version of English outlaw's adventures. 23 illustrations by Pyle. 296pp. 6½ x 9¼. 22043-5 Pa. $4.00

TWO LITTLE SAVAGES, Ernest Thompson Seton. Adventures of two boys who lived as Indians; explaining Indian ways, woodlore, pioneer methods. 293 illustrations. 286pp. 20985-7 Pa. $3.00

HOUDINI ON MAGIC, Harold Houdini. Edited by Walter Gibson, Morris N. Young. How he escaped; exposés of fake spiritualists; instructions for eye-catching tricks; other fascinating material by and about greatest magician. 155 illustrations. 280pp. 20384-0 Pa. $2.75

HANDBOOK OF THE NUTRITIONAL CONTENTS OF FOOD, U.S. Dept. of Agriculture. Largest, most detailed source of food nutrition information ever prepared. Two mammoth tables: one measuring nutrients in 100 grams of edible portion; the other, in edible portion of 1 pound as purchased. Originally titled Composition of Foods. 190pp. 9 x 12. 21342-0 Pa. $4.00

COMPLETE GUIDE TO HOME CANNING, PRESERVING AND FREEZING, U.S. Dept. of Agriculture. Seven basic manuals with full instructions for jams and jellies; pickles and relishes; canning fruits, vegetables, meat; freezing anything. Really good recipes, exact instructions for optimal results. Save a fortune in food. 156 illustrations. 214pp. 6⅛ x 9¼. 22911-4 Pa. $2.50

THE BREAD TRAY, Louis P. De Gouy. Nearly every bread the cook could buy or make: bread sticks of Italy, fruit breads of Greece, glazed rolls of Vienna, everything from corn pone to croissants. Over 500 recipes altogether. including buns, rolls, muffins, scones, and more. 463pp. 23000-7 Pa. $4.00

CREATIVE HAMBURGER COOKERY, Louis P. De Gouy. 182 unusual recipes for casseroles, meat loaves and hamburgers that turn inexpensive ground meat into memorable main dishes: Arizona chili burgers, burger tamale pie, burger stew, burger corn loaf, burger wine loaf, and more. 120pp. 23001-5 Pa. $1.75

LONG ISLAND SEAFOOD COOKBOOK, J. George Frederick and Jean Joyce. Probably the best American seafood cookbook. Hundreds of recipes. 40 gourmet sauces, 123 recipes using oysters alone! All varieties of fish and seafood amply represented. 324pp. 22677-8 Pa. $3.50

THE EPICUREAN: A COMPLETE TREATISE OF ANALYTICAL AND PRACTICAL STUDIES IN THE CULINARY ART, Charles Ranhofer. Great modern classic. 3,500 recipes from master chef of Delmonico's, turn-of-the-century America's best restaurant. Also explained, many techniques known only to professional chefs. 775 illustrations. 1183pp. 6⅝ x 10. 22680-8 Clothbd. $22.50

THE AMERICAN WINE COOK BOOK, Ted Hatch. Over 700 recipes: old favorites livened up with wine plus many more: Czech fish soup, quince soup, sauce Perigueux, shrimp shortcake, filets Stroganoff, cordon bleu goulash, jambonneau, wine fruit cake, more. 314pp. 22796-0 Pa. $2.50

DELICIOUS VEGETARIAN COOKING, Ivan Baķer. Close to 500 delicious and varied recipes: soups, main course dishes (pea, bean, lentil, cheese, vegetable, pasta, and egg dishes), savories, stews, whole-wheat breads and cakes, more. 168pp. USO 22834-7 Pa. $2.00

COOKIES FROM MANY LANDS, Josephine Perry. Crullers, oatmeal cookies, chaux au chocolate, English tea cakes, mandel kuchen, Sacher torte, Danish puff pastry, Swedish cookies — a mouth-watering collection of 223 recipes. 157pp.

22832-0 Pa. $2.25

ROSE RECIPES, Eleanour S. Rohde. How to make sauces, jellies, tarts, salads, pot-pourris, sweet bags, pomanders, perfumes from garden roses; all exact recipes. Century old favorites. 95pp.

22957-2 Pa. $1.75

"OSCAR" OF THE WALDORF'S COOKBOOK, Oscar Tschirky. Famous American chef reveals 3455 recipes that made Waldorf great; cream of French, German, American cooking, in all categories. Full instructions, easy home use. 1896 edition. 907pp. 6⅝ x 9⅜ .

20790-0 Clothbd. $15.00

JAMS AND JELLIES, May Byron. Over 500 old-time recipes for delicious jams, jellies, marmalades, preserves, and many other items. Probably the largest jam and jelly book in print. Originally titled May Byron's Jam Book. 276pp.

USO 23130-5 Pa. $3.50

MUSHROOM RECIPES, André L. Simon. 110 recipes for everyday and special cooking. Champignons à la grecque, sole bonne femme, chicken liver croustades, more; 9 basic sauces, 13 ways of cooking mushrooms. 54pp.

USO 20913-X Pa. $1.25

THE BUCKEYE COOKBOOK, Buckeye Publishing Company. Over 1,000 easy-to-follow, traditional recipes from the American Midwest: bread (100 recipes alone), meat, game, jam, candy, cake, ice cream, and many other categories of cooking. 64 illustrations. From 1883 enlarged edition. 416pp.

23218-2 Pa. $4.00

TWENTY-TWO AUTHENTIC BANQUETS FROM INDIA, Robert H. Christie. Complete, easy-to-do recipes for almost 200 authentic Indian dishes assembled in 22 banquets. Arranged by region. Selected from Banquets of the Nations. 192pp.

23200-X Pa. $2.50